Nations Abroad

Nations Abroad

Diaspora Politics and International Relations in the Former Soviet Union

EDITED BY

Charles King
and Neil J. Melvin

Westview Press
A Member of the Perseus Books Group

Copyright © 1998 by Westview Press, A Member of the Perseus Books Group

Published in 1999 in the United States of America by Westview Press, 5500 Central Avenue, Boulder, Colorado 80301-2877, and in the United Kingdom by Westview Press, 12 Hid"s Copse Road, Cumnor Hill, Oxford OX2 9JJ

A CIP catalog record for this book is available from the Library of Congress
ISBN 0-8133-9015-X (cloth) — ISBN 0-8133-3738-0' (pb)

21207860

The paper used in this publication meets the requirements of the American National Standard for Permanence of Paper for Printed Library Materials Z39.48-1984.

10   9   8   7   6   5   4   3   2   1   7772

Contents

A Note on Usage

There has never been a consensus on the anglicization and transliteration of east European and Eurasian proper nouns. This difficulty is compounded here by the fact that this volume deals with a vast array of historical periods and geographical regions. In most instances proper nouns are given according to the evolving English-language conventions based on indigenous usage; hence, Belarus rather than "Belorussia" or "Byelorussia," Kyiv rather than "Kiev." Normally, the forms remain the same regardless of the period under discussion. It seems to us unduly cumbersome (and, in some cases, simply inaccurate) to use different spellings for the Soviet and post-Soviet periods. Inconsistencies must inevitably arise, but the editors stress that they intend nothing political in the conventions employed here. Names and titles from languages that use non-Latin writing systems are transliterated according to simplified versions of the Library of Congress conventions; the Ukrainian apostrophe, however, is rendered with double quotation marks ("). Names and terms that now have a generally accepted form without diacritical marks in English are given as such in the text; hence, Wroclaw, Gdansk, Kazan, Chisinau, Perm, glasnost, etc.

Glossary

ADL	Armenian Democratic Liberal Party (Ramkavars)
akim	Kazakhstani regional administration head
ANC	Armenian National Committee of America
AO	autonomous *oblast'*
ARF	Armenian Revolutionary Federation (Dashnaks)
ASSR	Autonomous Soviet Socialist Republic
catholicos	Leader of the Armenian Apostolic Church
CIS	Commonwealth of Independent States
CPSU	Communist Party of the Soviet Union
FBIS	Foreign Broadcast Information Service daily report
guberniia	Russian imperial province
HOK	Aid Committee for Armenia
HSDP	Hnchakian Social Democratic Party (Hnchaks)
Ittifak	Unity (Volga Tatar organization)
Qazaq Tili	Kazakh Language Association
korenizatsiia	nativization
krai	administrative territory
kurultai, qurultai	assembly or congress (among Turkic peoples)
medreseh	Islamic school
Milli Medzhlis	"national parliament" (among Volga Tatars)
NATO	North Atlantic Treaty Organization
oblast'	administrative region
okrug	administrative area
OMRI	Open Media Research Institute (Prague)
OSCE	Organization for Security and Cooperation in Europe
polk	Cossack regiment or regimental district
PRI	Institutional Revolutionary Party (Mexico)
raion	administrative district
RFE/RL	Radio Free Europe/Radio Liberty (Munich)

rossiiane	citizens or inhabitants of Russia
RSFSR	Russian Soviet Federative Socialist Republic
russkie	ethnic Russians
russkoiazychne	Russian-speakers
sblizhenie	rapprochement, convergence (of nations)
sliianie	fusion, assimilation (of nations)
sootechestvennik	compatriot
SSR	Soviet Socialist Republic
spiurk	the Armenian diaspora
SWB	BBC Summary of World Broadcasts daily report
TIKA	Turkish Cooperation and Development Agency
TPC	Tatar Public Center
WCT	World Congress of Tatars
zhuz	hundred or horde (Kazakh kin group)

Acknowledgments

The editors would like to thank Georgetown University, which hosted a workshop in June 1997 at which earlier drafts of the individual chapters were presented. Ian Bremmer and the Association for the Study of Nationalities graciously agreed to co-sponsor the workshop. Additional resources were provided by Leeds University. Dan Abele, Dominique Arel, Oded Eran, Pål Kolstø, Azade-Ayşe Rorlich, and Roger Kangas kindly served as external readers for the case studies, but the authors and editors bear sole responsibility for the final product. Jennifer Garrard and Jeanette Rébert provided research and technical assistance. Laurie Beans and Cheryl Chriss Sawyer of Georgetown's Center for Eurasian, Russian, and East European Studies stepped in to provide invaluable assistance with the workshop. The editors especially thank Sue Miller for her support and encouragement at this project's inception, and Marcus Boggs of Westview for seeing the book through to completion.

About the Contributors

Sally N. Cummings is a doctoral candidate in the Department of Government, London School of Economics and Political Science, and an analyst for the Jamestown Foundation. Her research, supported by grants from the Leverhulme Trust and the Economic and Social Research Council, focuses on political elites in Kazakhstan. She has written on Kazakh domestic politics and foreign policy for such publications as the *Former Soviet South Briefing Papers* (Royal Institute of International Affairs) and the *Journal of Communist Studies and Transition Politics*. She is currently completing a book on *Kazakhstan since Independence* for Harwood Academic Press.

Zvi Gitelman is Professor of Political Science and Preston Tisch Professor of Judaic Studies at the University of Michigan. He has served as director of the Center for Russian and East European Studies at the University of Michigan, and is currently director of the university's Frankel Center for Judaic Studies. He is the author or editor of nine books, including *Bitter Legacy: Confronting the Holocaust in the Soviet Union* (Indiana University Press, 1997). His current research is on Jewish identities in post-Soviet Russia and Ukraine.

Katherine E. Graney is completing a doctoral dissertation on national identity in Tatarstan and Bashkortostan in the Department of Political Science, University of Wisconsin–Madison. She is the recipient of a John D. and Catherine T. MacArthur Foundation Fellowship for Peace and Security in a Changing World, as well as fellowships from the Social Science Research Council and the International Research and Exchanges Board.

Charles King holds the Ion Ratiu Chair in Romanian Studies at Georgetown University, with a joint appointment in the Department of Government and the School of Foreign Service. He was previously a research fellow at Oxford University and a research associate at the International Institute for Strategic Studies. He has published widely on nationalism, the Balkans, and the former Soviet Union, with articles in *Foreign Policy*, *Slavic Review*, *International Affairs*, *Ethnic and Racial Studies*, and other journals.

Neil J. Melvin is Lecturer in Politics at the University of Leeds. He has held positions as a British Academy fellow at the London School of

Economics and Political Science and as a research fellow at the Royal Institute of International Affairs. His areas of research include Russian politics, regionalism, and foreign policy. He is the author of *Russians Beyond Russia: The Politics of National Identity* (Pinter, 1995).

Razmik Panossian works on national identity in the Transcaucasus in the Department of Government, London School of Economics and Political Science. He is the editor (with Donald V. Schwartz) of *Nationalism and History: The Politics of Nation Building in Post-Soviet Armenia, Azerbaijan and Georgia* (University of Toronto Centre for Russian and East European Studies, 1994).

Tim Snyder, a historian, wrote his contribution while a National Security Fellow at the Olin Institute for Strategic Studies, Harvard University. His research interests include the interplay between varieties of nationalism and foreign policy choices, as well as Poland's eastern policy since 1989. He is the author of *Nationalism, Marxism, and Modern Central Europe: A Biography of Kazimierz Kelles-Krauz, 1872–1905* (Harvard University Press, 1997) and articles in *East European Politics and Societies*, *Nations and Nationalism*, and other publications.

Andrew Wilson is Lecturer in Ukrainian Studies at the School of Slavonic and East European Studies in London. He has published widely on various aspects of Ukrainian and post-Soviet politics and ethnic relations. His books include *Ukrainian Nationalism in the 1990s: A Minority Faith* (Cambridge University Press, 1997) and, with Graham Smith, Vivien Law, and Annette Bohr, *Nation–Building in the Post-Soviet Borderlands: The Politics of National Identities* (Cambridge University Press, 1998).

1

Introduction: Nationalism, Transnationalism, and Postcommunism

Charles King

Ethnic groups have long played an important role in international politics. Whether as advocates of specific policies affecting their ethnic homelands or as objects of "pan" movements aimed at the unification of all members of a distinct ethnic community within a single state, these populations have had an influence on the formulation of foreign policy, the actions of political parties at home and abroad, and the evolution of interstate relations in the spheres of trade, aid, and security cooperation. The 1980s and 1990s, though, have seen a remarkable increase both in the awareness of trans-border ethnic groups as independent foreign policy actors, as well as the demonstrable importance of these groups in interstate relations. India's failed intervention in Sri Lanka in 1987 was fueled by calls from the large Tamil population in southern India to aid ethnic Tamils in their battles with the government in Colombo. The vocal and well-organized Cuban community in the United States played a major role in pressing the U.S. Congress to pass the controversial "Cuban Liberty and Democratic Solidarity Act of 1996," or Helms–Burton Law, which sought to restrict external investment in Cuba. Similar points could be made about Irish-Americans and the conflict in Northern Ireland, American Jews and the peace process in Israel and the Occupied Territories, the overseas Chinese and economic development in the Asia–Pacific region, and east European diaspora communities in Europe and North America and their impact on debates over the enlargement of the North Atlantic Treaty Organization (NATO).

In many regions, the traditional ethnic homelands—or "kin-states"—of such groups have begun to take a more active role in cultivating a sense of community with co-ethnic populations living in foreign "host-states." Kin-states can reach out to their ethnic diasporas by sponsoring sports teams

1

and cultural exchanges, or by lobbying for increased opportunities for bilingual education among co-ethnic immigrants. Entities such as the Turkish Cooperation and Development Agency (TIKA), which sponsors cultural and development programs among Turkic populations in the former Soviet Union, and Mexico's Program for Mexican Communities Abroad, which defends bilingual education and civil rights for Mexicans and Mexican-Americans in the United States, are illustrative of the interest of kin-states in building bridges to co-ethnic populations. In other instances, though, the policies of both kin-states and host-states can be less benign. Since 1991 the Russian Federation has taken on the mantle of defender of ethnic Russians in its "near abroad" and, on at least one occasion, has used this status to justify military intervention in the newly independent states of Eurasia. In east central Europe, the problems surrounding ethnic Hungarians in Romania, Slovakia, and Yugoslavia; ethnic Greeks in Albania; ethnic Turks in Bulgaria; and ethnic Serbs and Croats in Bosnia have highlighted the intimate links between foreign policy, trans-border ethnic groups, and regional security concerns.

Despite the clear importance of these forms of "internationalized ethnicity," understanding the web of relations among kin-states, host-states, and trans-border ethnic groups has remained elusive. How precisely do diasporas and other trans-border communities influence foreign policy making? How does the impact of long-established diasporas, such as Jews and Armenians in the United States, differ from that of ethnic groups separated from their ostensible homelands by more recent changes in political borders? Are diasporas necessarily a source of insecurity, or can both kin-states and host-states learn to use their diasporas as tools of nation and state building without threatening the interests of neighboring countries? What role do diasporas play in the identity politics of newly independent states?

This book examines these questions by focusing on the political salience of trans-border ethnic populations for the domestic politics and international relations of the Soviet successor states. The essays in this volume examine an issue that is crucial to understanding the international politics of the post-Soviet space: the effort by the successor governments to buttress both their national identities and their national borders by reaching out to a co-ethnic population abroad. Since the collapse of the Soviet federation, ethnic diasporas have been discovered—and in some cases constructed—by their ostensible ethnic homelands and used as sources of political capital. The relatively weak states that emerged from the rubble of the Soviet system have in many cases learned the value of diasporas, using their cultural and linguistic ties with co-ethnic communities abroad as instruments of both domestic politics and foreign policy.

While some of these issues have been addressed in the case of the region's largest diaspora—ethnic Russians or "Russian-speakers"—this volume offers a comparative study of several different trans-border populations and their influence on the international politics of eastern Europe and Eurasia.[1] As the chapters in this volume illustrate, the study of trans-border ethnic populations has important implications not only for post-Sovietology, but for the study of comparative politics and international relations more broadly. These studies focus on issues of boundaries in two senses. First, they examine the boundaries between the former Soviet republics themselves, which overnight were transformed from internal administrative borders into international frontiers, and the ways in which these boundaries are likely to remain points of contestation among several post-Soviet political actors. Second, they explore the increasingly permeable boundary between domestic politics and foreign policy, a subject of central concern to both academics and policy makers.

Studies situated along what James Rosenau has termed the "domestic–foreign frontier" have proliferated in the 1990s, but the international dimensions of ethnicity have not normally been of central concern.[2] However, the post-Soviet case demonstrates the potential uses of ethnicity as a political instrument in both domestic politics and foreign policy. In 1991 Russians, Ukrainians, and many of the Soviet Union's other ethnic groups became "nations abroad," instant diasporic communities separated from states that came to see themselves as the homelands of distinct, culturally defined nations. These new diasporas have become a fundamental issue in discussions over minorities policy in the Soviet successor states, as well as in relations between the independent republics themselves. As the studies here make clear, there is now a variety of overlapping and at times conflicting sources of identity and loyalty available to the panoply of ethnic groups in the former Soviet republics. How these new diasporas and their self-defined ethnic homelands are coping with these changes is the major theme of the chapters that follow.

This introductory chapter seeks to place the discussion of trans-border ethnic populations in the former Soviet Union in a broader conceptual context, highlighting the importance of diaspora issues both for post-Sovietologists and for scholars of comparative politics and international relations in general. At a time when the boundary between comparativists and international relations specialists is increasingly indistinct, the study of trans-border ethnic groups is central to debates on such topics as the future of the nation-state, the bounds of national sovereignty, the determinants of national identity, and the challenges posed by "transnational" policy issues such as immigration, crime, and the arms trade. Since the early 1980s, students of comparative politics, dissatisfied with the relative lack of attention paid to institutions in mainstream American political science, have worried about bringing the state and its institutions back in; many international relations experts, faced with the proliferation of non-state actors in world politics, have at the same time stressed the need to get the state out.[3] The study of trans-border ethnic groups, in some sense, seeks to do both at the same time. By exploring the relationship between ethnic communities, the states in which they reside, and other states that can claim a special cultural or political interest in them, the study of diaspora issues focuses precisely on the contested boundaries, identities, and institutions that lie at the nexus of comparative politics and international relations.

This chapter begins with a discussion of terminology and the literature on ethnic diasporas before going on to examine in greater detail the components of what we term "diaspora politics." The chapter defends the use of the label "diaspora" even for ethnic communities that have arrived "abroad" only because of sudden changes in international frontiers. A final section assesses the place of diaspora issues in post-Soviet politics in particular, and the peculiar legacy of the Soviet Union for ethnic groups and borders in the Commonwealth of Independent States (CIS) and other post-Soviet republics.

Ethnicity, Borders, and Foreign Policy

In the United States, the links between ethnic groups and state policy have long been of interest to social scientists. Students of American politics have examined the role of American diasporas—Jews, Irish, Italians, Greeks, and others—as important interest groups affecting political outcomes in both federal and state institutions.[4] Since the 1950s a substantial literature has also emerged on the impact of domestic ethnic groups on U.S. foreign policy.[5] Historians, anthropologists, and sociologists have likewise explored such issues as group solidarity, intergenerational identity, and the maintenance of communal institutions among both archetypal diasporas, such as American Jews, and groups newly constructed as diasporic communities, such as African-Americans.[6]

Since the late 1980s, there has been an increasing interest in the comparative study of trans-border ethnic populations outside the United States. Gabriel Sheffer, Thomas Sowell, and others have charted the economic and political impact of such archetypal diaspora communities as the Greeks, Indians, and overseas Chinese,[7] while Rogers Brubaker has begun the task of building a conceptual framework within which to analyze the relationship between a diaspora population, its ethnic

acting as protectors

homeland, and the state in which its members reside.[8] In 1991 a scholarly journal was established with the aim of promoting the study of diaspora issues in what the editor, in the inaugural issue, described as the world's new "transnational moment."[9]

This new awareness of ethnic diasporas as important political agents acting within and beyond the boundaries of individual states has been the result of at least three inter-related developments. First, in terms of international law, the treatment of ethnic minorities is now a decidedly transnational—or more accurately, a trans-state—issue. Since at least the 1970s, states have become more willing to subordinate their domestic politics to the scrutiny of foreign states and multilateral institutions; nowhere has this become clearer than in the case of minorities that can claim an external "protector" state beyond the borders of the country in which they reside. Second, democratization and marketization in Europe and elsewhere have opened up new channels of influence for ethnic groups that span international frontiers. Ethnic solidarity has long extended beyond the boundaries of individual states, but the international environment today allows well-organized ethnic populations to play a role in influencing politics within both their ancestral homelands and the states in which they live. Global communications networks have likewise increased the ability of non-state actors to affect domestic politics from abroad. Democratization has created more transparent and open political systems that ensure that a variety of actors—domestic, international, transnational—are able to influence political outcomes.

Finally, the proliferation of new, "nationalizing" states in Europe has highlighted issues of ethnicity and borders. From Croatia to Kazakhstan, newly independent states have been engaged in tortuous processes of defining their own sense of nationhood and staking out unique proprietary claims to territories that are home to a manifestly heterogeneous population. In all of these countries, there is a certain tension between an inclusive vision of the state, in which citizenship and nationality are considered to be coterminous, and a more exclusive conception of the state as "*of* and *for* a particular ethnocultural 'core nation' whose language, culture, demographic position, economic welfare, and political hegemony must be protected and promoted by the state." [10] However, domestic debates over such issues as citizenship laws, state symbols, and language policy no longer take place in a vacuum; they are increasingly shaped by the "triadic nexus" of the nationalizing state, national minorities within the state itself, and external homelands claiming a special interest in the fate of "their" minorities abroad.[11] All politics may still be local, but in the 1990s it is also multi-local.

"Diaspora" as Condition and Process

Despite the growing interest in trans-border ethnic groups, conceptual-
izing the object of study has been a major source of disagreement.
Definitions of even the term "diaspora" are legion.[12] John Armstrong
produced perhaps the broadest definition with his view that a diaspora
constitutes "any ethnic collectivity which lacks a territorial base within a
given polity," that is, a diaspora is any dispersed ethnic minority which
is relatively evenly distributed within a single state.[13] Milton J. Esman, on
the other hand, has argued for reserving the term "diaspora" for ethnic
groups whose minority status results from migration, not from arbitrary
changes in state boundaries; the key fact that distinguishes diasporas
from ethnic minorities in general is the experience of forcibly or voluntarily leaving a homeland and residing more or less permanently
abroad.[14] Gérard Chaliand and Jean-Pierre Rageau have likewise focused
on the experience of migration as a basic feature of diaspora communities, but further qualified the term by arguing that true diasporas arise
from forced dispersion, have a distinct collective cultural memory, and
resist assimilation to the dominant non-diaspora culture.[15] Similarly,
William Safran has argued against using the term "diaspora" to cover
such diverse groups as expatriates, political refugees, immigrants, and
ethnic minorities in general. Instead, for Safran, the term should be used
only for those groups that approximate the ideal type of the Jewish
diaspora, that is, "expatriate minority communities" that: (1) have been
dispersed from a specific original region; (2) retain a collective vision or
myth of the homeland; (3) believe they will forever be at least partially
alienated from the society in which they reside; (4) see their ancestral
homeland as their ideal home; (5) believe they should be committed to
the maintenance, protection, or restoration of the homeland; and (6)
relate personally or vicariously to the homeland and see such a relationship as a key part of their identity.[16]

Archetypal Diaspora Populations

While specific criteria differ, until recently most discussions have focused
on four general traits of diasporic populations, drawn from the histories
of archetypal diaspora peoples such as the Jews, Armenians, and
Lebanese. First is the experience of dispersal or "scattering"—the original
meaning of the Greek verb *diaspeirein*—and the impact of this experience,
whether immediate or mediated by historical memory, on group consciousness and cohesion. The connection, as James Clifford notes,

between "roots and routes" is often paramount in the self-conception of a diasporic community.[17] The lived experience of having left an ancestral kin-state or the historical myth of dispersion from a homeland, it is often argued, is fundamental; this migratory memory serves to distinguish diasporas from ethnic groups in general, including those separated from their ethnic confreres by perhaps equally traumatic but less historically cataclysmic alterations of international borders.

Second, diasporas seem to differ from other kinds of ethnic groups in displaying a remarkably high level of ethno-communal organization. Cultural groups, political parties, schools, social-service organizations, and other institutions sustained by the community serve to shore up a sense of group identity and discourage group members from further assimilation to the dominant culture of the state of residence. Diasporas often differ from ordinary immigrants, many of whom may see assimilation as the quickest route to economic advancement and acceptance within their state of residence. Moreover, the diaspora experience itself, along with its distinctive culture, traditions, and institutions, may become the focus of group loyalty for generations far removed from the original diasporic migration. The *shtetl, barrio, ghetto,* and *mahalla* can themselves become independent objects of romantic attachment, quite apart from diaspora members' loyalty to their ancestral homelands.

Third, a diaspora is said to differ from other ethnic minorities in that its members reside more or less permanently outside the borders of the ethnic homeland. Refugees, seasonal migrants, asylum-seekers, and other groups do not have the political clout of established immigrant communities and are therefore not able to influence the policies of their state of residence to the same extent as true diaspora populations.

Fourth, the diaspora's permanent presence in a "foreign" state is always, in principle, in conflict with the community's attachment to an ethnic homeland. A commitment to the homeland's protection and prosperity—or liberation, if the homeland is not an independent state—is often an enduring feature of diaspora communities' sense of collective identity, a feature that seems to set diasporas apart from ethnic groups with no clear territorial attachment outside the state of residence. This identity is, moreover, normally in conflict with the need to demonstrate political loyalty to the government and laws of the state in which they find themselves; diasporas, therefore, are permanent outsiders, pulled in one direction by sentiment and in another by the exigencies of surviving in a country which, in some sense, is not their own.

Hence, diasporas are said to be a distinct form of ethnic minority and their relationship with kin-states and host-states a distinct kind of minorities problem. The migratory memory, strong inter-generational solidarity buttressed by communal institutions, permanent residence outside the historic or mythic homeland, and a sense of divided loyalty between the state of residence and the homeland (whether an independent state or part of a larger political entity) are often highlighted as qualities that distinguish diasporas from other types of ethno-cultural communities.[18]

Broadening the Diasporic Label

However, while archetypal diasporas clearly form an analytically distinct kind of ethnic community, there are several reasons for including under the diaspora rubric other ethnic communities whose political loyalties, communal identities, and perhaps economic interests are in some sense divided between two or more states. Strictly speaking, it may indeed do violence to the term to categorize every trans-border ethnic group as a "diaspora," but there are compelling reasons for analyzing relations between states and trans-border ethnic groups, of whatever type, within a common framework. In fact, it is only when we see traditional diasporas as a sub-set of a broader array of trans-border communities that the most interesting and important features of internationalized ethnicity become evident.

In the first place, what is often most intriguing about diaspora issues, and indeed about questions of ethnic or national identity in general, is the semantic malleability of the diaspora label itself—its appropriation by a variety of vastly different ethno-cultural groups, many of which actually fit few or none of the "objective" criteria sketched above. In the United States and the United Kingdom, black intellectuals and community leaders since the 1960s have constructed a vision of African-American and Afro-Caribbean communities whose histories and identities owe as much to the multicultural politics of these states as to the historical memory of dispersal from Africa. A diasporic identity has been appropriated and a distinct diasporic narrative encouraged as symbols of African-American and Afro-Caribbean distinctiveness and as sources of cultural pride and solidarity. While there is no debate about the fact of the historical dispersal of Africans to western Europe and the New World, the transformation of historical facts into a relatively coherent narrative of dispersal has been a recent occurrence.[19]

The "migration" of the term "diaspora" should not be surprising. As Robin Cohen has noted, even the supposedly well-established histories and symbols of classic diasporic peoples such as the Jews are actually highly contentious narratives; it does not take a great deal of excavation to reveal competing visions of the diaspora experience among groups seen as paradigmatic, "objective" diasporas. Therefore, "to mount a defence of an orthodox definition of diaspora, which in any case has been shown to be dubious, is akin to commanding the waves no longer to break on the shore."[20] Indeed, as James Clifford has argued:

> we should be wary of constructing our working definition of a term like *diaspora* by recourse to an "ideal type," with the consequence that groups become identified as more or less diasporic . . . . [A]t different times in their history, societies may wax and wane in diasporism, depending on changing possibilities—obstacles, openings, antagonisms, and connections—in their host countries and transnationally.[21]

Moreover, in the case of the former Soviet Union, "diaspora" is now the term normally used by local political leaders to describe co-ethnic populations outside the borders of the homeland, regardless of whether these communities were formed as a result of migration or changes in international borders.

The symbols and myths according to which ethnic communities define themselves and against which they define their neighbors are always in flux. Today's labor migrants may be tomorrow's ethnic minority, while today's ethnic minority may turn out to be an "incipient diaspora."[22] These processes, of course, do not occur randomly. There may be a variety of clear material and psychological incentives for such identity shifts, and the presence or absence of articulate ethnic entrepreneurs can be another major determinant of the strength and durability of such changing conceptions of the community. The key point, however, is that diasporic identities are not given, but arise as a result of the complex interaction between a particular ethnic population, the policies of the state in which it resides, and the existence—whether imagined or real— of a homeland beyond the borders of the state of residence. Hence, whether the diaspora label is analytically serviceable should be determined primarily by the degree to which given states and ethnic populations act as if a diasporic relationship exists, not by the extent to which the ethno-cultural community possesses a prescribed list of static cultural or historical traits.

States can engage in the construction of co-ethnic populations abroad as diasporic, a process which only becomes evident when we enlarge our conception of what kinds of groups count as diasporas. Both newly independent and established states can reach out to populations that already feel an affinity toward their ethnic homeland through electoral rules, constitutional provisions, regulations on the repatriation of assets, citizenship laws, and other legal structures to facilitate the participation of co-ethnic groups in the politics of their putative kin-state. Both states and non-state actors in the ethnic homeland may also shore up ties with co-ethnics abroad by encouraging investment from co-ethnic business elites, by using the population as a source of influence in the state in which it resides, or by forming links with criminal syndicates associated with distinct ethnic communities abroad.

Mexico's relationship with Mexicans in the United States is an illustrative example of some of these processes. In late 1996 the Mexican Congress approved a constitutional provision on dual nationality, allowing an estimated five million or more Mexicans who qualify for U.S. citizenship to retain their Mexican passports and own property in Mexico. The constitutional change removed a major cultural and administrative hurdle to Mexicans who had declined to take U.S. citizenship for fear that they would thereby sever their ties with Mexico, becoming what many Mexicans refer to as *pochos*, isolated and culturally denuded individuals without ties to hearth and home. Interestingly, the new legislation distinguished between the notion of "nationality" and "citizenship," maintaining that even first- or second-generation Mexican-Americans would still be considered part of a territorially dislocated Mexican nation. Mexicans abroad send an estimated $4 billion a year back to Mexico, and by promoting ties between these populations and their "ethnic" homeland, the government clearly hoped to encourage the continuation of remittance payments and the cultivation of foreign investment.[23]

At the same time, however, the restriction of the "nationality" category to passports and property rights also meant that the Mexican state and the ruling Institutional Revolutionary Party (PRI), could block any direct influence that Mexican-Americans might have on Mexican domestic politics. A traditional stronghold of opposition parties, Mexican communities in the United States have in the past been staunch supporters of anti-PRI presidential candidates; they would clearly alter the balance of Mexican domestic politics were they to be given voting rights in addition to their rights as passport-holders. Similar points about homeland–diaspora relations could be made about competition between the Republic of China and the People's Republic of China for influence among overseas Chinese communities; the policy of Germany with respect to the *Aussiedler*, ethnic Germans from eastern Europe and the former Soviet Union; and the effort by Turkey to increase its influence among Turkic and Muslim populations in the Balkans, Caucasus, and Central Asia.

While host governments may be concerned about the interest of foreign kin-states in the status of "their" minorities abroad, constructing co-ethnic populations as diasporas need not necessarily be a source of insecurity and rivalry between ethnic homelands and states of residence.

Indeed, imbuing a co-ethnic population with a diasporic identity and creating institutions to deal with the affairs of co-ethnic communities abroad can in fact be a way of defusing outstanding territorial issues between states. Irredentism is a charge often made against states that express an interest in co-ethnic communities located on the other side of international boundaries. The claim is that the state's interest in the cultural or political rights of "its" co-ethnics is merely a mask for historical or legal claims to territory and an effort to redeem lands lost through war or international treaty. Diaspora claims, however, are rather different. Instead of asserting that the population should return to the fold, labeling a co-ethnic group as a diaspora often implies that its existence outside the borders of the homeland is both a normal and permanent feature of its members' sense of self and community.

Political leaders are often eager to dissociate the question of their interest in the affairs of co-ethnic communities abroad from the prickly issue of interstate borders. One way of separating these issues is by expressing interest in the status of ethnic communities—the right to use national languages, the ability to travel to the homeland, the establishment of state-supported communal institutions, etc.—rather than forwarding overt claims to territory.

The cultivation of ties between an ethnic homeland and a trans-border ethnic group may also be aimed at ensuring that the diaspora remains diasporic, rather than becoming returnees. With the exception of countries with institutions that encourage diasporic return, such as Germany, Israel, and Ireland, kin-states generally have little desire to see the return of diasporic populations.[24] By separating the notions of nationality and citizenship—constructing a trans-border, diasporic nation out of what may have been disparate communities of labor migrants, or established settlements cut off through the vicissitudes of international politics—states can achieve a double goal: ensuring a connection with co-ethnic communities abroad and the influence and economic power that they represent, while reducing their impact on the domestic politics of the homeland itself.

Conceptualizing Diaspora Politics

Ethnic diasporas can clearly influence state policy, whether within the states in which they live or within their putative ethnic homelands. Assessing the precise relationship between diasporas and political institutions—parties, foreign ministries, and quasi-governmental agencies—is a major theme of the chapters in this volume. Following from the discussion above, we have eschewed attempts to arrive at a

single definition of "diaspora" or to elaborate a set of criteria for distin-
guishing "true" diasporas from other types of ethnic communities. Our
main interest in this book is the process by which states attempt to
construct ethno-cultural communities as diasporic, a process that we
identify as *diaspora politics*.

A Terminology for Diaspora Politics

We understand diaspora politics to be the interactive process by which
states, acting in the international arena, forge a conception of a co-ethnic
community extending beyond the boundaries of the state itself—a
process that might be called, for lack of a better term, *diasporization*—and
by which bounded, self-conscious, ethnic communities abroad relate to
the domestic politics and foreign policy of a state or other political entity
conceived as coterminous with or representative of an ethnic homeland.[25]
    The *homeland*, in turn, is defined as a piece of territory having a fun-
damental symbolic connection with the identity of a given ethnic group.
Often, homelands are coterminous with what we term a *kin-state*, that is,
an internationally recognized state (or distinct political unit within a
larger recognized state) that can be perceived as having a special political
interest in the affairs of ethnic communities abroad that are linked by
history, culture, or tradition with the kin-state. The states in which
members of these diasporic communities reside, more or less permanently, we term *host-states*. A *diasporic state*, then, can be understood as a
kin-state whose identity in some sense rests on its self-conception as the
homeland of a territorially dispersed ethnic group, and which to some
extent sees itself as the defender of the interests of "its" co-ethnic
population abroad.
    Clearly, each of these terms is less than ideal. Archetypal diasporas
may be confused by the application of "diaspora" to less solidary
communities that do not display a migratory memory. Ethnic minorities
may object to the implication that they are merely "guests" in a state that
has arrogated to itself the label "host." Communities with little affinity
for an ostensible ethnic homeland may balk at their being linked by
"kinship" with another state. Ethnic groups separated by sudden
changes in international borders may resent their being labeled diasporas, as if the land on which they reside were somehow not an area of
traditional (and legitimate) ethnic settlement. But for all their imperfec-
tions, these terms can be useful in the analysis of trans-border ethnic
communities and state policies toward them.

Charting Diaspora Politics

Broadly speaking, diaspora politics occurs in three major spheres. First, diasporas may directly influence the making of foreign policy by placing political pressure on the host-state, the kin-state, or both. They may advocate that the host-state take a particular foreign policy line in an area not affecting the kin-state, in which case the influence of the diaspora population is little different from that of any other domestic interest group. Alternatively, they may pressure the host-state to adopt a specific policy orientation with respect to the kin-state, as with Jewish-American support for Israel and Greek-American support for Greece in its disputes with Turkey and Macedonia. Conversely, diasporas may directly influence the general foreign policy of the kin-state, such as when members of the diaspora community return to take up key roles in the kin-state's foreign policy establishment. In yet another variant, they may persuade the kin-state to adopt a particular policy *vis-à-vis* the host-state, effectively acting as lobbyists on behalf of their host-state. The effectiveness of diasporas in each of these variants depends on the diaspora's level of communal organization and material resources, the "opportunity structure" of the political system in both host-state and kin-state, and the willingness of the diaspora to maintain solidarity and exert sustained influence in a particular policy direction.[26]

Second, a diaspora community may become an issue in relations between kin-state and host-state, even though members of the community may themselves have little direct influence on the shape or evolution of relations between the two countries. In this case, the mere existence of the diaspora exerts influence on foreign policy formulation, quite apart from the political inclinations or activities of the diaspora population itself. As in the case of Hitler and the Sudeten Germans, leaders within the kin-state may find it politically expedient to focus on the plight of their ethnic kindred in a neighboring state, and may claim a right to defend the interests of the diaspora community, even though members of the community may not be actual citizens of the kin-state. In turn, the host-state may focus on the ostensibly divided loyalties of the diaspora population, framing the diaspora as inimical to the stability and territorial integrity of the host-state itself. In such situations, international actors may also become involved, as with the efforts of the French "Balladur initiative" of 1995, which was aimed at shoring up relations between states in east central Europe at odds over the issue of trans-border ethnic populations. The fundamental determinant of the foreign policies of the host-state and the kin-state in these circumstances, however, is not the actions of the diaspora itself; the diaspora population may be the object of foreign policy wrangling, but it does not on its own exert direct influence on the policy making process.

Third, host-states and kin-states may use diasporas as a source of political capital, either in relations with each other or in relations with third parties. This case differs from the one described above in that the primary focus of foreign policy is not the diaspora, but rather the potential benefits the host-state and kin-state hope to accrue by shoring up relations with each other or by establishing stronger ties with a third party. Local politicians may rhetorically portray the diaspora as a "bridge" between the host-state and kin-state. They may also use radical diaspora nationalists as a foil against which to stake out their own, more pragmatic position on interstate relations.

For example, if politicians in both states perceive that they have an interest in improved relations, they may point to the existence of the diaspora as an important political and societal link between the two countries. Leaders may even use members of the diaspora as intermediaries in situations in which direct negotiations on improved ties remain politically risky. Similarly, a radicalized diaspora population—calling, at the extreme, for secession from the host-state and union with the kin-state—may be used as a kind of political compass with which leaders can chart their own positions on relations between kin-state and host-state. Politicians in both countries can label the diaspora as extremists, finding in the trans-border population a common opponent and a point of departure for talks on improved interstate relations. In all these cases, the diaspora serves more than a purely symbolic role. Its existence and particular political profile can exert a strong influence on foreign policy, even though members of the ethnic community themselves may not be directly involved in the policy making process.

There are a variety of rhetorical and institutional innovations that can signal a state's engaging in diaspora politics. Within a kin-state, citizenship laws may be changed to allow for dual nationality. Legal provisions on the right of "return" to the homeland may be put in place. Firms within the kin-state may be given economic incentives to cooperate with co-ethnic communities abroad. The state may establish cultural centers or consulates in foreign countries with sizable co-ethnic populations. The kin-state may advocate the rights of co-ethnics in international forums and among non-governmental organizations, or may intercede directly with the host-state to ensure that the cultural, linguistic, and political rights of the co-ethnic minority are respected.

At the same time, host-states may also seek to exploit diasporic populations in their midst, exploring the ways in which the diaspora population can be instrumentalized in order to achieve desired policy goals with respect to the community's kin-state. For example, the host-state may encourage dual citizenship or facilitate the right of return. It may encourage local ethnic groups to establish economic links and joint ventures with co-ethnic business people in the ethnic homeland. In each of these instances, the focus for both states is on discovering the uses of diversity—the ways in which ethnic heterogeneity can actually open up foreign policy options that might not exist in relatively more homogenous polities.

Diaspora Politics and Political Transition

Political transitions offer a clear opportunity for diaspora politics to come to the fore. In the May 1993 elections in Cambodia, for example, eight of the contesting parties were headed by Cambodian-Americans.[27] In El Salvador, remittances from Salvadorans in the U.S. helped lay the groundwork for economic reconstruction after twelve years of civil war.[28] Similar developments can be expected in Cuba after the demise of the Castro regime, as some Miami Cubans inevitably flock to the island to stake out their own position in a postcommunist Cuban state.[29] Such diasporic returnees often offer a level of political sophistication and an array of international contacts and material resources not found in the homeland. Especially when returning to their homelands from already democratic states, they often display a remarkable ability to "market the democratic creed abroad."[30] Their involvement in the politics of a democratizing kin-state can be a major guarantor of the success of political and economic reforms. Indeed, the willingness of co-ethnic communities abroad to return to their homelands, especially in cases in which political oppression was the primary impetus for departure in the first place, can be seen as a barometer of the entire transition process.[31] On the other hand, returnees can also contribute to instability in instances in which the diaspora's key aim is to promote its own political agenda rather than contribute to the growth of stable, democratic institutions. Croatian and Serbian returnees, for example, were among the strongest supporters of expansionist policies in Croatia and the Federal Republic of Yugoslavia after 1990.

The return of diasporic populations to their homelands has been especially evident in postcommunist Europe.[32] Milan Panić, a California pharmaceuticals magnate, was named prime minister of Yugoslavia in 1992; Alexander Eiseln, an American army colonel, took up the post of Estonian defense minister in 1993; and Valdas Adamkus, a Lithuanian-American who moved to Lithuania in 1997, was elected the country's president the following year. In Armenia, at one stage the president

(Levon Ter-Petrossian), foreign minister (Raffi Hovannisian), and energy minister (Sebouh Tashjian) were all diaspora returnees, the first from Syria and the other two from California.[33] George Soros, the American financier who made a fortune during the devaluation of the British pound in 1992, is a unique example of the diaspora "returnee:" Instead of returning to his native Hungary to take up a position in the postcommunist government, he instead invested hundreds of millions of dollars in educational and development projects throughout eastern Europe, a series of programs that has amounted to a privatized American foreign policy in the region.

Of course, diaspora issues have long played an important role in the foreign policies of the states of east central Europe and the former Soviet Union. First, ethnic communities in Canada, Australia, France, the United Kingdom, and particularly the United States exerted considerable influence on the governments of these countries during the communist period. The structure of U.S. immigration law reflected a preference for admitting citizens of east European communist states, since the outflow of people from the communist bloc was considered both an indication of the lack of legitimacy of the region's one-party governments and an important propaganda tool that the west could use against them. From 1952 to 1980 a "refugee" was defined in U.S. law as any person fleeing either the Middle East or "a Communist-dominated country or area," and the Jackson–Vanik Amendment to the Trade Act of 1974 specifically prohibited the granting of most–favored–nation status to "non-market" countries which limited the rights of their citizens to emigrate.[34] As a result of these policy orientations, the voices of east European diaspora leaders were often heard in Washington and elsewhere.

Second, apart from established emigre communities, other trans-border ethnic groups were no less important during the Cold War. Especially after the 1970s, labor migrants provided needed cash for some east European governments. From 1977 to 1987, the volume of remittances from Yugoslav workers abroad rose from $2.4 billion to $4.3 billion per year, much of it returned from workers residing in West Germany, Austria, Sweden, and the Netherlands. In 1988 the gross foreign remittances to Yugoslavia represented 21 percent of the country's total exchange revenues and 38 percent of the total value of its commodity exports—and almost two and a half times its total foreign revenues from tourism.[35]

Third, debates over the status of territorially compact diasporas—such as the large numbers of ethnic Hungarians in Czechoslovakia, Yugoslavia, and Romania—stood in stark contrast to the avowals of unity within the socialist camp. Minority populations with links to neighboring states were often considered a potential fifth column by communist governments, even when these diasporas' kin-states and host-states found themselves nominal allies. Especially in the Balkans, as countries such as Romania, Albania, and Yugoslavia sought to distance themselves from Moscow and other socialist states from the late 1940s, the question of ethnic groups that stretched across international borders assumed even greater significance. Controversies between Belgrade and Tirana over ethnic Albanians, between Bucharest and Budapest over ethnic Hungarians, and between Sofia and Belgrade over ethnic Macedonians were an enduring, if at times muted, feature of intra-bloc politics.[36]

Political transitions in eastern Europe have provided windows of opportunity for diaspora influence. Diaspora returnees, the legacy of trans-border ethnic problems, and the continuing interest in relations between homeland and host-state beyond the Cold War are important features of the region's ethno-politics. There is, however, a more fundamental dimension to diaspora politics in a period of political and social transformation. As new elites seek to redefine the interests of states during transitions—from one regime to another, or from one form of statehood to another—questions about the identity of the state and its constituents inevitably arise. The proper locus and boundaries of state sovereignty—in the physical sense of territorial borders and in the more conceptual sense of the relationship of the new authorities to political emigres, governments–in–exile, and co-ethnic populations abroad—are called into question.[37] Since 1991 this situation has been especially acute among the former Soviet republics, where the legacies of Soviet communism and the emerging international relations among the European and Eurasian successor states have placed diaspora issues on the political agenda.

The Soviet and Post-Soviet Contexts

Diaspora politics plays a special role in the context of the fifteen successor states to the Soviet Union, their relations with their former sister republics, and their bilateral and multilateral relations with states and organizations outside the post-Soviet space. Soviet communism bequeathed an array of incentives for the mobilization of diaspora interests. The Soviet federation was a political system in which ethnic affiliation was both reified and valorized; although rhetorically committed to the withering away of ethnic allegiances, the system itself—by creating a congeries of isomorphic institutions in the non-Russian republics organized along ethnonational lines—privileged ethnicity and underscored ethnic identity as a focus of group solidarity. The Soviet Union was divided into a shifting territorial hierarchy of union republics, autonomous republics, regions (*oblasts*), areas (*okrugs*), territories (*krais*), districts (*raions*), and councils (*soviets*), many defined at various times according to ethnic, linguistic, or ethno-religious criteria. Within the republics, other institutional structures, from local parliaments and councils of ministers to dance troupes and "national" restaurants, reinforced the image of the fifteen republics as the homelands of distinct historical nations.

These institutions, however, were "national" in an administrative, not a demographic, sense. From the inception of the Soviet state, policies of forcible resettlement, internal labor migration, haphazardly drawn borders, and what has become known simply as "ethnic cleansing" ensured that there was little correspondence between the ethnically defined, administrative constituents of the Soviet federation and the demographic boundaries of the ethnic groups that they claimed to represent. In 1989 a quarter of all Soviet citizens (over 73 million people) lived outside the borders of the administrative regions defined as the homeland of their respective ethnic groups.[38]

The enthusiasm with which Soviet officials supported the flowering of ethno-national allegiances waxed and waned during the seven decades of Soviet power, alternating between touting the Soviet Union as a state in which national affiliations could reach their highest fulfillment, to a new historical community formed from the convergence (*sblizhenie*) and fusion (*sliianie*) of national differences. But policy shifts notwithstanding, the institutional structure of the Soviet state encouraged the development of distinct national identities and the association of those identities with a set of distinct "national" institutions within the republics and other territorial units. As Ronald Suny has observed, regardless of Marxist-Leninist views on nationalism, the Soviet Union was not a melting pot for old nations but rather an incubator for new ones.[39] Individuals and entire populations were defined, for purposes both praiseworthy and pernicious, in terms of their ethnic affiliation—an affiliation that was itself in many instances actively constructed by Soviet ethnographers, linguists, and historians in the early years after the Bolshevik revolution.[40]

During the perestroika period, it was not surprising that a form of group cohesion encouraged by the system should prove so powerful when other cross-cutting allegiances—class, party, and state—began to weaken. What had initially been calls on the part of Lithuanian, Ukrainian, and other elites for greater provision for native-language education and control over local resources rapidly became demands for national self-determination. Much of the institutional structure through which such claims could be articulated—territorial boundaries supposedly defined according to ethnic criteria, and a set of internal institutional structures of administration and mobilization—had been in place since the 1920s.[41]

Moreover, as elites in each of the fifteen republics breathed life into "national" institutions, the problem of diaspora politics quickly arose: If the newly sovereign states were in fact the national homelands of their respective nationalities, what was to become of ethnic groups who, because of changes in political borders, suddenly found themselves beyond the frontiers of "their" national states? Thus, at the end of 1991, the Soviet Union gave way not only to an array of newly independent states, but to a mass of newly stateless diasporas as well—populations that were suddenly separated from states now defined as their proper national homelands.

Since the collapse of the Soviet federation, the former Soviet republics have all been, in Rogers Brubaker's term, "nationalizing states:" countries in which there is an uneasy relationship between, on the one hand, the imperative of building a supra-ethnic community defined primarily through citizenship, and on the other hand, an equally strong desire to craft a polity whose boundaries and institutions reflect its status as the homeland of a single, ethnically defined community. Like all nationalizing states, the post-Soviet republics are thus engaged in a remedial project, attempting to correct either the borders of the state itself or the internal state institutions and symbols (or both) so as to rectify the perceived disadvantages of the titular nationality.

The ethno-politics of the former Soviet Union is thus also the politics of diasporas. As states address the relationship between political boundaries, political identities, and the state's constituent ethnic communities, the position of groups beyond the state who share cultural and linguistic traits with the titular ethnic group is of crucial importance. In addition to being nationalizing states, however, the successor republics are also weak states, existing precariously within a relatively uncertain and sometimes hostile regional sub-system. Many have found that having co-ethnic populations abroad—either within neighboring states or even farther afield—can provide needed links to other states and potential targets of foreign and economic policy.

Diaspora issues matter for one final reason as well. For the first time in history, many of the former Soviet republics are emigre-producing states. They now send individuals and families to live, work, and perhaps permanently reside abroad. All fifteen states now have ties with populations that only a few of the republics could claim to have before the advent of Soviet power—diasporic communities, both foreign-based and increasingly foreign-born, whose members have some sense of loyalty to and affinity toward their new homelands. Diaspora politics thus works at a number of interrelated levels. Not only are post-Soviet states reaching out to co-ethnic communities in their former sister republics, but governments in the region are increasingly finding both opportunities and dangers in the array of new diasporic communities produced by the easing of restrictions on travel abroad. Labor migrants, scholarship grantees, and even criminal networks form yet another type of post-Soviet diaspora group which the former Soviet republics are likely to find offer both unique instruments of foreign policy as well as unique threats to the stability of the state.

Conclusion

The essays that follow focus on a crucial element in the emerging international relations of the post-Soviet space: the effort by the successor governments to construct and legitimate cultural and political identities and buttress national borders by reaching out to ethnic diasporas beyond their frontiers. The aim in this volume is not to attempt a comprehensive catalogue of diaspora issues in the post-Soviet republics. Rather, the cases of Russians, Jews, Armenians, Ukrainians, Kazakhs, Volga Tatars, and Poles have been chosen because, collectively, they illustrate the diversity of motivations and outcomes in the diaspora politics of the former Soviet Union, and underscore the malleability of the diaspora label for kin-states, host-states, and trans-border ethnic groups themselves. Many of the post-Soviet republics are, in this sense, emerging diasporic states, conceived as the political representation of a territorially dislocated and culturally defined nation. Connecting with these diasporas—through economic policy, cultural policy, foreign relations, and other instruments—has become an important theme in relations within and outside the former Soviet Union.

The contributors to this volume have therefore been asked to focus on four sets of problems:

1. *Nation and State Building.* How have states in the former Soviet Union used their diaspora(s)—however defined—in the processes of post-Soviet state and nation building? What has determined the variable effectiveness of diaspora policies?
2. *Ethnicity and Interstate Relations.* How has the existence of the diaspora shaped relations among the former Soviet republics, and among these republics and external powers?
3. *Diasporas and Domestic Politics.* How have diasporas influenced domestic politics and policy making within the successor

states? What has determined the variable salience of diaspora politics in individual states?
4. *The Post-Soviet Region in Perspective.* What might diaspora issues in the former Soviet Union reveal about state power, identity, and interstate relations more broadly?

As the case studies show, the experience of the new "nations abroad" in the former Soviet Union can shed light on the complexities of democratic transitions, the boundaries of collective identity, and the instruments of statecraft in newly independent states. How state policies toward transborder ethnic groups have emerged since 1991, what they reveal about the international relations of the region, and in what directions they are likely to develop in the future are questions addressed in the chapters that follow.

Notes

The author would like to thank Erin Brunson, Joe Lepgold, Neil J. Melvin, Tim Snyder, and the other contributors to this volume for helpful comments on an earlier version, and Jennifer Garrard and Jeanette Rébert for research assistance. Drafts of this chapter were presented at the Woodrow Wilson International Center for Scholars and at the 1997 Annual Meeting of the American Political Science Association.

1. On the Russian case, see Neil Melvin, *Russians Beyond Russia: The Politics of National Identity* (London: Pinter, 1995); Vladimir Shlapentokh, Munir Sendich, and Emil Payin, eds., *The New Russian Diaspora: Russian Minorities in the Former Soviet Republics* (Armonk: M. E. Sharpe, 1994); Paul Kolstoe, *Russians in the Former Soviet Republics* (Bloomington: Indiana University Press, 1995); Jeff Chinn and Robert Kaiser, *Russians as the New Minority: Ethnicity and Nationalism in the Soviet Successor States* (Boulder: Westview, 1996); David D. Laitin, *Identity in Formation: The Russian-Speaking Populations in the Near Abroad* (Ithaca: Cornell University Press, 1998).

There is also a substantial literature that attempts to place post-Soviet state building in the comparative context of post-imperialism and federal collapse. See Richard R. Rudolph and David E. Good, eds., *Nationalism and Empire: The Habsburg Empire and the Soviet Union* (New York: St. Martin's, 1992); W. Raymond Duncan and G. Paul Holman, Jr., eds., *Ethnic Nationalism and Regional Conflict: The Former Soviet Union and Yugoslavia* (Boulder: Westview, 1994); Reneo Lukic and Allen Lynch, *Europe from the Balkans to the Urals: The Disintegration of Yugoslavia and the Soviet Union* (New York: Oxford University Press, 1996); Karen Barkey and Mark von Hagen, eds., *After Empire: Multiethnic Societies and Nation-*

Building (Boulder: Westview, 1997); and the two multi-volume series edited by Bruce Parrott and Karen Dawisha for M. E. Sharpe (*The International Politics of Eurasia*) and Cambridge University Press (*Authoritarianism and Democratization in Postcommunist Societies*).

2. James N. Rosenau, *Along the Domestic–Foreign Frontier: Exploring Governance in a Turbulent World* (Cambridge: Cambridge University Press, 1997). The exception has been the study of "ethnic conflict," its spread across international borders, and the role of international organizations in its termination. See, for example, Raymond C. Taras and Rajat Ganguly, *Understanding Ethnic Conflict: The International Dimension* (New York: Longman, 1998); David Carment and Patrick James, eds., *The International Politics of Ethnic Conflict* (Pittsburgh: University of Pittsburgh Press, 1997); Michael E. Brown, ed., *The International Dimensions of Internal Conflict* (Cambridge: MIT Press, 1996); Milton J. Esman and Shibley Telhami, eds., *International Organizations and Ethnic Conflict* (Ithaca: Cornell University Press, 1995); Michael E. Brown, ed., *Ethnic Conflict and International Security* (Princeton: Princeton University Press, 1993).

3. For important discussions of these issues in comparative politics and international relations, see Joel S. Migdal, "Studying the State," in Mark Irving Lichbach and Alan S. Zuckerman, eds., *Comparative Politics: Rationality, Culture, Structure* (Cambridge: Cambridge University Press, 1997), 208–35; Peter Evans, "The Eclipse of the State? Reflections on Stateness in an Era of Globalization," *World Politics* 50, no. 1 (1997): 62–87; Thomas Risse-Kappen, *Bringing Transnational Relations Back In: Non-State Actors, Domestic Structures and International Relations* (Cambridge: Cambridge University Press, 1995); David J. Elkins, *Beyond Sovereignty: Territory and Political Economy in the Twenty-First Century* (Toronto: University of Toronto Press, 1995); Peter B. Evans, Dietrich Rueschemeyer, and Theda Skocpol, eds., *Bringing the State Back In* (Cambridge: Cambridge University Press, 1985); Thom Kuehls, *Beyond Sovereign Territory: The Space of Ecopolitics* (Minneapolis: University of Minnesota Press, 1996); Gene M. Lyon and Michael Mastanduno, eds., *Beyond Westphalia? State Sovereignty and International Relations* (Baltimore: Johns Hopkins University Press, 1995); Michael J. Shapiro and Hayward R. Alker, *Changing Boundaries: Global Flows, Territorial Identities* (Minneapolis: University of Minnesota Press, 1996); Hendrik Spruyt, *The Sovereign State and Its Competitors: An Analysis of System Change* (Princeton: Princeton University Press, 1994).

4. The classic study is Nathan Glazer and Daniel Patrick Moynihan, *Beyond the Melting Pot* (Cambridge: MIT Press, 1963).

5. Alexander DeConde, *Ethnicity, Race and American Foreign Policy: A History* (Boston: Northeastern University Press, 1992); Lawrence H. Fuchs, "Minority Groups and Foreign Policy," *Political Science Quarterly* 74, no. 2 (1959): 161–75; Louis L. Gerson, *The Hyphenate in Recent American Politics* (Lawrence: University of Kansas Press, 1964); Charles McC. Mathias, Jr., "Ethnic Groups and Foreign Policy," *Foreign Affairs* 59 (Summer 1981): 975–98; Abdul Aziz Said, ed., *Ethnicity and U.S. Foreign Policy* (New York: Praeger, 1977); Yossi Shain, "Ethnic Diasporas and U.S. Foreign Policy," *Political Science Quarterly* 109, no. 5 (1994–95): 811–41;

Robert Tucker et al., eds., *Immigration and U.S. Foreign Policy* (Boulder: Westview, 1990).

6. Michael L. Coniff and Patrick J. Carroll, eds., *Africans in the Americas: A History of the Black Diaspora* (New York: St. Martin's Press, 1994); Vincent Bakpetu Thompson, *The Making of the African Diaspora in the Americas, 1441–1900* (New York: Longman, 1981); Sidney Lemelle and Robin D. G. Kelley, *Imagining Home: Class, Culture and Nationalism in the African Diaspora* (London: Verso, 1994); W. D. Davies, *The Territorial Dimensions of Judaism* (Minneapolis: University of Minnesota Press, 1992); Paul Gilroy, *The Black Atlantic: Double Consciousness and Modernity* (Cambridge: Harvard University Press, 1993).

7. Joel Kotkin, *Tribes* (New York: Random House, 1992); Thomas Sowell, *Migrations and Cultures: A World View* (New York: BasicBooks, 1996); Dimitri C. Constas and Athanasios G. Platias, eds., *Diasporas in World Politics: The Greeks in Comparative Perspective* (London: Macmillan, 1993); Gabriel Sheffer, ed., *Modern Diasporas in International Politics* (London: Croom Helm, 1986); Lynn Pan, *Sons of the Yellow Emperor: A History of the Chinese Diaspora* (Boston: Little Brown, 1990); Sterling Seagrave, *Lords of the Rim: The Invisible Empire of the Overseas Chinese* (New York: Putnam, 1995);

8. Rogers Brubaker, *Nationalism Reframed: Nationhood and the National Question in the New Europe* (Cambridge: Cambridge University Press, 1996). See also his *Citizenship and Nationhood in France and Germany* (Cambridge: Harvard University Press, 1992).

9. Khachig Tölölyan, "The Nation-state and Its Others: In Lieu of a Preface," *Diaspora* 1, no. 1 (1991): 3–7.

10. Brubaker, *Nationalism*, 103.

11. Brubaker, *Nationalism*, 67.

12. For a critical overview, see Khachig Tölölyan, "Rethinking Diaspora(s): Stateless Power in the Transnational Moment," *Diaspora* 5, no. 1 (1996): 3–36.

13. John Armstrong, "Mobilized and Proletarian Diasporas," *American Political Science Review* 70, no. 2 (1976): 393.

14. Milton J. Esman, "Diasporas and International Relations," in Sheffer, ed., *Modern Diasporas*, 333.

15. Gérard Chaliand and Jean-Pierre Rageau, *The Penguin Atlas of Diasporas* (New York: Viking, 1995), xiv–xvii.

16. William Safran, "Diasporas in Modern Societies: Myths of Homeland and Return," *Diaspora* 1, no. 1 (1991): 83–84.

17. James Clifford, "Diasporas," *Cultural Anthropology* 9, no. 3 (1994): 308.

18. For an elaboration of these features, see Gabriel Sheffer, "Ethno-national Diasporas and Security," *Survival* 36, no. 1 (1994): 61

19. See Stuart Hall, "Negotiating Caribbean Identities," *New Left Review* (January–February 1995): 3–14; and Paul Gilroy, *"There Ain't No Black in the Union Jack:" The Cultural Politics of Race and Nation* (London: Hutchinson, 1987).

20. Robin Cohen, *Global Diasporas: An Introduction* (London: UCL Press, 1997),

21. Cohen himself, however, would not include all trans-border ethnic groups under the diaspora label.

21. Clifford, "Diasporas," 306.

22. Myron Weiner, "Labor Migrations as Incipient Diasporas," in Sheffer, ed., *Modern Diasporas*, 47–74. On labor diasporas, see also Milton J. Esman, "The Political Fallout of International Migration," *Diaspora* 2, no. 1 (1992): 3–41.

23. Mark Fineman, "Lawmakers in Mexico Approve Dual Nationality," *Los Angeles Times*, December 11, 1996, p. 1; Sam Dillon, "Zedillo Courting Mexicans in the U.S.," *International Herald Tribune*, December 11, 1995, p. 6.

24. In all three countries, however, there have been major changes and controversies surrounding return policies in the 1990s.

25. We learned after arriving at this inelegant term that Robin Cohen had already used it to describe a rather different process—the creation of dislocated ethnic populations through migration. We use the term to refer to the process by which states attempt to portray ethnic communities as diasporic, regardless of whether they are "really" diasporas in the classic sense of the term. See Cohen, *Global Diasporas*, 175.

26. Esman, "Diasporas," 337.

27. Yossi Shain, "Marketing the Democratic Creed Abroad: U.S. Diasporic Politics in the Era of Multiculturalism," *Diaspora* 3, no. 1 (1994): 102.

28. Edward Orlebear, "Killings Cloud El Salvador Poll," *Financial Times*, March 8, 1994.

29. See Maria Cristina Garcia, *Havana USA: Cuban Exiles and Cuban-Americans in South Florida, 1959–1994* (Berkeley: University of California Press, 1996); and David Rieff, "From Exiles to Immigrants," *Foreign Affairs* (July–August 1995): 76–89.

30. Shain, "Marketing," 85–111; and idem, "Multicultural Foreign Policy," *Foreign Policy* (Fall 1985): 69–87.

31. See Yossi Shain, "Democrats and Secessionists: US Diasporas as Regime Destabilizers," in Myron Weiner, ed., *International Migration and Security* (Boulder: Westview, 1993), 287–322.

32. For an insightful overview, see Michael Radu, "Western Diasporas in Post-Communist Transitions," *Problems of Post-Communism* (May–June 1995): 57–62.

33. "Eastern Europe's Diasporas," *The Economist*, January 8, 1993, p. 53. Ter-Petrossian, however, barely counts as a returnee, since he "returned" to Armenia as a child.

34. Michael S. Teitelbaum, "Immigration, Refugees, and Foreign Policy," *International Organization* 38, no. 3 (1984): 429–50.

35. V. Grecic, "The Importance of Migrant Workers' and Emigrants' Remittances for the Yugoslav Economy," *International Migration* 28, no. 2 (1990): 203.

36. See Robert R. King, *Minorities Under Communism* (Cambridge: Harvard University Press, 1973).

37. See Yossi Shain, ed., *Governments–in–Exile in Contemporary World Politics* (New York: Routledge, 1991). See also idem, *The Frontier of Loyalty: Political Exiles in the Age of the Nation-State* (Middletown: Wesleyan University Press, 1989).

38. On relations between homelands and ethnic groups in the Soviet and immediate post-Soviet periods, see Robert J. Kaiser, *The Geography of Nationalism in Russia and the USSR* (Princeton: Princeton University Press, 1994).

39. Ronald Grigor Suny, *The Revenge of the Past: Nationalism, Revolution and the Collapse of the Soviet Union* (Stanford: Stanford University Press, 1993), 87. See also Brubaker, *Nationalism*, 23–54

40. On nation building in the Soviet period, see Yuri Slezkine, "From Savages to Citizens: The Cultural Revolution in the Soviet Far North," *Slavic Review* 51, no. 1 (1992): 52–76; idem, "The USSR as a Communal Apartment, or How a Socialist State Promoted Ethnic Particularism," *Slavic Review* 53, no. 2 (1994): 414–52; Gerhard Simon, *Nationalism and Policy Toward the Nationalities in the Soviet Union* (Boulder: Westview, 1991), especially chapter 2; Michael Kirkwood, ed., *Language Planning in the Soviet Union* (London: Macmillan, 1989); Michael Smith, "The Eurasian Imperative in Early Soviet Language Planning: Russian Linguists at the Service of the Nationalities," in Susan Gross Solomon, ed., *Beyond Sovietology: Essays in Politics and History* (New York: M. E. Sharpe, 1993), 159–91.

41. See Richard Pipes, *The Formation of the Soviet Union*, rev. ed. (Cambridge: Harvard University Press, 1964); Hélène Carrère d'Encausse, *The Great Challenge: Nationalities and the Bolshevik State, 1917–1930* (London: Holmes and Meier, 1992).

2

The Russians: Diaspora and the End of Empire

Neil J. Melvin

Following the collapse of the Soviet Union in 1991, the Russian diaspora emerged as one of the critical issues shaping political developments in many of the post-Soviet republics, particularly the Russian Federation.[1] High levels of tension around the issue of the russified communities in the Baltic states and Ukraine, a bloody conflict in Moldova, rising political mobilization among the russified settlers in Kazakhstan, and a sizable out-migration from Central Asia pointed to the diaspora issue as a defining element of the post-Soviet order.[2] Uncertainty about the loyalty of the settlers, the location of settler populations in important geostrategic locations, and their potential to serve as a "fifth column" for an aggressive Russian foreign policy toward the former Soviet republics caused concern within the newly independent states and among members of the international community. Indeed, the political crisis that appeared to be developing around the settler issue in the early 1990s led several authors to draw parallels between the situation of the Russian communities outside the Russian Federation and that of the German diaspora prior to the Second World War.[3]

The issue of the russified settlers has a number of dimensions, but it primarily concerns the definition of the Russian national community and the relationship of this community to the newly independent states of the former Soviet Union, especially the Russian Federation. The russified settler question has acquired particular importance because the modern history of Eurasia has been marked by the development of the Russian community around a hybrid of imperial, statist, civic, and ethnic identities. Determining the nature of the contemporary Russian state's relationship to the russified settler communities is, therefore, at the heart of the project to fashion a post-imperial Russian nation.[4] Inevitably, the forms of political engagement that develop between Russia and the

27

"diaspora" will have a crucial impact on the other states and national communities of the region.

Despite concerns that the Russian diaspora would serve as the basis for conflict between the newly established states, the form of diaspora politics that has developed around the russified communities in the initial period of independence has not fundamentally threatened the largely peaceful evolution of a post-Soviet political order. Examination of the Russian case suggests that the relatively benign role of the Russian diaspora within the contemporary interstate politics of the region is in large part the legacy of the close relationship that developed between the Russian community and the imperial regimes that dominated Eurasia from the sixteenth century onward.

The fusion of Russian identity first with the Russian imperial order and then with the Soviet state was critical to the expansion of these two political orders and to their ability to dominate events on the Eurasian land mass. While Russian culture furnished the core symbols and identity of the Russian empire, the migration of large numbers of settlers from the European, particularly Russian, heartland to the periphery of the empire served to cement political control over conquered lands. In addition, the settlers operated as agents of cultural change, most importantly through linguistic russification. Although important differences existed between the Russian empire and the Soviet Union, within the Soviet order the Russian population continued to fulfill functions similar to those it had performed in the tsarist system. During the Soviet era, the high mobility of the russified population and the policies of the regime ensured that the Russian community dominated key geographic and socio-economic positions throughout the territories subordinated to Moscow's rule.

The symbiotic relationship that existed between the Russian community and the dominant political regimes of Eurasia served primarily to strengthen the colonial state and its institutions rather than to develop a distinct Russian ethnic and national identity. Indeed, to a significant degree, the cohesion of the Russian imperial and Soviet orders rested on ensuring that the borders of the Russian community had a relatively fluid and porous quality. Thus, while the boundaries of most ethnic and national communities became more rigid under Soviet rule, the margins of the Russian community retained a high degree of plasticity. With the collapse of the Soviet system, the interdependent relationship that had existed between the Russian community and the hegemonic political regime was severed in many important respects. In particular, the political order that had structured the Russian community in a geographical, socio-economic, and political sense, and provided Russian identity with its central role as the core culture of the empire, was shattered.

Once the Russian community was deprived of the support of an imperial state, the ambiguous nature of Russian identity and its weakness as a basis for political mobilization were exposed. On the one hand, the russified settlers outside the Russian Federation were divided in their response to the creation of the post-Soviet states. While a minority of the settlers sought to defend the Soviet system, others offered support for independence and the promotion of a civic definition of citizenship in the newly established states. On the other hand, the political mobilization of key sections of Russia's numerous minority populations challenged narrow conceptions of the Russian nation, encouraging the emergence of a territorial rather than ethnic definition of the Russian people. Fears of an aggressive Russia's using the issue of the russified settler populations for the purposes of rebuilding an empire, therefore, overlooked the structural legacy of the colonial era, which made the concepts of the Russian national and ethnic community extremely problematic in the immediate post-Soviet era.

The Russian Community and Imperial Expansion

Following Mongol conquests of Slav lands in the thirteenth century, the Great Russians gradually emerged as a group with a distinct cultural identity. The defeat of the Mongols and the unification of European territories under a single sovereign, the tsar of Muscovy, provided further momentum to Russian cultural consolidation. The expansion of the Russian empire, however, presented a challenge to Russian domination of the imperial state. As the borders of the empire advanced beyond the original core lands, an increasingly diverse range of minorities was brought under imperial control.

With the conquest of Kazan in 1552, a sizable Muslim group—the Volga Tatars—joined the Finno-Ugric minority populations already within the empire. Two years later, a second Muslim community, the Astrakhan Tatar khanate, was taken. These conquests marked the opening of a prolonged period of imperial expansion accompanied by the incorporation of different peoples, which was to reach its high-water mark with the Soviet Union's territorial annexations during the Second World War. The solution that developed to managing and controlling the rising numbers of non-Russians within the empire was twofold.

First, while the imperial system drew heavily upon and supported the development of a distinct Russian culture (notably the Russian language) for the core elements of the political order, until at least the late nineteenth century Russia was defined not as the land of the Russians but as the territory of the Russian empire-state. The political legitimacy of the Russian political system rested not on popular sovereignty expressed through the Russian nation or ethnos, but on a commitment to the Russian state. The Russian elite was bound to the state or fatherland (*otechestvo*), rather than to the homeland (*rodina*). Thus, although the expansion of the Russian empire diluted the territorial sense of Russia, it did not pose a direct threat to the underpinnings of the political system.[5]

Second, Russian identity was developed as an inclusive concept. Notions of Russianness hinged on allegiance to the tsar, the political system that he commanded (autocracy), and the Russian Orthodox church. The concept of Russian identity that emerged from this period became a powerful means by which to assimilate or partially assimilate other communities that came into contact with the expanding empire. The central role performed by the Russian community in integrating new lands and peoples into the imperial system, however, stunted the development of a distinct Russian national identity and also discouraged the growth of a politicized Russian ethnic consciousness.[6]

At the height of its power, the Russian empire consisted of a vast territory bound together by a complex pattern of economic, administrative, political, and ethno-cultural arrangements. Critical to the consolidation of the Russian imperial state in newly acquired territories was an extensive movement of population from core to the new periphery.[7] The relentless expansion of the borders of the Russian empire was reinforced by the waves of migrants—Cossacks, peasants, administrators, bureaucrats, and professionals—that washed outward from the imperial heartland as a result of demographic pressures within European Russia, the prospect of economic opportunities in the new territories, and state policies promoting migration.[8] Over four centuries, tens of millions were transferred to the conquered lands, often setting down deep roots in the new territories.[9] The establishment of settler communities across the empire provided a critical link that bound together many of the diverse elements of the imperial order.[10]

Toward the end of the nineteenth century, as the tsarist system began to seek new forms of legitimacy, the Russian imperial state became involved in promoting a form of Russian nationalism. At the same time, the growth of nationalist sentiments among Ukrainian, Georgian, Baltic, and Turkic intelligentsias and rising ethnic consciousness among the masses as a result of urbanization, rising literacy, industrialization, and Russian migration into the borderlands prompted a drive by the imperial authorities to russify and acculturate non-Russians. The increased emphasis on linguistic russification notwithstanding, there is little indication that the nationalizing process in this period had a predominantly ethnic dimension.[11] The drive to alter the relationship between the imperial state and the population of the empire took the form of an attempt to foster an identification among the minority communities with the tsarist system through assimilation into a broadly civic Russian national identity.

The fusion of the Russian ethnic and national community with the colonial state, however, had a significance that went beyond the ability of the Russian imperial order to dominate the territory and peoples of Eurasia for three hundred years. The dovetailing of Russian identity with the prevailing political regime established the preconditions for a process of identity formation among the indigenous populations of Eurasia. The imperial order served as a crucible within which the identities of conquered peoples were recast into national forms. Opposition to imperial control was frequently framed in terms of anti-Russian sentiments, with resistance mobilized in response to policies and perceptions of russification, Russian migration, Russian dominance of prestigious positions in society, and Russian control over economic resources.

The effort to shift the legitimacy of the Russian imperial regime onto a new national basis was ultimately to fail. Instead, the nationalization drive, coupled with the migration of russified populations to the imperial periphery, helped to foster a reactive ethno-nationalist mobilization in many parts of the Russian empire. The rise of separatist nationalisms challenged a Russian empire critically weakened by the First World War and the Bolshevik revolution, leading eventually to the disintegration of the imperial system.

From Imperial Settlers to Soviet *Kulturträger*

The collapse of the Russian imperial order and the civil war that followed called into question the territorial unity that had been established within the Russian empire. One of the principal early successes of the Bolshevik leadership was to remake the Russian empire, but in a new form.[12] Within the new political order, Russian identity was redefined in relation to the Bolshevik state. While the link between the Russian community and the Soviet state was rebuilt in ways different from that which had existed in the Russian empire, there were also important elements of continuity.[13] The manipulation of Russian symbols, language, and history to provide a core culture for the state and a reliance on russified settlers to consolidate control over large areas of territory were of particular significance.

The Bolsheviks' ability to reconstitute Russian imperial territories as the Soviet Union initially relied upon the introduction of a set of policies to curb "Great Russian chauvinism." Indeed, the new Soviet federal state was presented as a means to provide minority communities with protection from Russian domination. Stalin's rise to power and the consolidation of the Soviet state, however, were accompanied by the introduction of a political agenda that relied heavily upon russification and assimilation of non-Russian groups—a reversal of the policies of nativization and equalization among national groups that had previously prevailed.

From the late 1920s, the Soviet regime promoted Russian as a *lingua franca*, the language of success, and a means to destroy "local nationalisms" and replace them with policies of "internationalization." Schools employing native languages were closed or restricted, while Russian became the principal language of education. The Soviet regime also expropriated elements of Russian culture to help provide a core cultural identity for the Soviet system. These processes were greatly accelerated during the Second World War (the "Great Patriotic War") when Russian nationalism was incorporated as an important part of the regime's legitimacy.[14]

Despite the Soviet regime's avowed aim of supplanting national self-identities with an all-encompassing "inter-national" one, ethnicity was institutionalized as a basic organizing principle of the state. The creation of an ethnically defined federal system and a set of administrative practices based on ethnic identity established an ethno-political environment within which the Russian community acquired a more distinct set of boundaries than had existed within the Russian empire. Russian identity, however, continued to operate as a far more open system of identification than most other national identities within the Soviet Union, particularly as the Soviet state endured.

The significant advantages enjoyed by those conversant with Russo-Soviet culture, coupled with the replacement of the policies that gave preference to non-Russian populations in the 1920s with russification in the 1930s, ensured that Russian identity exerted a strong pull on the rest of the population of the Soviet Union. As many as ten million non-Russians may have transferred to a Russian identification from the late 1920s to the late 1930s.[15] At the same time, Soviet policies of acculturation and assimilation (which included compulsory military service and educational policies) helped to promote intermarriage and bilingualism. The expansion of the Russian cultural community that had undergirded Russian imperial expansion continued, therefore, for much of the Soviet period.

By the end of the Second World War, Russians had gained the status of first among equals or "elder brothers," and sovietized Russian culture was ascendant. This position continued into the 1980s. The fusion of Soviet Marxism with elements of Russian culture, which together defined the elements of an internationalist consciousness, gave Russian-speakers an important advantage, but not guaranteed privilege. Although non-Russians were expected to adopt the Russian language and a heavily russocentric version of history and politics, even ethnic Russians had to accept the ambiguous fusion of national and multinational visions of the Soviet polity, and strenuous efforts were made to repress ethnic Russian nationalism.

While Russian culture and language formed core elements of Soviet identity, the loyalty of russified settler communities to the state and the migration of settlers to new areas undergirded Moscow's control over the Soviet territories. State policies and the high degree of mobility within the Russian community enabled russified populations to dominate urban areas, key professions, and strategic geographical regions throughout the Soviet Union.

During the Soviet period, there was an important numeric and geographic expansion of the russified settler communities—often building upon the patterns of settlement established within the Russian empire. Although the migration of russified populations to Central Asia and Transcaucasia slowed from the 1950s, population movement continued to the Baltic states and the western borderlands well into the 1980s.[16] The Soviet regime depended on the settler populations to dilute the power of the titular nationalities within the republics and to enhance Soviet rule. Migrant communities were encouraged to see themselves as political and economic benefactors and as *Kulturträger* for the ambiguous meld of Soviet and Russian culture.

The settler communities were not, however, composed solely of ethnic Russian migrants, although they usually formed the core and the largest group. Nor were ethnic identities primary in the settler-dominated areas. Russians formed the nucleus of highly sovietized, predominately urban, and largely industrial settler communities that included a variety of ethnic groups—the particular correlation of groups depended on the region of settlement (although Ukrainians and Belarusians often formed the core group along with the Russians).[17] The identity of the settler communities was primarily defined in socio-cultural rather than ethnic terms. The social and cultural identity of the settler communities was further reinforced by their position in the Soviet political and economic system. Although geographically scattered, the settlers were at the heart of the Soviet political economy. The russified communities were generally tied more to the all–union economy rather than the local economy, and to the Communist Party of the Soviet Union (CPSU) rather than to republican-level Communist party structures.

In the final decades of the Soviet order, rising nationalist mobilization among the titular populations of the Soviet republics appeared to foster a heightened sense of ethnic distinctiveness within the Russian settler communities.[18] Despite these pressures, the close historical link between Russian identity and the imperial state, coupled with the complex of institutions, cultural values, and political relationships at the core of the Soviet Union, ensured that the Russian–Soviet relationship remained durable. As the Soviet system disintegrated in the late 1980s and early 1990s, however, this intimate relationship was split apart.

The reforms of the perestroika era and nationalist mobilization within many of the Soviet republics, including the Russian Federation, had a fundamental effect upon the Russian community.[19] The relationship that had developed over centuries between the imperial state and the Russians was challenged from two directions. The emergence of powerful ethno-nationalist independence movements in a number of republics undermined Russian cultural and linguistic dominance in many areas and called into question the presence of Russian communities in these regions. At the same time, the development of an anti-Soviet political movement in the Russian Federation, which was largely based on a territorial notion of Russian nationhood, broke the historic link between the russified settlers and political power centered within Russia.

While titular nationalist movements relied heavily on ethnic identity as a basis for mobilization and often articulated anti-Russian sentiments, when the Soviet center weakened the russified communities could not draw upon well-articulated ethno-political structures to organize resistance to the process of change. Composed of a variety of groups arranged in diverse patterns and relationships, characterized by high levels of intermarriage and geographic mobility, and dominated by Soviet institutions (particularly the Communist party), the russified communities had little in the way of indigenous political or cultural institutions upon which to rely for mobilization.

The most active resistance to the growth of titular nationalist and independence movements came in the form of Interfronts, the "internationalist" organizations that sprang up in heavily sovietized enclaves situated outside the Russian Federation.[20] While support for these movements was drawn predominantly from the russified communities, defense of the Soviet system rather than promotion of the Russian nation formed the basis for the activities of the Interfronts. Historically defined by their political relationship to the imperial state, the Russian communities remained wedded to the Soviet order to a greater degree than any other group.

The emergence of a powerful anti-Soviet political movement led by Boris Yeltsin within the Russian Federation further isolated the russified settlers. The Russian democratic movement campaigned within a civic and territorial notion of Russian nationhood and in loose alliance with independence movements in the other republics. Tied to the collapsing Soviet state and outside the ethno-nationalist and independence movements within the republics, the russified settlers were largely bypassed by the political developments of the Gorbachev era.

Diaspora Politics After Communism

The collapse of the Soviet Union at the end of 1991 produced a dramatic transformation in the position of the russified settlers. In place of the Soviet order, the Russian Federation emerged as an independent state, although not necessarily a Russian homeland. At the same time, the relationship of the russified settlers to the new states was fundamentally different from the one that had historically existed between settler and state: The settlers became minorities.

Although the russified settler communities received little attention during the Gorbachev era, in the early years of independence the "Russians abroad" quickly became one of the critical issues in the post-Soviet order. The reasons for the transformation of the settler issue were threefold. First, the relationship between the russified settler communities and the Russian state became a central issue in the struggle for power between members of the political elite in the Russian Federation. Second, in the early independence period, titular nationalists in the post-Soviet republics frequently identified russified settler communities as elements of the "colonial" and "imperial" past and potential fifth columns for Russian neo-imperialism. Finally, the newly independent states set in motion official and informal political, economic, and socio-cultural changes that directly challenged the positions of prominence that the settler communities had previously enjoyed.

At the end of 1991, the notion that a Russian diaspora existed within the territory of the former Soviet Union was largely absent from political and popular discourse. In the late perestroika period, the openness of intellectual life that accompanied the policy of glasnost led to the widespread discovery by the Soviet public of the works of intellectuals who had fled or been expelled from the Soviet Union. The generations that had left the Soviet Union were, however, seen as having little connection to contemporary Russia. The emigres, particularly those who had left in the early years of the Bolshevik regime, were viewed more as a lost civilization than an organic part of the new Russia.

Within a few months of independence, however, the fate of the russified settler communities in the former Soviet territories emerged as a critical issue within the domestic and interstate politics of the Russian

Federation. The settler communities became a defining element in the struggle to determine Russia's national identity, which in turn formed a core part of the struggle between competing post-Soviet Russian political elites. In the course of these contests, the status of the settler communities was transformed into that of a Russian diaspora—a constituent part of the Russian nation—and the Russian Federation emerged as the homeland for this diaspora. The development of Russia's relationship with the russified settler communities in this important early period of independence passed through four stages.[21]

The Atlanticist Vision

In the struggle with Gorbachev and the Soviet center, the Russian democratic movement advocated a so-called Atlanticist vision of Russia's place in the world: a political agenda based primarily upon the integration of Russia into the international community, particularly its economic aspects, with attention focused on Russia's relationship with the western powers. As a result of the adoption of this set of foreign policy priorities, in the first phase of independence (autumn 1991–autumn 1992) the Russian government lacked a developed set of policies with respect to the newly independent states of the former Soviet Union.

Implicit in the democratic movement's conception of the Russian polity and its vision of the new Russia was a territorial (*rossiiskii*) rather than ethnic (*russkii*) definition of the Russian nation. While there were historical and personal ties to the russified settler communities, and economic and military links remained important, initially the priorities of the Russian government and the concentration on policy toward the "far abroad" ensured that there was no political link between the Russian Federation and the russified settlers. Instead, the primary concern of the Russian government with regard to the settler communities was the prospect of an uncontrolled mass migration from the "near abroad." The main response to this fear was the creation of the Federal Migration Service in September 1992—in order to regulate migration to Russia from the diaspora—rather than any attempt to manipulate the settlers for political purposes.[22]

As opposition to the new government emerged, the issue of the settlers and Russia's responsibility toward these communities became a focus of the battle for political power. Policy toward the settlers became the key issue in a far broader struggle to determine the nature of the new Russian state and its place in the world. Conflict between the president and the parliament served as an important forum for debate about the settler communities and provided the opposition with an opportunity to exploit the lack of a state policy toward the russified population outside Russia.[23] Criticism of the failure of the government to declare Russia's right to "protect" the diaspora was not, however, confined to communists and extreme nationalists. A powerful group of critics among the government's supporters, the so-called statists (*gosudarstvenniki*), developed an extensive critique of Russia's external policies focused on the absence of a policy toward the settlers.

Under sustained political attack, the Russian government's initial vision of Russia's relationship with the world was revised at the end of 1992. Leading exponents of the "Atlanticist" vision of external relations were removed from the government. Alongside the previous set of priorities, relations with the former Soviet republics were given greater emphasis. Significantly, the assertion that Russia had an obligation and a right to protect the settler populations emerged as a leading element in the new foreign policy agenda.

The Construction of the Diaspora

The first phase of the development of post-independence Russian foreign policy concluded with an important shift in Russia's external orientation; relations with the former Soviet republics began to receive more attention from the end of 1992. Central to this shift was an acceptance among the Russian political elite of the principle that the Russian state was organically linked to the settler communities and bore responsibility for their well-being. Before this idea could have practical significance, however, the basis of Russia's relationship to the settlers needed elaboration. In the second phase of Russian diaspora politics (winter 1992–autumn 1993), the ideas that the Russian government's critics had earlier articulated about Russia's responsibility to the settler communities coalesced as official policy. As part of this process, the status of the settler communities was transformed into that of a "Russian diaspora."

An important problem that faced those who sought to develop a policy toward the settler populations was the difficulty of establishing just whom exactly Russia was claiming a special right to protect. The ill-defined nature of the Russian ethnic and national community and the complex socio-economic and cultural basis of the settler populations meant that the boundaries of the diaspora were unclear. Although many Russian nationalists spoke of an ethnic Russian diaspora (*russkaia diaspora*), this narrow definition failed to capture the multi-ethnic linguistic, economic, and political essence of the settler communities.[24]

In response to the important cultural–linguistic character of the settler communities and to policies which aimed to weaken the position of the Russian language in the newly independent states, a linguistic definition of the diaspora also enjoyed popularity among many journalists and politicians. The ambiguity inherent in the term "Russian-speakers" (*russkoiazychne*), and the fact that the vast majority of the Soviet population could be considered Russian-speaking (including many of those thought to be threatening the settlers), meant that for the purpose of developing policy such a definition of the diaspora was largely meaningless.

While the complex ethnic and socio-cultural basis of the settler communities ensured that developing a clear definition of the diaspora proved difficult, the uncertain nature of Russian identity within the Russian Federation also placed considerable restraints on Russia's ability to define a Russian diaspora. The powerful challenge to centralized state authority within the Russian Federation mounted by ethnic communities such as the Tatars and the Chechens made the development of an inclusive and territorially defined notion of modern Russian nationhood and statehood imperative.[25]

With the Russian Federation propelled into operating with a largely civic notion of the Russian nation, the task of developing a single term to define the diaspora and establish Russia's link to the settlers was further complicated. Was the Russian state to defend all ethnic groups with a homeland within Russia, for example, Lezgins in Azerbaijan? If the diaspora was to be defined more narrowly—Slavs and Europeans—how could this be reconciled with the multi-ethnic and multi-confessional character of the Russian Federation? The tension at the heart of competing notions of the diaspora led initially to the adoption of the oxymoron "ethnic citizens of Russia" (*etnicheskie rossiiane*) to describe the settlers in Russian policy documents.[26] Nevertheless, despite the ambiguous nature of the "Russian" communities and of Russia's links to the settlers, in the second phase of diaspora politics the notion of Russia's innate obligation to its diaspora became widespread and uncontested in Russian domestic politics.

Russia as Kin-State

In the third phase of diaspora politics (winter 1993–winter 1995), a concerted effort was made to promote Russia's ties to the russified communities through a series of policy initiatives. The success of Vladimir Zhirinovsky in the parliamentary elections of December 1993 prompted the Russian government to adopt a far more active policy toward the settler communities.[27] In autumn 1994 support for a definition of the Russian nation that included the russified settlers was signaled by the introduction of a comprehensive government policy toward the Russian diaspora.[28] Henceforth, the Russian state was to have a direct responsibility for the well-being of the newly invented diaspora.

The emergence of an explicit commitment to the settler communities was matched by progress in defining the nature of the diaspora. The term "compatriot" (*sootechestvennik*) now emerged as the standard official term to describe members of the diaspora. Although ambiguous, it held advantages over other terms. "Compatriot" is neutral in an ethnic and cultural sense and draws instead upon the notion of fatherland (*otechestvo*). By linking the diaspora to the Russian state rather than directly to the problematic Russian nation, employing this term restored the political element that had previously defined the settler communities.[29]

The politico-historical definition of the diaspora also dovetailed with the effort to construct a civic notion of the Russian nation in the Russian Federation. Within this project, citizenship (*grazhdanstvo*) rather than ethnicity formed the basis for defining the Russian national community.[30] From early 1994, securing agreements on dual citizenship with the post-Soviet states therefore became the main priority of Russian diaspora policy.[31] Ultimately, however, only the Central Asian states of Turkmenistan and Tajikistan agreed to such arrangements, although Kazakhstan and Kyrgyzstan adopted highly flexible citizenship arrangements with the Russian Federation.[32] Russian citizenship was offered to all former citizens of the Soviet Union, leading to the emergence of sizable populations of Russian citizens in some areas, notably in Estonia and Crimea.[33]

The Waning of Diaspora Politics

The final major period of change in the development of the diaspora issue in the Russian Federation (spring 1996–summer 1997) was characterized by a less assertive approach to the diaspora by the Russian government. With the settler communities tied to the Russian state and defined, however uncertainly, as a part of the Russian nation, the symbolic value of the diaspora declined within Russian domestic politics. Unable to criticize the government over policies toward the settlers, the opposition began to focus on other issues.[34]

Although the settler question receded from political debate, the diaspora and Russia's ties to the Russian communities continued to exert an

Diaspora becomes a tool of many areas of F.P – border disputes, NATO expansion, CIS integration, domestic affairs of CIS countries

Neil J. Melvin

important influence on political relationships in the former Soviet Union. Russia's responsibility for the diaspora became an uncontested principle of Russian interstate policy and an element that frequently served to legitimate Russia's other political, military, and economic interests, including border disputes with Estonia, NATO expansion, and integration within the CIS.[35] On occasion, Moscow also sought to influence the domestic affairs of the other post-Soviet states where new policies caused alarm within the settler communities.[36]

little of substance done in last 5 years

Despite the formal commitment to the development of relations with the diaspora signaled in the government program of 1994, lack of resources and uncertainty about just who constituted the diaspora meant that very little in the way of concrete measures was undertaken in the first five years of independence. In response to this inaction, some sections of the Russian legislature sought to keep the settler issue on the political agenda.[37] In December 1995 dissatisfaction about progress in relation to the diaspora prompted the Duma to pass a "declaration in support of the Russian [*rossiiskii*] diaspora and Russian compatriots."[38]

495 – broader definition

Discontent with official notions of the diaspora, and particularly the over-reliance on citizenship as the means of establishing a link to the settlers, led the framers of the declaration to seek to broaden the definition of the diaspora. In the declaration it was stated that "the Russian [*rossiiskii*] diaspora" consists of all of those who (1) have "issued from [*vykhodets*]" the Russian empire, Russia, the RSFSR, and the Soviet Union, and their direct descendants irrespective of their national or ethnic affiliation, their occupation, place of residence, or citizenship, and (2) recognize a spiritual or cultural–ethnic link with the Russian Federation or any of its subject territories.

where '97 bill

In early 1997 an attempt was made to build on the declaration of December 1995 by introducing legislation on the diaspora that would force the Russian government to take a more active approach to the settler issue.[39] The draft legislation utilized the broad definition of the Russian diaspora proposed in the declaration and incorporated extensive rights for members of the diaspora. Disagreement between liberal and communist factions in the Duma about the details of the legislation and the priorities of parliament's activities—as well as opposition from the Council of the Federation and the executive on the grounds of the costs involved in the legislation and the likelihood that the law would stimulate mass migration to Russia—eventually led to the failure of the bill. The collapse of legislation on the diaspora left Russia's links to the settler communities lacking a clearly defined basis and with little in the way of concrete substance.

Despite the lack of progress in the development of a coherent set of policies toward the russified settler communities, the diaspora issue nevertheless played a vital role in post-Soviet politics. Diaspora politics did not, however, lead to the emergence of a developed relationship between Russia and the settler communities. Instead, the significance of the diaspora issue lay in its links with elite politics in the Russian Federation and in the struggle conducted by elements of the political elite to determine the future trajectory of Russia's development.

In the early years of independence, Russian domestic politics provided the crucible for forging a new notion of the Russian nation and for establishing the role of the Russian state in the post-Soviet world. Central to this process was transforming the russified settler communities into a Russian diaspora and linking these communities to the Russian Federation, which became a homeland for the diaspora. The notion of Russia as a diasporic state became a central element of modern Russia's identity—a nation and state with extensive responsibilities to protect and enhance the Russian diaspora across the Eurasian land mass. With such responsibility, of course, came the burden of being a "great power" and of having to provide "leadership" and "guidance" to neighboring states.

Most significantly, the post-Soviet Russian political elite embraced the settler communities as an extension of the Russian nation and an important responsibility of the Russian state. The development of the concept of the diaspora served to help cement a new ruling elite; it provided a common sense of identity and purpose, and justified the assertion that Russia had a leading role to play in the postcommunist world.[40] Reflecting this evolving vision of Russia's connection to the settler communities, in the early years of independence a range of organizations and institutions was created within the executive, legislature, and society at large in order to provide links to the diaspora.[41] The institutionalization of Russia's relationship to the diaspora ensured that the development of a new Russia was shaped by its image as a diasporic state.[42]

However, as Zevelev has noted, "Contrary to the belief that Russian policy in the 'Near Abroad' has been imperialistic and aggressive over issues concerning the new Russian diaspora, we find that Russian policy has instead been reasonably moderate in some of its features and tremendously ineffective in others."[43] While the desire of key members of the Russian government to develop interstate relations on the basis of international law, rather than through ethno-nationalism, contributed significantly to the moderate direction of Russian policy, the colonial legacy also played a critical role.

The weakly articulated nature of Russian ethnic and national identity, along with the multi-ethnic nature of the Russian Federation, established a political environment in which a strategy of nation and state building within the borders of present-day Russia was the most viable solution to domestic problems.[44] At the same time, the russified settler communities proved largely incapable of organizing themselves because they lacked effective indigenous ethno-cultural or political identities and institutions. The new states and societies of the former Soviet Union, however, also played a leading role in shaping the issue of the russified settler communities.

The Russian Diaspora and the Newly Independent States

During the perestroika period, the nationalizing processes that had been initiated within the Russian empire and Soviet Union were accelerated. Ethnic and national identities were enhanced, often within the context of an ethno-nationalist mobilization against "Russian" rule and the instruments and symbols of that rule: the russified settler communities, Russian culture, the Russian language, and a russocentric version of history. From the late 1980s, republican laws on citizenship and naturalization, language and education, political and social organization, the control of economic resources, and state service redefined the relationship of the settler communities to the states of the region.

The creation in 1991 of new states principally legitimated by the right of the titular nations to self-determination marked a dramatic reversal of fortune for the russified settlers and a challenge to the primacy of Russian culture and language. Along with state-induced change, the actions of societal actors and conflicts at the local level also helped to transform the situation of the settlers. As a result of these dramatic changes, the leading position that settlers had previously enjoyed was challenged in fundamental ways. In response, new links developed between the settler communities and the Russian Federation .

Although the settlers faced a range of problems, the combination of issues, the degree to which each community experienced a particular problem, and the form of settler response to the new situation varied considerably. The perception within the Russian Federation that Russian diaspora communities faced a sustained and comprehensive set of threats disguised the emergence of a complex pattern of problems, relationships, and reactions to the changes of the perestroika and independence periods among the settler communities within each republic.[45]

The Baltic States

To a significant degree, the emergence of a notion of the diaspora was a response to the situation that developed around the russified settler communities in the Baltic states of Latvia and Estonia in the early 1990s. As a result of the intense nationalist mobilization that occurred in the Baltic states in the late 1980s, which was in large part a response to high levels of russified settler migration to the region, the newly independent states of Latvia and Estonia developed sets of policies intended to transform the position of the settler communities. Most important was the introduction of laws based on restrictive definitions of citizenship, definitions that subsequently served as the basis for the allocation of economic, political, and employment rights.[46] These laws created a formidable set of practical and psychological hurdles for the settlers to cross if they were to become equal members of the Baltic societies.

Russia's accusation that the settlers faced discrimination as a result of the introduction of these laws was not substantiated by the international community, although the Baltic states were required to redraft some legislation to meet international norms. Nevertheless, there can be no doubt that laws adopted in Estonia and Latvia were intended to prevent the majority of the settler community from integrating into the newly independent societies. The economic prosperity of the Baltic region compared to the rest of the former Soviet Union, however, helped to offset the discomfort felt by the settler communities, and the region experienced relatively low levels of settler out-migration following independence.

The large number of settlers who adopted Russian citizenship but elected to remain resident in the region is testimony to the complex relationship that exists between the russified settlers and the Baltic states. Moreover, the presence of settler enclaves with chronic socio-economic problems and a strong residue of pro-Soviet identity (notably in the northeastern region of Estonia) has ensured that the Baltic governments continue to face important obstacles in their drive to establish economically prosperous, politically stable, and pro-western societies.[47]

The Western Borderlands

The experience of settler communities in Moldova, Ukraine, and Belarus was, after Estonia and Latvia, the most significant in shaping notions of the Russian diaspora and Russian policy toward the settler communities. Within the Soviet Union, the integration of the Russian communities within the western republics was generally high. In Ukraine and Belarus, the close cultural and linguistic links between Russians, Ukrainians, and Belarusians ensured that migrants to these republics had little or no sense that they were settling in alien lands. The establishment of independent states affected perceptions of the settler communities in two distinct ways.

First, a military conflict in 1992 (interpreted in Russia as an ethnic conflict) in the Transdniester region of Moldova and rising tension in Ukraine around the issue of the Russian language, the status of the Crimean peninsula, and fears of ukrainianization enhanced the sense of an external Russian community under threat—a view of events that had already been established by developments in the Baltic region. Second, in contrast to the cases of Ukraine and Moldova, Belarus confirmed a sense in Russia that Slav lands were an inextricable part of Russia, artificially divided by anti-Russian nationalists. Within Belarus, the absence of a strong Belarusian identity permitted the emergence of a movement for integration with the Russian Federation. In this context, there is very little sense that the Russians in Belarus constitute a diaspora community.

Belarussian Russians don't constitute a diaspora (?)

Central Asia

Immediately following independence, the sizable settler communities in Central Asia did not figure to any significant degree in the debate about the Russian diaspora. Although the Central Asian states introduced laws on language and sovereignty in 1989 and 1990, these measures were largely in response to initiatives taken elsewhere in the Soviet Union. The relatively low level of ethno-nationalist mobilization in Central Asia during perestroika ensured that the settler communities did not face the same pressures that were manifest in the western regions. Subsequently, however, Central Asia emerged as one of the key arenas for the development of diaspora politics. The form of settlement in the region compared to other parts of the former Soviet Union and the instability that characterized the region following independence provided the basis for this shift.

The main thrust of settlement by Slavs and Europeans in Central Asia took place over a hundred and fifty years, with intensive settlement at the turn of the nineteenth century and in the years immediately following the Second World War. The settlers in Central Asia, with the exception of those in northeast Kazakhstan, did not develop the strong sense of attachment to territory found in regions of Ukraine, Moldova, and the Baltic states. The lack of an association between communities and territory within Central Asia in part explains why settler demands for territorial autonomy were muted.[48]

The settler communities that developed within Central Asia during the Russian and Soviet periods functioned as melting pots for Slavic and European migrants, particularly where the settlers concentrated in enclaves. The cultural differences between the settler communities and the native populations, and the myths of superiority and civilization that were propagated within the settler communities, ensured that barriers between settler and native populations were often greater than in other regions under Moscow's control. The gulf between the two communities was further reinforced by the employment structure in the region, with the settlers occupying the more advanced and high-status sectors of society while the native population was concentrated in the rural areas.

From the 1960s the russified settlers began to face increased competition from upwardly mobile indigenes as a result of demographic shifts in favor of the native population, rural–to–urban migration, and the penetration of representatives of the native population into leading republican-level political and economic institutions. The challenge to the local settler communities brought about by these changes fostered an out-migration from the region that preceded the upheavals of the 1980s and reversed the dynamic of settlement that had been established in the early nineteenth century.

With independence, the issue of the settler populations in Central Asia began to develop in directions different from those found in other regions of the former Soviet Union. While the policies pursued by states in the region toward the settlers were of a generally inclusive nature—with broadly defined citizenship laws, favorable legislation on the status of the Russian language, some provision for dual citizenship, and public support from Central Asian leaders for a continued Russian presence—in the early years of independence there were significant out-migrations from the Central Asian states.[49] Ethnic conflicts involving other groups in the region, the collapse of the state in Tajikistan and Afghanistan, an Islamic renaissance, and poor economic prospects caused concern among the settlers. Formal and informal policies of nativization also threatened to displace the settlers from their previous domination of high-status employment, encouraging professionals, specialists, and the younger generation to migrate to the Russian Federation or farther abroad.[50] Although the situation stabilized after the initial wave of migration, a further flight from the region cannot be excluded.

Transcaucasia

The Transcaucasus region did not initially play a significant role in the debate about the Russian diaspora because of the nature of Russian settlement in the area. While Russian military conquest of the region wa similar to that undertaken in Central Asia, the form of colonial control was different. Whereas Central Asia became a magnet for skilled urban

Slavs and Europeans from the end of the nineteenth century onward, Transcaucasia did not experience such a large migration. Instead, a relatively small group of russified settlers arrived in the region to undergird Moscow's control.

With the exception of Baku, which became the center for a sizable settler community, the settlers did not dominate the indigenous populations to the same extent as elsewhere in the Soviet Union. In comparison to Central Asia, the societies in the Transcaucasus region were more advanced, particularly with respect to the development of notions of nationalism. As a result, russified migrants to the region faced strong indigenous competition for high-status positions almost from the moment of their arrival. Competition with the settlers intensified during the 1970s and 1980s, prompting an out-migration from the region well before the events of the late 1980s.

In the early 1990s, the strong ethno-nationalist character of the independence movements in the region, the Armenia–Azerbaijan war, armed conflicts in Georgia over Abkhazia and South Ossetia, and general political instability in Georgia and Azerbaijan fostered a further out-migration of russified settlers. The rise of nationalist sentiments in the region did, however, have an important impact on the development of the notion of the Russian diaspora. Some of the first explicitly Russian diaspora organizations in the former Soviet Union were created in the Transcaucasus, and it was these groups that made contact with political figures in the Russian Federation in the early 1990s.[51]

Determinants of Russian Diaspora Politics

Despite large emigrations from the Russian empire beginning in the late nineteenth century, the notion of a Russian diaspora only emerged after the collapse of the Soviet system. The development of this idea has been complex, and behind it lies a highly variegated set of processes and outcomes across the territory of the former Soviet Union. Indeed, close examination of the russified settler communities suggests that it is difficult to talk of a single diaspora. Instead, there are competing and imprecise definitions operating simultaneously and reflecting the situation in different locations and the aims and perspectives of different actors.

The Policies of the Russian State

The development of a Russian diaspora was crucially shaped by the historic links between the Russian community and the hegemonic states of

Eurasia. Within the colonial political system, the Russian community served to support the extension of the imperial state into new areas, tethering conquered territory to the imperial core and partly assimilating minorities as they were incorporated into the empire. With the collapse of the Soviet order, finding a formula to re-establish a link between Russia and the settlers initially proved difficult.

The territorial notion of Russia that underlay the Russian democratic movement's political agenda appeared to undermine the notion that Russia could have a diaspora. Reflecting the historic growth of the Russian community within the Russian and Soviet imperial orders, the Russian government sought to solve this dilemma by defining the diaspora primarily in terms of a relationship to the Russian state rather than to a Russian ethnic group. The basis for Russia's relationship to its diaspora, however, remained problematic, with important areas of tension between competing territorial and ethnic understandings of Russia and the diaspora.

Initially, the construction of a diasporic community in the imaginings of Russian politicians was not matched by the emergence of a diaspora in reality. Instead, the needs of elite consolidation provided the primary driving force behind the development of diaspora politics. The emergence of a consensus in Russian domestic politics on the existence of a diaspora served as the prelude to the transformation of the Russian Federation into a diasporic state. The establishment of this image of Russia served a twofold end. The development of the concept of the diasporic state helped to establish a broad consensus among the Russian elite about Russia's place in the world. At the same time, the idea of a diaspora provided a foundation for Russia to construct new policies toward the former Soviet republics following the breakdown of colonial control over these territories.

The emergence of the Russian Federation as a diasporic state, with a range of external commitments stemming from the presence of a section of the Russian nation outside Russian borders, also provided the basis for the Russian state and society to be shaped as a Russian homeland. With the establishment of the infrastructure of a diasporic state, Russia launched a series of activities to diasporize the russified settler communities themselves. State policy, institutions, public associations, and political parties within Russia were created to help foster a diaspora identity within the settler communities.

The activity of Russian state and public organizations toward the settlers helped to foster a sense among the settler communities that they indeed belonged to a *rossiiskii* diaspora and that the Russian Federation constituted their homeland. The nationalizing process induced by Russian policy was, however, hampered by the ethno-cultural structure of the settler communities, Russia's limited resources, and some resistance to the diaspora as a foreign policy priority among sections of the Russian elite. The nationalization of the settlers was not, however, solely a product of Russian actions and interstate relations. Indeed, in most respects developments within the newly independent states were more important to the emergence of a diaspora identity within the settler communities.

The Post-Soviet Environment

From the late 1980s, the socio-economic position, cultural identity, and political organization of the settler communities were redefined by the activity of the governments and populations of the newly independent states. The particular forms that the russified settler communities adopted in the former Soviet republics were shaped by the interaction of three sets of factors: the form of settlement that developed in a particular region during the Russian/Soviet empire, the range of policies adopted to structure ethnic relations, and developments in inter-ethnic relations at the societal level.

Of particular significance to the development of the russified communities from the late 1980s was the type of settlement that was undertaken within the Russian and Soviet orders. The size of the settler communities, the history of migration to a particular region, the ethnic composition of the settler communities, the socio-economic position of the settlers within each society, and the degree of cultural cleavage with the indigenous community all played critical roles in the settler issue.

While forms of settlement shaped developments from the late 1980s, the policies pursued by the new governments of each republic were equally important in fashioning ethnic and national identities after independence. Definitions of citizenship, laws on language and education, and specific policies designed to promote various ethno-cultural identities arose in response to the various nation and state building projects in the former Soviet republics.

The final set of factors that influenced the development of the settler communities was the broad and often long-term processes of social and economic change in each republic. Demographic shifts, intensification of rural–urban migration patterns, and "bottom–up" processes of nativization, economic dislocation, and religious and cultural revival all occurred in the former Soviet republics, although to different degrees and in differing combinations.[52]

The Settler Response

Collectively these factors, along with the activity of Russia, produced diverse responses among the russified settlers, as well as competitive conceptions of "Russianness." The russified settlers reacted to their changing situation in three broad patterns: flight, integration, and resistance.[53] From the late 1980s there was a substantial out-migration of russified settlers from the former Soviet republics. For potential migrants, however, uncertainty about the homeland (should Ukrainians in Kazakhstan move to Russia or Ukraine?), their resettlement rights, and prospects for integrating into a new community created obstacles.[54]

In most republics, forms of co-existence between the settler communities and the new political regimes emerged. The fundamentally new situation following independence, however, involved significant readjustments within the settler communities. Even under the most benign regimes, settlers were required to adjust to a new citizenship, declining opportunities for monolingual Russian-speakers, and increased competition for the high-status positions in society.

Finally, in a number of the newly independent states the settler communities, or parts of the communities, undertook active resistance to change. In the most extreme cases, confrontation and even conflict developed. The settlers, however, faced difficulties in following the path of resistance because they lacked the ethno-cultural forms necessary for political mobilization that were available to other groups. The heterogeneous nature of the migrants from the Russian imperial core ensured that the settler communities developed around complex and diverse patterns of linguistic, ethnic, and socio-economic interaction, and functioned as ethnic melting pots within the colonial order. This was particularly the case in the Soviet period when supranational communist and Soviet identities served as alternatives to full assimilation to Russian culture. Establishing organizations and cultural identities common to all settlers often proved difficult. In a number of cases, Slavic cultural organizations provided a basis for political mobilization (e.g., *Lad*, a Slavic political movement established in Kazakhstan in the early 1990s), but the political cohesion that such groups could provide proved short lived.

Initially, the settler economic elite in some regions provided the basis for a more active resistance to the nationalizing policies of the newly independent states (e.g., the regions of Transdniester in Moldova and Narva in Estonia). The opportunities for such resistance declined as privatization and economic decline struck at the basis of the settler economy (the former all–union economy). Lacking the ethno-cultural basis for political opposition, integrated elites, and economic resources, the settler populations often adopted a passive acceptance of the changes that were imposed upon them.

Conclusion

Although the development of the Russian diaspora from the late 1980s did not bear out the pessimistic predictions of some writers, the issue nonetheless played a critical role in determining the trajectory of the post-Soviet states. Moreover, the Russian diaspora question is far from resolved. To a significant degree, the relatively stable development of the settler issue has been contingent upon the weak nature of Russian identity. Since the late 1980s, both the former Soviet states and the Russian Federation have been engaged in projects to remake identity and loyalty within the settler populations through a range of policies. These policies have begun to forge alternative notions of Russian identity that may become the basis for more effective forms of political mobilization in the future. *how useful are the various versions of ied?*

Notes

1. The scale of Russian settlement across the Eurasian land mass meant that with the creation of the post-Soviet states, sizable russified communities found themselves separated from the former imperial metropole by new state borders. In the 1989 Soviet census, 25 million individuals resident outside the Russian Federation identified themselves as ethnically Russian, and millions more claimed a Russian linguistic affiliation. For a review of the size and distribution of the settler communities, see Chauncy Harris, "The New Russian Minorities: A Statistical Overview," *Post-Soviet Geography* 34, no. 1 (1993): 1–27.

2. In this chapter the term "russified settler communities" is preferred to "russophones," "Russian diaspora," or simply "Russians," terms which are more usually employed to describe these communities in the former Soviet Union. "Russified settlers" is used here for a number of reasons:

First, the "Russian" communities are in fact composed of a variety of ethnic groups, but Russian language and culture are dominant.

Second, the russified communities were not primarily organized around ethnicity. In the imperial system, the form and function of the russified communities were primarily political. The settler communities developed as a basic element of imperial expansion and consolidation. This history continues to exert an important influence on contemporary developments. Ethnic and national identities remain ill-defined among the settlers, and describing these communi-ties as Russian is, therefore, both inaccurate and misleading.

Third, understanding the potential for political mobilization within the set-tler communities involves identifying structures that might serve as potential bases for political action. The second-order significance of Russian ethnicity and the complex interaction of various ethnic communities within the settler popula-tions have meant that ethnicity has not functioned as a political resource. In-stead, issues such as threats to Russian language rights have been the primary impetus for mobilization across ethnic boundaries.

Fourth, the use of the term "Russian diaspora" often has a tendentious char-acter. The emergence of the idea of a Russian diaspora has served various politi-cal interests.

Fifth, while the Russian language is clearly a central element in the settler communities, to term these populations "russophone" can be misleading. Lan-guage is only one dimension of identity formation among the settlers, and it is not simply challenges to Russian language rights that have prompted political activism within settler populations. Policies that undermine the economic posi-tion of the settlers have also caused significant reaction. In addition, in some areas (for example, Kazakhstan), Russian is the dominant language among the indigenous elite as well as the Slavic/European/Russian populations, suggest-ing a linguistically based interpretation of politics in these areas would be inac-curate.

To use the label "russified settlers" is not to claim that the right of these communities to reside in the new states is any less than that of the titular popu-lations. Nor is it to deny that some "settler" communities are based on popula-tions that have deep historic roots or, indeed, may be considered indigenous in a region (for example, Belarus and Ukraine). The term "russified settlers" is em-ployed because it more clearly captures the political character and functions of these communities within the modern imperial history of Eurasia and the con-tinued relevance of this history for the contemporary period. Any term used to categorize these communities will inevitably have disadvantages. Moreover, as the newly independent states develop and the russified settler populations are altered as a result of political and economic change, new terms that capture the essence of these communities will be required.

3. More than any other single phenomenon, the russified communities ap-peared to hold the key to a range of critical issues in the territory of the former Soviet Union, including the extent of the power to be wielded by the new states, the nature of nationalism in the region and the role of minority rights, the sig-nificance of international borders, and the form of relations among the newly independent states. Brubaker offers a considered analysis of the parallels be-tween the German and Russian diasporas. Rogers Brubaker, *Nationalism Re-framed: Nationhood and the National Question in the New Europe* (Cambridge: Cambridge University Press, 1996), 107–47.

4. While the focus of this chapter is on the "external diaspora" of Russian communities outside Russia, there are also important Russian communities within the non-Russian ethnic republics of the Russian Federation which devel-

oped with imperial expansion. The issues of the internal and external diaspora are interlinked, and together these two sides of the Russian diaspora are critical to the question of forging a new Russian national identity.

5. For an analysis of the competing and changing definition of Russia and Russian lands, see Ladis Kristoff, "The Geographical Image of the Fatherland: The Case of Russia," *Western Political Quarterly* 20, no. 4 (1967): 941–54; and Mark Bassin, "Russia between Europe and Asia: The Ideological Construction of Geographical Space," *Slavic Review* 50, no. 1 (1991): 1–17.

6. Historically, the boundaries between the three Slav communities of the Russians, Ukrainians, and Belarusians were often ill-defined. As Tishkov has noted, being baptized Russian Orthodox was often a sufficient qualification for being considered Russian, even if one's parents identified with a different ethnic group. Valery Tishkov, *Ethnicity, Nationalism and Conflict in and after the Soviet Union: The Mind Aflame* (London: Sage, 1997), 249. It is, however, important to note that a Russian identity became more significant in the late Russian imperial period, often accompanied by the suppression of other Slavic identities (notably Ukrainian). Within the Russian empire, the term "foreigners" (*inorodtsy*) was employed to categorize the less European, usually Muslim, and often nomadic and feudal communities of the south and east of the empire.

7. Rogers Brubaker, "Nationhood and the National Question in the Soviet Union and Post-Soviet Eurasia: An Institutionalist Account," *Theory and Society* 23, no. 1 (1994): 47–78; and idem, "Political Dimensions of Migration From and Among Soviet Successor States," in Myron Weiner, ed., *International Migration and Security* (Boulder: Westview, 1993), 39–64.

8. I thank Pål Kolstø for pointing out that the process of moving into the settler communities was itself a means to russify large numbers of non-Russian migrants, particularly those from regions within modern Ukraine and Belarus.

9. Paul Kolstoe, *Russians in the Former Soviet Republics* (London: Hurst, 1995), 14–40.

10. Jeff Chinn and Robert Kaiser, *Russians as the New Minority: Ethnicity and Nationalism in the Soviet Successor States* (Boulder: Westview, 1996), 44–51.

11. Although there were important ethno-nationalist elements to the nationalizing drive, there is evidence that the Russian national community at a popular level was developing around a multicultural and cosmopolitan view of Russianness. Jeffrey Brooks, *When Russia Learned to Read: Literacy and Popular Literature, 1861–1917* (Princeton: Princeton University Press, 1985), 216, 241. Indeed, Sunderland has noted that the complex relationship between Russian settler communities and the indigenous population, especially in border regions, led on occasion to the partial assimilation of the Russians by native peoples. Willard Sunderland, "Russians into Yakuts? 'Going Native' and Problems of Russian National Identity in the Siberian North, 1870s–1914," *Slavic Review* 55, no. 4 (1996): 806–25.

12. Richard Pipes, *The Formation of the Soviet Union: Communism and Nationalism, 1917–1923*, new rev. ed. (Cambridge: Harvard University Press, 1997).

13. For a discussion of the imperial character of the Soviet state, see Mark R. Beissinger, "The Persisting Ambiguity of Empire," *Post-Soviet Affairs* 11, no. 2 (1995): 149–84; Ronald Grigor Suny, "Ambiguous Categories: States, Empires and Nations," *Post-Soviet Affairs* 11, no. 2 (1995): 185–96; Walter Kolarz, *Russia and Her Colonies* (New York: Praeger, 1952); Dominic Lieven, "The Russian Empire and the Soviet Union as Imperial Polities," *Journal of Contemporary History* 30, no. 4 (1995): 607–36; Alexander J. Motyl, "From Imperial Decay to Imperial Collapse: The Fall of the Soviet Empire in Comparative Perspective," in Richard L. Rudolph and David F. Good, eds., *Nationalism and Empire: The Habsburg Monarchy and the Soviet Union* (New York: St. Martin's Press, 1992), 15–43; Karen Dawisha and Bruce Parrott, eds., *The End of Empire? The Transformation of the USSR in Comparative Perspective* (Armonk: M. E. Sharpe, 1997), 3–29, 65–93, 243–60.

14. Frederick Barghoorn, *Soviet Russian Nationalism* (New York: Oxford University Press, 1956), 3–91.

15. For rates of assimilation, see S. Bruk and V. Kabuzan, "Dinamika chislennosti i rasseleniia russkikh posle Velikoi oktiabr'skoi sotsialisticheskoi revoliutsii,' *Sovetskaia etnografiia*, no. 5 (1982): 3–21; and Robert Lewis, Richard Rowland, and Ralph Clem, *Nationality and Population Change in Russia and the USSR* (New York: Praeger, 1976), 216. Although the 1920s and early 1930s were a time of particularly significant re-identification to Russian ethnicity, this process was important throughout most of the Soviet period. The introduction of bureaucratic checks on re-identification during the 1930s, however, slowed the expansion of the Russian community through the assimilation of other groups.

16. Bruk and Kabuzan, *Dinamika*, 3–21; I. Gurich, "Sovremennye napravleniia etnicheskikh protsessov v SSSR," *Sovetskaia etnografiia*, no. 4 (1972): 16–33; and John B. Dunlop, "Will a Large-Scale Migration of Russians to the Russian Republic Take Place Over the Current Decade?" *International Migration Review* 27, no. 3 (1993): 605–29.

17. Szporluk has noted that as late as 1917 the Russian population remained divided along several fault lines, with the peasantry in particular lacking a developed Russian identity. Roman Szporluk, "The Fall of the Tsarist Empire and the USSR: The Russian Question and Imperial Overextension," in Dawisha and Parrott, eds., *The End of Empire?*, 73–74. The high geographical mobility that accompanied the Soviet modernization drive led to large numbers moving into urban areas and to new regions. In these new surroundings, a range of identities (including a Soviet one) was available over and above a Russian identity.

18. Iu. V. Arutiunian, ed., *Russkie: etno-sotsiologicheskie ocherki* (Moscow: Nauka, 1992).

19. Leokardia Drobizheva, "*Perestroika* and the Ethnic Consciousness of Russians," in Gail Lapidus, Viktor Zaslavsky, and Philip Goldman, eds., *From Union to Commonwealth: Nationalism and Separatism in the Soviet Republics* (Cambridge: Cambridge University Press, 1992), 98–113.

20. Estonia—especially Narva; Latvia—especially Daugavpils; Moldova—especially Transdniester; Ukraine—especially the eastern regions; and Kazakhstan—especially the northeast.

21. The transformation of the Russian settler populations into a diaspora community is described in Neil Melvin, *Forging the New Russian Nation: Russian Foreign Policy and the Russian-Speaking Communities of the Former USSR*, Discussion Paper 50 (London: Royal Institute of International Affairs, 1994). For the broader context of the debate about the diaspora, see Margot Light, "Foreign Policy Thinking," in Neil Malcolm, Alex Pravda, Roy Allison, and Margot Light, *Internal Factors in Russian Foreign Policy* (Oxford: Oxford University Press, 1996), 33–100.

22. The fears of a large-scale migration to the Russian Federation that pervaded the Russian government in the early years of independence were the product of the dire predictions about mass population movements that began to appear in the Russian press. For a more considered view of the potential for migration, see the article by Viktor Perevedentsev in *Moskovskie novosti*, no. 41 (October 1992): 9.

23. In this first phase of the evolution of post-independence policy, criticism of the government was strengthened by a series of developments within the post-Soviet states (notably the introduction in the summer of 1992 of a restrictive law on citizenship in Estonia, a conflict in Moldova centered on the Transdniester region, and growing tension around the status of the Crimean peninsula), which leading figures in the opposition movement were able to manipulate to their advantage.

24. See note 2.

25. Tishkov, *Ethnicity, Nationalism and Conflict*, 246–71.

26. The difficulty that Russian policy makers faced in developing a link between the Russian Federation and the settler populations was most clearly signaled in the presidential decree of November 1992 (*O voprosakh zashchity prav i interesov rossiiskikh grazhdan za predelami Rossiiskoi Federatsii*). The decree attempted the difficult, some might say impossible, task of linking a primarily ethnic notion of the Russian diaspora with a civic notion of the new Russian nation. The mechanism that was devised to achieve this end was the extension of Russian citizenship to all *etnicheskie rossiiane*. The Russian foreign ministry was then instructed to become more involved in the protection of the Russian citizens located in the CIS.

27. "Yeltsin Gives New Year Address With Pledge to Stand by Russian Citizens Abroad," *SWB-SU*, January 3, 1994. In a shorter address at the beginning of 1995, Yeltsin again picked out the Russians outside Russia for particular mention. "Yeltsin's New Year Address," *SWB-SU*, January 3, 1995. In a series of speeches at the beginning of 1994, the foreign minister made clear his conversion to the diaspora cause. "Kozyrev Details Russian Foreign Policy Agenda," *FBIS-SOV*, February 10, 1994, pp. 12–14; "Foreign Minister Kozyrev Outlines Parliament's Role in Foreign Policy," *SWB-SU*, February 5, 1994; "Kozyrev Warns Against Violations of Rights of Russian Minorities in Former USSR," *SWB-SU*, January 21, 1994.

28. "Ob osnovnykh napravleniakh gosudarstvennoi politiki Rossiiskoi Federatsii v otnoshenii sootechestvennikov prozhivaiushchikh za rubezhom," *Rossiiskaia gazeta*, September 22, 1994.

29. Andrei Edemsky and Paul Kolstoe, "Russia's Policy Towards the Diaspora," in Kolstoe, *Russians*, 261.

30. Russian citizens outside Russia were to form the core of the group that qualified as compatriots. See the interview with Abdullah Mikitaev, Chairman of the Presidential Commission for Questions of Citizenship, in *Diplomaticheskii vestnik*, no. 2 (1995): 52.

31. George Ginzburgs, "Citizenship and State Succession in Russia's Treaty and Domestic Repertory," unpublished paper, 1995.

32. The Ukrainian parliament adopted a new citizenship law barring dual citizenship in the republic. "Ukraine Tightens Citizenship Requirements," *OMRI Daily Digest*, November 4, 1996.

33. According to official Russian figures, in 1996 up to 800,000 people had citizenship of the Russian Federation and were resident within one of the former Soviet republics. "New Citizenship Figures Released," *OMRI Daily Digest*, January 29, 1997.

34. This was especially true when Evgenii Primakov replaced Andrei Kozyrev, the symbol of the Atlanticist viewpoint, as Russian foreign minister.

35. "Russia, Belarus Lecture Balts on Human Rights," *Jamestown Foundation Monitor*, November 25, 1996; "Developments in Russian Policy Signal Intensified Pressure," *Jamestown Foundation Monitor*, February 12, 1997.

36. For example, Russia pursued an active policy in relation to the future of the Russian language in Kazakhstan. "Kazakhhstan's Language Law Seeks to Equalize Native Language With Russian," *Jamestown Foundation Monitor*, November 26, 1996; "Kazakhh Premier Under Pressure in Moscow," *Jamestown Foundation Monitor*, November 27, 1996.

37. "Duma Backs Keeping Russian Troops in Moldova," *Jamestown Foundation Monitor*, November 14, 1996; "Federation Council Favors International Status For Sevastopol," *RFE/RL Newsline*, April 18, 1997.

38. *Deklaratsiia o podderzhke Rossiiskoi Federatsiei rossiiskoi diaspory i o pokrovitel'stve rossiiskim sootechestvennikam* (passed by the Duma on December 8, 1995).

39. *O gosudarstvennoi politike v otnoshenii sootechestvennikov v gosudarstvakh-uchastnikakh Sodruzhestva Nezavisimykh Gosudarstv, Latvii, Litvy, Estonii i drugikh stranakh (Proekt)*. In 1993 the nationalist politician Sergei Baburin had attempted to pass legislation on the diaspora. With the destruction of the Supreme Soviet in the autumn, the legislation was lost.

40. Neil Melvin, *Russians Beyond Russia: The Politics of National Identity* (London: Pinter, 1995), 22–24.

41. A range of state and semi-public institutions and organizations was established in the Russian Federation as a result of the diaspora issue, or became closely involved in the issue, after 1991. These include: the Duma Committee for CIS Affairs and Compatriots; sections of the presidential apparatus and the min-

istries of nationalities, foreign affairs, and CIS affairs; the Congress of Russian Communities political movement; the Russian Institute of Diaspora and Integration (Institute of the Near Abroad); and a large number of pressure groups.

42. The mechanisms by which the diasporic image was institutionalized within the Russian state were complex and involved competition around a diverse set of interests. For analysis of some of the key individuals and institutions in this process, see Edemsky and Kolstoe, "Russia's Policy," 268–80.

43. Igor Zevelev, "Russia and the Russian Diasporas," *Post-Soviet Affairs* 12, no. 3 (1996): 265–66.

44. John Barber, "Russia: A Crisis of Post-imperial Viability," *Political Studies* 42, special issue (1994): 46–48.

45. Reports on the diverse experience in the individual republics can be found in Chinn and Kaiser, *Russians*, 93–267; Kolstoe, *Russians*, 105–258, Pål Kolstø, "The New Russian Diaspora—An Identity of Its Own? Possible Identity Trajectories for Russians in the Former Soviet Republics," *Ethnic and Racial Studies* 19, no. 3 (1996): 622–32; and Melvin, *Russians*, 25–123.

46. Erik André Andersen, "The Legal Status of Russians in Estonian Privatization Legislation 1989–1995," *Europe–Asia Studies* 49, no. 2 (1997): 303–16.

47. "Latvian President Warns of Growing Ethnic Tension," *RFE/RL Newsline*, July 11, 1997.

48. Northern and eastern regions of Kazakhstan are important exceptions. The size and history of colonial settlement of these areas have established a strong commitment to the northern steppe territories among the russified settlers.

49. Tishkov, *Ethnicity, Nationalism and Conflict*, 115–34. Heleniak has suggested that the decline in the percentages of Russians in the Central Asian republics between 1989 and 1996 was: 3.8 percent in Kazakhstan; 5.9 percent in Kyrgyzstan; 4.2 percent in Tajikistan; 2.9 percent in Turkmenistan; and 2.7 percent in Uzbekistan. Timothy Heleniak, "Going Home: Migration Among the Soviet Successor States," *ACE: Analysis of Current Events* 9, no. 6 (1997): 5. For a discussion of the causes of Russian out-migration from Central Asia, see *Russkie v novom zarubezh'e: Kirgiziia* (Moscow: Russian Academy of Sciences, 1995).

50. Vladimir Mesamed, "Interethnic Relations in the Republic of Uzbekistan," *Central Asian Monitor*, no. 6 (1996): 24.

51. Dmitrii Rogozin, the leader of the Congress of Russian Communities, established contact with Russian organizations in Abkhazia as early as 1992. See the Archive of the Congress of Russian Communities (Moscow) on these early contacts.

52. Smith and Wilson combine a "top–down" focus on how the state, political system, and opportunity structure have affected the possibility for collective action by the russified settler communities within Ukraine and Estonia, with a "bottom–up" analysis of cultural, material, and formal organizational resources available for political mobilization. Graham Smith and Andrew Wilson, "Rethinking Russia's Post-Soviet Diaspora: The Potential for Political Mobilization in Eastern Ukraine and North-east Estonia," *Europe–Asia Studies* 49, no. 5 (1997): 845–64.

53. For a detailed analysis of the identity types of the Russian diaspora, see Kolstø, "The New Russian Diaspora," 613–22.

54. Dunlop, "Will a Large-Scale Migration," 605–29. Many settlers lack the finances for a move, do not have family links in the Russian Federation, have not got a clear place to move to, and face opposition from the local populations and difficulties with registration in Russia.

3

The Jews:
A Diaspora Within a Diaspora

Zvi Gitelman

Jews are the archetypical "diaspora" people. Exiled from their state and homeland, first in 722 and 586 B.C.E., and then in 70 C.E., they remained without a state until 1948. However, long before the Balfour declaration of 1917 promised Jews a "national home for the Jewish people" in Palestine, they regarded *Eretz Yisrael* (the Land of Israel) or Palestine not only as their historic homeland but as a place to which they would return. To others in Christian Europe, the dispersion and statelessness of the Jews confirmed that they were being punished for killing the Christ. Just as the first murderer, Cain, was marked and condemned to be a "wanderer on earth," so too were the Jews, who were judged guilty of deicide, condemned to be without a place of their own. Some Jews saw their dispersion as punishment for their sins, as the Hebrew prophets had foretold, but they were comforted by the prophetic promise of redemption and return. In the last half of the twentieth century, the Jewish diaspora has been shrinking and the Jewish population of the homeland growing. Aside from the Holocaust, which destroyed about a third of world Jewry and led many survivors to immigrate to the historic homeland, Palestine/Israel, the major cause of this trend has been the emigration of over one million Jews from the Soviet Union and its successor states, about two-thirds of whom have settled in Israel. This chapter explores the emergence of what may be a new diaspora of ex-Soviet Jews within the larger Jewish diaspora and suggests some implications of the existence of this new sub-diaspora for the larger diaspora and for Israel, as well as for the Jews remaining in the former Soviet Union.

In the nineteenth century the traditional sense of being in exile (*galut* in Hebrew, *golus* in Yiddish) was denied by assimilationists who seized upon the emancipation of west European Jewry to argue that Jews could now solve their "problem" by melding into the nations among whom they lived and finding their homelands there. Reform Judaism, which arose in the early nineteenth century in central Europe as an attempt to stem the tide of assimilation, argued that Jews were no longer a nation but were nationals of the countries in which they resided, that they constituted a religious and not an ethnic or a national group, and that Palestine was only the historic "homeland" and had no claim on Jews' affections. Rather, the homelands of Jews were now their countries of residence; Berlin was the new Jerusalem. Later, in eastern Europe, "territorialists" asserted that Jews should accept the diaspora as a permanent condition but should carve out territories for compact settlement in different parts of the diaspora. At the same time, the Jewish Labor Bund, founded in 1897, also confirmed the diaspora as a legitimate and permanent mode of Jewish existence, but looked to a world socialist revolution to solve the "Jewish problem." In the same year, the world Zionist organization was founded. Zionists rejected the diaspora as "abnormal" and the various "solutions" to the "Jewish problem" as unworkable. Only an independent state, which most Zionists understood as being located in Palestine, could solve the Jews' problems, whether political, economic, social or cultural. Zionists translated the religious ideal of a "return to Zion" into the fashionable romantic nationalist ideal of the establishment of a state for each nation. In opposition to assimilationists and Reform Jews, Zionists had no doubt that Jews constituted a nation. They advocated a state for the Jewish nation, which, unlike many of the peoples of Europe then clamoring for statehood, had once had a state and, through the medium of religion, had maintained allegiance to that state.

Religion and Ethnicity

Judaism is a "tribal" rather than "universal" religion. Unlike Christianity or Islam, which are practiced by many peoples the world over, Judaism is associated exclusively with Jews. That is, religion and ethnicity are fused, though citizenship is a distinct category. Thus, anyone who practices Judaism is assumed to be Jewish ethnically, though he or she may be French, American, Israeli, etc., by citizenship. Jews emerged in the ancient Near East where the distinction between religion and ethnicity was largely unknown. The fusion of religion and ethnicity among Jews survived the modern separation of the two identities. Therefore, religion and its attendant culture—rituals which become "national" customs or practices—were the nexus of the Jewish diaspora. The Jewish "imagined community" long predated "print capitalism;" Jews do not fit Benedict Anderson's model of the development of nationhood.[1] The "imagined community" was maintained in specific places by a combination of its cultural content and the boundaries that it and non-Jews erected to define Jewry.[2] However, trans-state national consciousness was and is maintained by religious content as well as by shared boundaries (prohibitions on intermarriage, a single faith). It is telling that while no one challenges the Jewishness of a Jewish-born atheist, the Supreme Court of Israel, a secular body, decided in 1961 in the "Brother Daniel" case that anyone who actively practices a faith other than Judaism places himself beyond the boundaries of the Jewish people.[3] The trans-state culture and religion enabled rabbis in Morocco and Poland, who had no other common culture or language, to correspond in Hebrew about a common body of law, one which regulates all aspects of life and makes Judaism a comprehensive way of life rather than a compartmentalized religion.

Secularism, which developed in eastern Europe in the late nineteenth century, began to undermine the religious nexus of the diaspora. The leading ideologue of Yiddishist secularism, Chaim Zhitlovsky, confidently asserted that a "complete revolution . . . the secularization of Jewish national and cultural life," had occurred and had been made possible by the substitution of Yiddish language and culture for religion. "The great significance of this Yiddish culture sphere is that it has succeeded in building a 'spiritual–national home,' purely secular, which can embrace Jews throughout the world . . . ." (Whether Zhitlovsky seriously thought that Sefardic Jews would adopt Yiddish, or whether he simply ignored their existence, is not clear, but telling). For Zhitlovsky, Yiddish had become the content of Jewishness. "The Yiddish language form becomes for us a content of great weight, a fundamental."[4]

An ethnic group is one whose members "share a sense of common origins, claim a common and distinctive history and destiny, possess one or more distinctive characteristics, and feel a sense of collective uniqueness and solidarity."[5] Thus, Zhitlovsky's conception posited language for the first time as the "distinctive characteristic" of the Jews, as the nexus connecting them.

At the same time, Zionism advocated the liquidation of the diaspora and the re-establishment of a Jewish state, so that the nexus would be nationhood and statehood. By 1917 there was a multilateral struggle on the nature of Jewishness: Jewish assimilationists and well-motivated non-Jews, such as Lenin, who wished to solve the "Jewish problem," advocated the disappearance of the Jews through their merger into the societies in which they lived; Reform Judaism argued that Jewishness was a religious identity only; Yiddishists such as Zhitlovsky, autonomists such as the historian Shimon Dubnov, territorialists, and Bundists affirmed the legitimacy and viability of Jewish life in the diaspora; and Zionists negated it, advocating national revival, not assimilation, as the solution to the "Jewish problem."

Jewish Identity and the Jewish Diaspora in the Soviet Period

The Bolsheviks denied that the homeland of the Jews was the historic Land of Israel and even denied the existence of a Jewish nation. As Lenin remarked as early as 1903, "The Jews have ceased to be a nation, for a nation without a territory is unthinkable."[6] Thus, he denied the existence of diaspora nations in general, and the nationhood of Jews in particular. "The idea of a Jewish nationality runs counter to the interests of the Jewish proletariat, for it fosters among them, directly or indirectly, a spirit hostile to assimilation, the spirit of the 'ghetto.'"[7] For Lenin, there was no Jewish nation, only a "Jewish problem." That "problem" could be solved by the assimilation of the Jews, meaning their acceptance by the societies in which they lived, but at the cost of their abandoning a distinct culture and identity.

The Bolshevik revolution eliminated the Zionist, Bundist, territorialist, and religious ideologies and movements, and left the Jews of Soviet Russia with two options: assimilation, recommended for all Jews in the long run and prescribed for the more "progressive" elements immediately, and a transitory secular, socialist Soviet culture based on Yiddish for those who would be slower in arriving to the promised land of socialism.[8] Either option effectively cut Soviet Jews off from the rest of the diaspora, most of which shared neither the assimilationist nor the Soviet dream (though acculturation and acceptance into the larger society were increasingly the goals of many in eastern Europe, let alone the Jews of western Europe and the immigrant masses in North and South America and Australia).

In the 1920s, parallel to the Bolsheviks' retreat from the radical ideals of "war communism" and the introduction of the New Economic Policy (NEP), there was a stepping back from the belief in instant assimilation (*sliianie* in Soviet terminology) and the immediate solution of the "Jewish problem." Some attempted to create a viable if "temporary" diaspora culture which, they argued vehemently, had nothing to do with the rest of the diaspora and its cultures, since Jews in each country had nothing in common except a distant past (irrelevant to forward-looking communists) or, for the believers, a religion (which had no place in a socialist society). Jewish communists felt obliged to differentiate the Soviet position on Yiddish from what they called "bourgeois Yiddishism" in order to prove that this was a genuinely new, Soviet Jewishness, not a reincarnation of Zhitlovsky's "spiritual–national home." They had to demonstrate that Yiddish was simultaneously an authentic Jewish expression, and hence a force for continuity, and yet a radical innovation, a distinctly Soviet phenomenon breaking with the bourgeois past.

It proved to be impossible to square the circle, though the effort was made. The new Yiddish orthography, which tried to mask the Hebrew origin of many Yiddish words and to make the language purely phonetic, was asserted to be "a kind of revolutionary symbol . . . . It shows immediately that there is a difference between the old Yiddish . . . and the new one . . . . Let people see that revolutionary means revolutionary in everything."[9] The shapers of linguistic policy were well aware of the tension between tradition and revolution. As Nochum Shtiff put it, the orthographic reform was "imbued with the spirit of October, the spirit which conducts a cultural revolution [without] being afraid of tradition."[10]

Some activists of the Jewish Sections of the Communist party claimed that a new culture, having nothing to do with pre-revolutionary Yiddishism, was being created.[11] As ideological "vigilance" increased toward the end of the 1920s, they repeated that they did not view Yiddish as *Yidish hakoidesh* (the Holy Tongue), that they were not advocating "linguistic fetishism" or "pan-Yiddishism," and that they had nothing to do with the Yiddishists of Poland, Argentina, or North America. Language, one writer asserted, is "an active means of implementing this or that class ideology." Therefore,

> struggle in the area of language is, in the final analysis, a reflection of class struggle. Yiddishism is not a linguistic school but a political tendency with a bourgeois, anti-proletarian tendency [*shtrom*]. The same is true of Hebraism, which is Zionism translated into a linguistic form. The struggle against Hebraism and Yiddishism is the struggle against bourgeois nationalism . . . an organic part of our struggle for proletarian internationalism, for Leninist nationality policy, against Zionism, Bundism . . . .[12]

The attempt to create a "proletarian" Jewish culture and cut off Soviet Jews from the rest of the diaspora—not only politically, socially, and economically, but also culturally—was doomed to failure. The overwhelming majority of Soviet Jews preferred Russian culture (or, to a lesser extent, Ukrainian, Georgian, or Central Asian culture) to the ersatz, sovietized "Jewish" culture promoted by the regime. Russian was the key to social and economic mobility. While traditional Jewish culture was thought by most to have lost its relevance, the new Soviet Jewish culture had little to recommend it—it was neither a link to tradition nor a conduit to the future. By the 1930s, when the emphasis in Soviet nationalities policy had shifted from the "flowering of the nationalities" to Russian culture and language, the regime, too, gave up on the substitute culture. The arrest of its leading creators in 1948, and the execution of many of them in 1952, destroyed this unique diaspora culture.

Another attempt was made to separate Soviet Jews from the rest of the diaspora, and indeed to destroy the perception that Jews were in a diaspora at all, by constructing a Soviet Jewish "homeland." In the 1920s the Soviet government and the Communist party had begun to settle Jews on land in Belarus, Ukraine, and the Crimea, with the aim of rehabilitating economically the *shtetl* Jewish population that had been ruined by war, revolution, and the nationalization of trade and commerce. By the late 1920s, these efforts were replaced by a much-publicized campaign to settle large numbers of Jews in Birobidzhan, just north of Manchuria. The true aim of the plan is not clear to this day, but it is reasonable to assume that Stalin, in particular, sponsored the project in order to settle a region threatened by Chinese and Japanese incursions, and perhaps to put an end to Jewish agricultural settlement in the European areas of the Soviet Union, where it was running into opposition from the local peasantry. Some have argued that Stalin knew quite well that the Jewish masses would not abandon the cities and towns of Belarus and Ukraine and the large cities of the RSFSR, from which they had been barred before 1917, for an undeveloped and remote region thousands of miles from the centers of Jewish population. His real agenda was to enlist foreign financial and political support while insuring that the plan would never come to fruition. Nevertheless, as one Jewish woman was reported to have exclaimed, Birobidzhan would be "Eretz Yisroel in unzer land!" ("The Land of Israel in our own country!").[13] If for the Reformers of a century before, Berlin was the new Jerusalem, Birobidzhan would be the new Zion for Soviet Jews. The new "homeland" attracted a great deal of publicity, both in the Soviet Union and abroad, but few settlers. Many of the pioneers who came out to Birobidzhan soon returned to their original homes. The purges of the 1930s devastated the political and cultural leadership of the area, which was declared in 1934 a Jewish autonomous region (*oblast'*) and was spoken of as a "future Jewish republic." Despite a brief flurry of settlement during and after the Second World War, Birobidzhan remained a Jewish backwater. The Jewish population of the region was never more than nine percent in the post-war era. Ironically, in the 1990s there has been substantial emigration from the Soviet Jewish homeland to the historic Zionist homeland, Israel.[14]

By the 1940s any discussion of Jewish nationhood was not only politically heretical but life-threatening. Leading Soviet Jewish cultural and social figures who proposed that, following the huge losses of the Holocaust, surviving Jews be permitted to settle in compact areas of the Crimea were purged, accused of being "bourgeois Zionists."[15] Indeed, for the most part Soviet Jews thought of the Soviet Union as their only homeland. It was only when the authorities marginalized Jews after the Second World War—accusing them of disloyalty, removing them from responsible positions, and barring their entry to military academies, political, and security posts, and many areas of higher education—that large numbers of Jews began to question whether their motherland had disowned them, whether they were political orphans or had a "real" motherland elsewhere. Stalin's charge that Jews were "rootless cosmopolitans" crystallized their dilemma: While Israel was not supposed to be their homeland, and few thought of it as such, the Soviet Union had disowned them, though they had proved their loyalty to the country and its system. They saw themselves as without a homeland after all.

Ironically, it was the vigorous anti-Zionist campaign of the 1960s and 1970s that sparked an association with the Zionist homeland among increasing numbers of Soviet Jews. When the Soviet Union unequivocally supported the Arab states in the run-up to the 1967 war, during the war itself, and during the subsequent Arab–Israeli war of 1973, people began to ask themselves how they could remain in a country which, after the murder of six million Jews in the Holocaust, supplied weapons and training to those whose avowed aim was the destruction of the Jewish state. "Until June 1967 Soviet Jews had illusions about co-existence with the regime, despite the fact that it wanted to spiritually destroy the Jews. But suddenly they realized that the Soviet government identifies with the people who want to destroy the Jewish state 'and then we knew that we would never be able to live under such a regime.'"[16] The Holocaust had led some to the conclusion that Jews could not remain in the diaspora; Soviet anti-Israel policies convinced others that they could not remain in the Soviet Union.

Though Soviet authorities tried to minimize contacts between Soviet Jews and the rest of world Jewry and, as we have seen, had even tried to deny the bases for connections between them, world Jewry did not disown the Jews of the Soviet Union. Indeed, in the 1960s world Jewry turned its attention to what it perceived as the plight of Soviet Jews, decrying the denial of educational, cultural, and religious opportunities to them and the antisemitic discrimination that they suffered from both state and society.

World Jewry became attentive to Soviet Jewry for several reasons. At a time when civil rights movements became prominent, Soviet Jewry became the "civil rights" cause of world Jewry. Second, diaspora attention to Soviet Jewry was spurred by public discussions of how world Jewry had failed to rescue European Jewry in the 1930s and 1940s.[17] Rightly or wrongly, many Jews felt that Soviet Jews needed to be "rescued" and were motivated by guilt for the failures during the Second World War. Third, western Jews—highly educated, urban, and politically involved—were generally more concerned with international affairs than most other groups in the population. Fourth, the great majority of west European and American Jews could trace their ancestry to the old Russian empire and saw Soviet Jews as their kin. More generally, there is an old tradition of transnational solidarity among Jews, including the religious obligation of *pidyon shvuyim*, the rescue of captives. The Rothschilds and such figures as Sir Moses Montefiore, who in the nineteenth century used his influence in England on behalf of Russian, Polish, Syrian, and Palestinian Jews, embodied this tradition. In that same century, English and American Jews protested the tsars' treatment of their Jewish subjects and persuaded the American government to abrogate a treaty with Russia because of Russia's treatment of Jews. Finally, like support for Israel, Soviet Jewry was a consensus issue—one of the very few—around which world Jewry could unite.[18]

World Jewry's ability to become involved with Soviet Jews, despite official efforts to discourage such involvement, was facilitated by secular shifts in the international arena. Today, more actors are included in world politics than ever before. Once the preserve exclusively of states and their leaders, international affairs and domestic affairs of foreign countries have come on to the agenda of citizens' groups, multinational corporations, international organizations, and concerned individuals. Issues such as Soviet Jewry are no longer handled by a small elite which formulates a policy and presents it as a *fait accompli* to a politically inert public. Policies are forged through the interaction of individuals, interest groups, states, and publics affected by these policies. As James Rosenau puts it, "There is a decentralized, multi-centric world functioning interactively with, but independently of the state system under conditions in which complexity further confounds the lines of authority and reduces the utility of employing armed force."[19] Interactions among the expanded number of actors are more rapid and intense than earlier thanks to new modes of communication and technology. Education and mass media have brought more people into awareness of and involvement in world affairs. There are prominent issues which cut across state boundaries (the drug trade, pollution, terrorism), so that even a state like the Soviet Union could not insulate itself from external actors and issues.

World Jewry's initial demands paralleled those of Soviet Jews: curbing antisemitism, giving Jews equal opportunities, and restoring Jewish cultural and religious rights. After 1967 emphasis shifted to the right to emigrate, especially to Israel (a right formally acknowledged by the Soviet Union in three international agreements). When Soviet leaders were interested in detente, limited, selective emigration was permitted. Thus, beginning in mid-1971 and continuing for about a decade, Jews, Germans, and Armenians were permitted to leave the Soviet Union on the grounds that historical circumstances had cut off these three peoples from their co-ethnics in the rest of the world and that the Soviet state was pursuing a humanitarian policy of "reunification of families." In this period, about 100,000 Soviet Jews emigrated, almost all to Israel.

Following the December 1979 Soviet invasion of Afghanistan and the worsening of east–west relations, it became much more difficult to obtain permission to emigrate. Moreover, as the first wave of committed Zionists departed the Soviet Union, mostly from the Baltic republics, Georgia, and western Ukraine (areas where Jewish traditions and culture survived to a greater extent than in the Slavic heartland), and as Israel's security and economic situations worsened following the October 1973 war, those Jews who did manage to leave the Soviet Union headed mostly to the United States. By the late 1980s, over 80 percent of all who emigrated went to the United States. These were more acculturated Jews whose families had lived under Soviet rule for two, three, and even four generations, in contrast to the *zapadniki* (westerners), those from the Baltic and western peripheries of the Soviet Union who had only recently been socialized into Soviet political culture and who remembered the vibrant pre-Soviet Jewish culture and political life.

In 1989, as a result of glasnost, perestroika, and the loosening of Soviet controls, grass-roots antisemitism became much more visible than at any time since the early 1920s. At the same time, many believed that the fabric of Soviet society was unraveling: The command economy was breaking down and was not being replaced by a smoothly functioning market economy; crime was increasing; political "order" was disappearing. But as a result of the reformist turn, emigration controls were substantially relaxed. The combination of these developments led to a "panic migration" among Jews. Between 1989 and the end of 1991, 464,000 Jews emigrated, an astounding one-third of all Jews enumerated in the January 1989 census. Equally astonishing is the fact that about 73 percent of them went to Israel, reversing the trend of the previous decade. This was due not to a sudden Zionist fervor sweeping Soviet Jewry, but to restrictions on Soviet immigration announced by the United States in mid-1989. Fleeing what they saw as a deteriorating situation wherein they were likely to play their historical role of scapegoats, Jews and their non-Jewish relatives who had never considered leaving the

Soviet Union, let alone for Israel, rushed through gates they thought might close once again.

A Diaspora Within a Diaspora

By 1992 the panic had died down. In subsequent years, Jewish emigration from the former Soviet Union has averaged about 65,000 a year to Israel, 25,000 a year to the United States, and a few thousand a year to Germany. Nearly 1.2 million Jews have emigrated (out of a population which numbered 2,268,000 in 1959 and which has had no natural growth for decades). Of the emigres, two-thirds resettled in Israel and most of the rest in the United States. The great irony is that the Soviet state, which opposed Zionism consistently from its inception, allowed no Zionist propaganda or recruitment, severely restricted tourism to and from Israel after 1967 when it unilaterally broke relations with Israel (not restored until the late 1980s), and even forbade the teaching of Hebrew— this is the state which, along with its successor states, has sent more Jews to Israel than any other in the world. Moreover, in the period after the Second World War, the largest Jewish immigration to the United States, the archenemy of the Soviet government during the long Cold War, has come from the Soviet Union and its successor states. Over 800,000 Soviet and post-Soviet Jews immigrated to Israel and about 325,000 to the United States.[20] The rest have gone mainly to Germany, Canada, and Australia.

Thus, a sub-diaspora of Jews has been created by the Soviet Jewish emigration. There are about 13 million Jews in the world, 95 percent of them concentrated in ten countries, and about five million live in Israel. In other words, the diaspora consists of about eight million Jews. About 800,000 live in the former Soviet Union and over a million others, including the three-quarters of a million in Israel, recently lived there.[21] Former Soviet Jews not only constitute a significant portion of the world Jewish population, but because of linguistic, cultural, family, and experiential ties may be said to form a diaspora of former Soviets within the Jewish diaspora.

In 1992 two Russian colleagues and I conducted a survey of 1,300 Jews in three Russian cities: Moscow, St. Petersburg, and Ekaterinburg. We found that while 90 percent of the respondents had never been to Israel, 47 percent claimed to have "close relatives" there; 63 percent had distant relatives; and 74 percent said they had friends there. As for the United States, 93 percent had never been there, but 27 percent averred that they had close relatives in America, nearly half had distant relatives, and 55 percent had friends there. In Ukraine, among 2,000 Jews we queried in five cities in 1993, 91 percent had not been to Israel, but 31 percent had close relatives, 72 percent distant relatives, and 85 percent friends in the Jewish state. Almost no one had been to America, but 18 percent had close relatives, 62 percent distant relatives, and 79 percent friends in the United States.[22] In just a few years, then, Jews in the former Soviet Union went from an isolated group with few family, cultural, or commercial ties to the rest of the Jewish diaspora and to the historic homeland, to a group with strong and multiple ties to the two largest centers of Jewish population in the world, Israel and the United States.

Do these ties indicate the emergence of a triangular "imagined community" of ex-Soviet Jews? If such an international sub-diaspora exists, what is its relationship to the overall diaspora and to the historic homeland? What are the implications of the existence of such a diaspora for Jews in the former Soviet Union, for Israel, and for world Jewry?

Fran Markowitz suggests that a community of Soviet and post-Soviet Jews now exists in three locales—the former Soviet Union, Israel, and the United States—and is a self-conscious entity.[23] This is obviously true, since there are strong family, linguistic, cultural, and experiential ties among them. When Soviet immigrants to America visit Israel—there are Israeli tour companies specializing in this kind of tourism—they often stay with relatives and friends. The developing market economy in the former Soviet republics, especially in Russia and the Baltic states, has attracted ex-Soviet Jews now living in America and Israel. In 1997, Natan Sharansky (Anatolii Shcharanskii), the Israeli minister of commerce and perhaps the most famous Soviet Jewish dissident, traveled to Russia and Ukraine to promote trade between those countries and Israel. There are American and Israeli citizens, born in the Soviet Union, who live and do business most of the year in their former homeland. Russian entertainers and artists travel regularly to Israel and the United States where they perform for appreciative audiences, the largest Russian-speaking diasporas outside the former Soviet states. They earn significant sums in these countries, enabling them to survive in their home countries, whose governments no longer support culture and the arts as the Soviet Union did.

However, the Soviet Jewish emigration is not a homogenous entity. Little except the experience of Soviet rule and use of the Russian language connects Bukharan Jews from Central Asia with their co-ethnics from the European regions of the Soviet Union; Ashkenazi Jews regard Georgian and Mountain Jews from the Caucasus as being ethnically different from themselves. In our Russian survey (1992), 68 percent of the respondents said they felt closer to the Russians of their city than to Georgian, Mountain, or Bukharan Jews. Strikingly, 46 percent even said they were closer to local Russians than to the Jews in Belarus or Ukraine. Only three percent of Ukrainian Jews said they felt closer to Bukharan Jews than to Russians or Ukrainians. Moreover, Soviet emigres take quite seriously the cultural and educational differences among them. Muscovites and Leningraders look down their noses at "provincials," who generally include former residents even of capitals of former Soviet republics. Educated emigres mock the accents and grammar of those with less education or those from the Caucasus, Central Asia, the Baltic, or even western Ukraine.

In Israel especially, but also in the United States, there are sometimes tensions between immigrants who came in the 1970s and early 1980s, and those who arrived beginning in 1989. Some of the former regard the latecomers as "greenhorns," just as generations of immigrants have done to those who came later than they. The *vatikim* (veterans) ask why they did not emigrate sooner and come for the "right" (i.e., Zionist) reasons; the more recent arrivals resent what they perceive as the materialism, selfishness, and indifference of those who have already established themselves in Israeli or American society. Those who arrived in the 1970s and 1980s generally resettled quickly and successfully, and soon became "invisible" in Israeli society as they learned Hebrew, found housing and employment, and generally adopted Israeli culture. By contrast, the huge wave of arrivals from 1989 to 1992 found it harder to find employment in their professions and to obtain permanent housing. A significant proportion were not Jewish and came because a family member was Jewish and had the right, under Israel's "Law of Return," to bring non-Jewish relatives, who were equally eligible for almost immediate citizenship. The more recent arrivals have clung to Russian culture more than their predecessors. Whereas there were only two Russian-language newspapers in the 1970s, one of which folded after a few years, by 1997 there were about half a dozen dailies, scores of magazines, and extensive Russian radio and television programs. There are Russian-language theaters, Russian nightclubs, and many immigrant organizations. A Russian-language subculture, hardly visible in the 1970s, is highly visible today. One reason a party of Soviet immigrants was formed in 1996 and, to everyone's amazement, got seven seats in the Israeli Knesset, was that more recent immigrants felt not only that the government neglected their needs, but that the earlier waves of immigrants had been so well "absorbed" into Israeli society that they were unconcerned with the fate of the newcomers.[24]

Though the immigrants have a high profile at present, it is likely that with the passage of time, as older immigrants pass on, younger immigrants become highly acculturated and assimilated into their new societies, and their children think of themselves as "Americans" or

"Israelis," consciousness of the ties forged in the Soviet crucible will fade. Among American Jews the tensions between *Litvaks* and *Galitzianer* have faded, the *landsmanshaftn* (immigrant associations) have all but disappeared, Yiddish is spoken only among the ultra-Orthodox, the immigrant press no longer exists, and the term "greenhorn" is no longer heard. It is reasonable to assume that the distinct identity of Soviet emigres and their ties across continents will likewise fade with time. Nevertheless, to the extent that Russian-language facility is transmitted to younger generations, they will be advantaged in doing business in the former Soviet Union and are more likely to maintain even minimal cultural and social ties with other Russian-speakers, particularly Jews, wherever they reside. Moreover, to the extent that children of immigrants maintain affection for and loyalty to Russian culture, as many of their parents do, a "Russian" identity may persist, if only as a sub-identity within a more compelling Israeli or American one.

Homeland and Diaspora:
Jews in the Former Soviet Union and the State of Israel

Until the late 1980s, the Soviet Jewish diaspora was very different from western Jewry. Though it was the second largest Jewish diaspora population and the third largest Jewish population in the world, it had not a single Jewish school of any kind; Hebrew could not be studied legally; and there were only a few Jewish theaters or synagogues, and no Jewish social, cultural, or civic organizations at all. There was no representative body of Soviet Jewry and no communal organization at the local, regional, or national levels. Soviet Jews did not have representation in international Jewish forums or anywhere else in the international arena.

Therefore, Soviet Jewry was regarded as a problem, an issue. The Zionist contention that the only solution to this problem was mass immigration to Israel was widely accepted in the diaspora, though the American Jewish establishment insisted that Soviet emigres be given free choice of country of immigration and resisted efforts by the Israelis to force Soviet emigres to move to Israel.[25] After 1991 and the collapse of the Soviet system, Soviet Jewry became a "normal diaspora." American Jews debated whether or not to dismantle the National Conference on Soviet Jewry, formed by two dozen major American Jewish organizations to fight for equal rights and the right of emigration for Soviet Jews. The Union of Councils for Soviet Jews, a grass-roots organization with aims similar to those of the National Conference but using more activist tactics, broadened its mandate to human rights generally. The Memorial Foundation for Jewish Culture, which supports Jewish cultural endeavors world wide, disbanded its Soviet Jewry committee. While Israelis clung to the Zionist principle of *shlilat hagalut* (negation of the diaspora, the belief that all Jews everywhere should move to the Jewish state and that Jewish life in the diaspora is not viable), Jews in the former Soviet Union and some outside of it began to consider ways of reconstructing Jewish communal life and creating a viable diaspora Jewish existence. Schools were established (there were in 1997 in the former Soviet Union about 40 Jewish all-day schools, four or five universities emphasizing Judaica, and about 200 Sunday or supplementary schools), clearly signaling a commitment to a consciously Jewish collective and individual future in the former Soviet region. Local communal organizations were formed. They began to regain former communal properties, such as synagogues and schools, set up welfare organizations to assist the large number of elderly and infirm, and sponsor social and cultural activities. Sports clubs, Jewish libraries, and research institutions were established.

Two attempts have been made to form an umbrella organization representing all Jewish communities in the former Soviet Union. The Va'ad, or Council, established in 1989 by Jewish activists from localities from the Baltic to the Pacific, tried to unite and represent all the communal organizations of Soviet Jewry, but foundered as a result of the break-up of the Soviet federation and the Va'ad's inability to raise its own funds and provide services. More recently, a Russian Jewish Congress, limited to the Russian Federation and supported by some of the most prominent "new Russians" (actually Jews), has tried to play the role of a national umbrella organization and representative body.[26] Meanwhile, the Jewish Agency, a formally non-governmental Israeli body whose main function is to encourage and organize immigration to Israel, and the "Liaison Office" of the Israeli government have been permitted to operate openly in all the former Soviet republics, though the Agency's activities were curtailed briefly in 1996. They do not explicitly negate the efforts at communal reconstruction, but their message is that as many Jews as possible should emigrate to Israel, no matter what effect this might have on the reconstruction of a viable diaspora community, because in the long run all Jews should live in a Jewish state. Moreover, they argue, the situation of Jews in the former Soviet republics will remain precarious as long as stable, prosperous democracies are not established on the ruins of the Soviet state. This posture has created some tension between, on the one hand, the Israelis, and on the other hand, local Jewish communities and organizations such as the American Jewish Joint Distribution Committee which try to assist them. However, since 1991 the two positions have co-existed; while some try to promote emigration and the "liquidation of the diaspora," others acknowledge emigration as a viable option but insist on the feasibility of Jewish life in most parts of the former Soviet Union, especially those republics that still have substantial Jewish populations—Russia, Ukraine, Belarus, and Latvia.

True, the demographic outlook is very bleak. The population is shrinking fast through low fertility, high mortality, intermarriage, and emigration. The average European Jewish family in the former Soviet Union has one child—not enough for replacement. Already in 1970, 25 percent of the Jews in Russia were over 60; in 1997, in the entire former Soviet Union, 24 percent were over 65 (compared with 11 percent of the general population and 17 percent among American Jews). In 1989 Jewish deaths exceeded Jewish births by a ratio of three–to–one. By 1991, when so many younger people were emigrating, that ratio climbed to an astounding seven–to–one in the Russian republic, which had the largest number of Jews in the Soviet Union. The median age of Jews in the former Soviet republics is now over 50. In America it is 37 and in Israel 28.[27]

In 1988, 47 percent of Jewish women and 58 percent of Jewish men who married in the Soviet Union that year married non-Jews. In Russia the figures were an astronomical 73 percent for men and 63 percent for women. Very few of their children are likely to identify as Jews, unless they want to leave the country. Even if efforts at re-creating and sustaining Jewish life continue unimpeded, will there be enough people to sustain them, especially since the young—who would produce the future generations—are disproportionately represented among the emigres? Even with this drastic decline, the Jewish population in the former Soviet Union is likely to be greater than that in England (which had 460,000 Jews in 1950 and fewer than 250,000 by the mid-1990s) if not in France, and far greater than that in the rest of Europe, Argentina, and South Africa, communities that are still seen as important centers of world Jewish culture. Moreover, there is the mathematical conundrum that the number of Jews does not seem to shrink through emigration because the more Jews leave, the more Jews seem to come out of the closet, having discovered or invented a Jewish grandparent. In most cases, this is the prelude to emigration. But the demographic problem is a serious one, as it is for the rest of the Jewish diaspora.

The Jewish Diaspora and the Former Soviet Union

Russia, Belarus, Georgia, Lithuania, Latvia, and Ukraine have "used" their Jewish populations in order to cultivate a favorable image in the west. They have done so by abandoning antisemitism as state policy, supporting—at least morally, and to a far lesser extent financially—Jewish communal and cultural revival. Since one criterion for admission to "Europe" is safeguarding human rights, including minority rights, treating well an ethnic group that has notoriously been the subject of discrimination—a group which, because of its extensive and strategically located diaspora has high visibility in the west—is an effective way of gaining credibility and generating good will both among western governments as well as among attentive western publics.

The Jewish diaspora has influenced post-Soviet states to some degree, in that it has played a major role in forcing them to abandon antisemitism. Building on the myth of Jewish wealth and power, diaspora Jews have conveyed the impression that western governments and companies will look more favorably on the successor states if local Jews are treated well. Moreover, as in Poland and Hungary, some leaders in the former Soviet republics expect major foreign Jewish investment. One could argue that it was the Soviet system itself that was antisemitic and that once the system disappeared there would be no governmental antisemitism. However, the depth of grass-roots antisemitism and the authoritarian tendencies of some post-Soviet regimes (Belarus, Uzbekistan) and the xenophobic postures of others (Latvia, Estonia) may have been conducive to official antisemitism. The west's watchfulness, itself largely a product of Jewish vigilance and pressure, may therefore have influenced these governments.

Furthermore, the Jewish diaspora has influenced politics by assuming that the norm should be inclusion of domestic Jews in the political life of the post-Soviet republics, thereby perhaps indirectly pressuring states such as Ukraine, Russia, and Belarus to define their state identities less in ethnic than in civic terms. The Jewish diaspora has not involved itself in shaping domestic politics and policy making directly, in contrast to, say, the Ukrainian or Baltic diasporas, because it claims no state in the former Soviet Union as its homeland. Its modest agenda has been to guarantee individual and communal rights and the ability to assist in communal reconstruction, as well as the international right to emigration.

As Jews of the former Soviet Union become reattached to the Jewish diaspora and the Jewish state, this will not weaken attachments of local Jews to their respective states, just as it has not among the Jews of the United States, Canada, and England—states that afford Jews equal rights, as opposed to countries that persecuted them (Iran, the Soviet Union, Syria) and therefore lost what were once powerful Jewish loyalties. Moreover, while there are diaspora-wide Jewish institutions and functions, the agenda of the Jewish diaspora is not to create states, except for those Zionists who believe that all Jews should emigrate to Israel. Diaspora Jewry will continue to deal with co-ethnics and coreligionists in the Soviet successor states without challenging the legiti-macy or functioning of those states themselves. The record shows that diaspora Jews work with the state, providing investment, hard currency, and political support, as in American Jewry's support for most–favored–nation status (MFN) for Romania, as long as the state allows domestic Jews to pursue their own cultural and religious agendas, assuming these agendas do not conflict with the state. The other side of the same coin is shown by American Jewish support for the Jackson–Vanik amendment, which denied MFN to the Soviet Union because it restricted emigration.

The Soviet Jewish diaspora in emigration may be thought of as a sub-diaspora that is likely to weaken and disappear within one or two generations. At present, however, it is an important part of the American diaspora. The 325,000 Soviet immigrants in the United States constitute about six percent of American Jewry. But the Jewish diaspora as a whole is shrinking and Israel will soon have the largest Jewish population in the world. Still, barring another Holocaust, the Jewish diaspora will be significant and in many places viable for a long time, including Russia and Ukraine, but not in Lithuania, Tajikistan, and other successor states.

Conclusion

There are several dimensions to the concept "diaspora" when applied to Soviet and post-Soviet Jewry. Because so many Jews in Israel, western Europe, and the Americas originated in the former Soviet Union and its predecessor states, and because the Jewish population of the former Soviet republics remains a significant proportion of the diaspora, world Jewry will continue to focus attention on the needs, aspirations, and interests of Jews in this region. This implies, in addition, that world Jewry will be attentive to the character and policies of the former Soviet republics, and may well be attracted to involve themselves in them economically, politically, and culturally. Involvement, in turn, inevitably means different and even competing goals. Some Hassidic groups (Lubavitch/Chabad, Karlin–Stolin) have invested considerable effort in "returning" to their types of Judaism the "lost" Jews of the former Soviet Union and those who have left it. Reform Judaism has tried to establish itself as a more appropriate alternative to Hassidic and non-Hassidic Orthodoxy. The American Jewish Joint Distribution Committee, on the other hand, has provided assistance for the needy and elderly, for the reconstruction of Jewish communal life, and for a broad range of Jewish educational and cultural activities whose specific character is determined by local Jews and which covers the spectrum of Jewish belief and non-belief. Israelis generally negate these efforts, arguing that the only goal should be the "return" of Jews from the former Soviet Union to their "true homeland." The governments and societies of the region are no doubt ambivalent about this issue: On one hand, many see emigration as a betrayal of the "motherland." On the other, they welcome the emigration of Jews whom they consider as aliens whose real homeland, if it exists, lies outside their own country. At the least, when Jews emigrate they free up housing and jobs for others, or so it is thought. From the perspective of world Jewry, while Soviet Jewish emigration forms a distinctive sub-diaspora, it is not likely to remain so as new generations are born far from the former Soviet host-states. The Soviet Jewish diaspora will thus continue to mean different things to different people, playing a variety of changing roles in political, cultural, and economic arenas.

Notes

1. Benedict Anderson, *Imagined Communities* (London: Verso, 1983). For a different view, which explains the Jewish case better, see Anthony D. Smith, *The Ethnic Origins of Nations* (Oxford: Basil Blackwell, 1986). Smith's ideas of Jewish ethnicity and nationhood are elaborated in his "The Question of Jewish Identity," in Peter Medding, ed., *A New Jewry: Studies in Contemporary Jewry VIII* (New York: Oxford University Press, 1992), 219–33.

2. Ethnic groups are defined both by their specific content and by the borders they and others construct in order to set themselves off. In some cases content plays a larger role than borders in group definition, and in other cases the reverse is true. See Stephen Cornell, "The Variable Ties that Bind: Content and Circumstance in Ethnic Processes," *Ethnic and Racial Studies* 19, no. 2 (1996): 265–89.

3. See Howard Sachar, *A History of Israel* (New York: Alfred Knopf, 1979), 604.

4. Chaim Jitlovsky, "What is Jewish Secular Culture?" in Joseph Leftwich, ed., *The Way We Think*, vol. 1 (South Brunswick: Thomas Yoseloff, 1969), 92, 93, 95.

5. Anthony D. Smith, *The Ethnic Revival* (Cambridge: Cambridge University Press, 1981), 66.

6. *Iskra*, no. 51, October 22, 1903.

7. *Iskra*, no. 51, October 22, 1903.

8. On the Soviet program for transforming Jewish culture from a religious and Zionist base to a secular Soviet one, see Zvi Gitelman, *Jewish Nationality and Soviet Politics* (Princeton: Princeton University Press, 1972).

9. *Der emes*, September 15, 1921, cited in Rachel Erlich, "Politics and Linguistics in the Standardization of Soviet Yiddish," in Joshua Fishman, ed., *Never Say*

Die! A Thousand Years of Yiddish in Jewish Life and Letters (The Hague: Mouton, 1981), 701.

10. *Ortografisher verterbuch* (1932) quoted in Erlich, "Politics and Linguistics," 702. For a recent discussion of some of the politically charged issues surrounding Yiddish in the Soviet Union, see Gennady Estraikh, "Yiddish Language Conference Aborted," *East European Jewish Affairs* 25, no. 2 (1995): 91–96.

11. *Komunistishe fon*, April 12, 1924. See also Mordechai Altshuler, *HaYevsektsia biVrit haMoetsot, 1918–1930* (Tel Aviv: Sifriat Poalim, Moreshet, Institute of Contemporary Jewry, 1980), 145–47.

12. Altshuler, *HaYevsketsia*, 92.

13. Cited in Gitelman, *Jewish Nationality*, 433.

14. On the Birobidzhan experiment and other Soviet schemes to settle Jews on land, see Yaacov Lvavi (Babitsky), *Hahityashvut hayehudit bebirobidzhan* (Jerusalem: Historical Society of Israel, 1965); Benjamin Pinkus, *The Soviet Government and the Jews, 1948–1967* (Cambridge: Cambridge University Press, 1984); Allan Laine Kagedan, *Soviet Zion: The Quest for a Russian Jewish Homeland* (New York: St. Martin's Press, 1994); Robert Weinberg, *Stalin's Forgotten Zion* (Berkeley: University of California Press, forthcoming).

15. See Yehoshua Gilboa, *The Black Years* (Boston: Little, Brown, 1971); Shimon Redlich, "The 'Crimean Affair,'" *Jews and Jewish Topics in the Soviet Union and Eastern Europe* 2, no. 12 (1990): 55–65; and Shimon Redlich, *War, Holocaust and Stalinism* (Luxembourg: Harwood Academic Publishers, 1995).

16. David Giladi, summarizing statements made by Soviet immigrants at the 28th Zionist Congress, *Haaretz*, January 25, 1972.

17. See, for example, Richard Breitman and Alan Kraut, *American Refugee Policy and European Jewry, 1933–1945* (Bloomington: Indiana University Press, 1987); David Wyman, *The Abandonment of the Jews: America and the Holocaust, 1941–1945* (New York: Pantheon, 1984); Haskel Lookstein, *Were We Our Brothers' Keepers?* (New York: Hartmore House, 1985); Henry Feingold, *The Politics of Rescue* (New Brunswick: Rutgers University Press, 1970); Arthur Morse, *While Six Million Died* (New York: Random House, 1967); Bernard Wasserstein, *Britain and the Jews of Europe, 1939–1945* (Oxford: Clarendon Press, 1979); Irving Abella and Harold Troper, *None is Too Many: Canada and the Jews of Europe, 1933–1948* (New York: Random House, 1983).

18. For an elaboration of these arguments, see Zvi Gitelman, "New Transnational Politics: The Case of Soviet Jewry," *Shvut*, new series, 1–2 [17–18] (1995): 194–217.

19. James Rosenau, *Turbulence in World Politics: A Theory of Change and Continuity* (Princeton: Princeton University Press, 1990), 275.

20. On the dimensions of Soviet Jewish immigration to the United States, see Steven Gold, "Soviet Jews in the United States," *American Jewish Year Book 1994* (New York: American Jewish Committee, 1994), 3–57. For a historical perspective, see Zvi Gitelman, "'From a Northern Country:' Russian/Soviet Jewish Immigration to America and Israel in Historical Perspective," in Yaacov Ro'i, ed., *Russian Jews on Three Continents* (London: Frank Cass, 1997), 21–44. The dimen-

sions and nature of Soviet immigration to Israel are explored in Zvi Gitelman, *Immigration and Identity: The Resettlement and Impact of Soviet Immigrants on Israeli Politics and Society* (Los Angeles: Wilstein Institute, 1995). Soviet Jewish immigration to Germany is discussed in Madeleine Tress, "Soviet Jews in the Federal Republic of Germany: The Rebuilding of a Community," *Jewish Journal of Sociology* 37, no. 1 (1995): 39–54.

21. Population estimates are taken from U. O. Schmelz and Sergio DellaPergola, "World Jewish Population, 1994," *American Jewish Yearbook 1996* (New York: American Jewish Committee, 1996), 434–63. Estimates of the Jewish population of the former Soviet Union vary considerably and depend in part on who is considered a Jew (e.g., a person having a Jewish father or only one who has a Jewish mother—the latter being the traditional rabbinic criterion rejected in recent years by Reform Judaism) and on political motivations. For example, there is reason to believe that the government of Israel and the Jewish Agency favor estimates at the high end because they imply a greater potential immigration to Israel. The very low fertility rates, high mortality rates, and high rates of marriage to non-Jews, not to speak of massive emigration, incline me toward the lower estimates.

22. The survey was designed by me, Valery Chervyakov, and Vladimir Shapiro, and supervised by Chervyakov and Shapiro. We used the 1989 census data for each of eight cities in order to construct a demographic profile of the local Jews, and then constructed local quota samples who were our respondents.

23. Fran Markowitz, "Criss-Crossing Identities: The Russian Jewish Diaspora and the Jewish Diaspora in Russia," *Diaspora* 4, no. 2 (1995): 201–10; and idem, "Emigration, Immigration and Culture Change: Towards a Transnational 'Russian' Jewish Community?" in Yaacov Ro'i, ed., *Jews and Jewish Life in Russia and the Soviet Union* (London: Frank Cass, 1995), 403–14.

24. See for example, Ella Fried, "Hakatseh hasmoli shel hakoalitsia," *Haaretz*, June 7, 1996. The article is about Marina Solodkina, now a member of the Knesset, who is one of the most outspoken critics of the earlier immigrants. See also Efraim Gur, "Pochemu repatrianty ne ob"ediniaiutsia," *Vesti*, April 3, 1996.

25. See Zvi Gitelman, "Recent Demographic and Migratory Trends Among Soviet Jews: Implications for Policy," *Post-Soviet Geography* 33, no. 3 (1992): 139–45.

26. Zvi Gitelman, "Jewish Communal Reconstruction in the Former Soviet Union," in Peter Medding, ed., *Values, Interests and Identity: Studies in Contemporary Jewry XI* (New York: Oxford University Press, 1995), 136–56.

27. Mark Tolts, "Trends in Soviet Jewish Demography Since the Second World War," in Ro'i, ed., *Jews and Jewish Life*, 365–82; and idem, "The Jewish Population of Russia, 1989–1995," *Jews in Eastern Europe* 3 (31) (1996): 5–19.

4

The Armenians:
Conflicting Identities and
the Politics of Division

Razmik Panossian

Where is my homeland? is a difficult question for most Armenians. The varying and overlapping answers are indicative of a community whose history over the past eighty years has not only been based on homeland–diaspora relations, but is also a reflection of contesting definitions of "homeland" and "Armenianness." The essential division within the Armenian nation, and within each major Armenian community, has been defined by the question of how to relate to (formerly Soviet) Armenia. This chapter examines the political history of this division and its contemporary manifestations.

Of course, the modern Armenian diaspora is much more than a mere extension of the homeland; it is an entity in its own right, with various sources of identity. Since the 1920s the core meaning of the term "diaspora" (*spiurk* in Armenian) has been not so much Armenian communities in the other republics of the Soviet Union, but Armenians living outside the Soviet federation—in the Middle East, Europe, and the Americas. This vision of the diaspora has remained unchanged since the creation of an independent Armenia in 1991.

Hence, throughout this chapter, the primary focus will be on the "external" (mostly western) diaspora rather than on the "internal" diaspora of ethnic Armenians in the other post-Soviet republics. This chapter first looks at the historical dimensions of the Armenian diaspora and then examines the relationship between Soviet Armenia and the diaspora up to 1988. The remaining sections concentrate on homeland–diaspora relations after 1988 before concluding with some thoughts on the challenges of contested identities.

The History of Diaspora

Dispersion has been a central element of Armenian history over the past millennium. In fact, the earliest indications of *modern* Armenian identity, and later nationalism, can be traced to major diasporic communities in Europe and Asia. Such centers became major sources of Armenian art, literature, and learning, (re)producing essential cultural markers for national identity. For example, the first modern Armenian political tracts were published in Madras, India, between 1772 and 1789. Meanwhile, the Mkhitarist Brotherhood in Venice (established there in 1717) was producing historical texts which conceived of Armenians as a nation, dispersed in reality but united in essence. Such activities, taking place outside the homeland of Armenia proper, provided the cultural basis of what was to follow in the nineteenth century: the politicization of identity and nationalist demands for the liberation of the homeland, where the bulk of the population still lived as subjects of the Ottoman empire.

By the latter part of the century, revolutionary activity emerged mostly among urban intellectuals in cities such as Constantinople, Baku, and Tiflis (Tbilisi). Along with workers, they began to mobilize around radical organizations with nationalist and socialist ideologies.[1] In the Russian empire, influenced by Marxism and populism, they reworked the Russian populist call of "going to the people" to mean "going to the homeland" (*tebi yergir*) and focused on the liberation of Armenians in the Ottoman empire. The two most prominent organizations founded for the dual purpose of national and socio-economic liberation were the Armenian Revolutionary Federation (ARF, the Dashnaks), founded in Tiflis in 1890, and the Hnchakian Social Democratic Party (HSDP, the Hnchaks), founded in Geneva in 1887. With a melange of nationalist and socialist ideologies, these two organizations engaged in propaganda and terrorist activities and set up self-defense units and revolutionary cells. They demanded security and autonomy for the Armenian population, as well as profound social changes, first in the Ottoman empire and then (after 1905) in the Russian empire. In response to the radicalism of such organizations, the reformist Democratic Constitutional Party was founded in Alexandria in 1908 and reorganized in Istanbul in 1921 as the Armenian Democratic Liberal Party (ADL, the Ramkavars). The Ramkavars were the party of the bourgeoisie but claimed to speak on behalf of the entire nation. Since their founding, all three parties have played important roles in diaspora politics and community structures.

While these organizations were working on behalf of the homeland, two fundamental turning points occurred in 1915 and 1918. The first was the emptying of Armenians from their traditional homeland in the Ottoman empire through genocide and mass deportations (which killed one to one and a half million Armenians). The second was the creation of an independent Armenian state in Russian Armenia (1918) and its subsequent sovietization in the period 1920–21. The consequences of the first event were manifold: It led to the creation of the modern Armenian diaspora, in the Middle East, Europe, and America—a diaspora predominantly of refugees and Genocide survivors for whom the homeland was literally "lost," with no possibility of return. In terms of its sheer size and location, this new post-Genocide diaspora eclipsed the traditional diasporic communities. Half of the nation was now in exile, forced to live in the diaspora condition; four-fifths of the historic homeland was depopulated of Armenians. The consequences of the second turning point, the establishment of an Armenian state five centuries after the collapse of the last independent Armenian kingdom, were manifold as well. Although it was only about twenty percent of "greater Armenia" in its land mass, and though it came to be part of the Soviet Union, it nevertheless remained the only tangible "homeland" for Armenians in this century and as such became the locus of national identity. Even though the diaspora's "real" homeland lay in western/Ottoman Armenia, the very existence of an Armenian state shifted the center of national consciousness, cultural work, and even nationalism (by the 1980s) from the diaspora to a kin-state.

It is estimated that in 1914 there were 2.5 million Armenians living in the traditional Armenian homeland, an area partitioned between the Russian, Persian, and Ottoman empires. Another 2.5 million lived in major centers within these empires (Istanbul, Tiflis) and 200,000 or so in the remainder of the diaspora (India, Europe, and elsewhere). In 1921, 150,000 Armenians were left in post-Genocide Turkey. Approximately half a million lived in the diaspora (the Middle East, Europe, and the United States). A little over one million lived in Soviet Armenia, and about half a million in other parts of the Soviet Union.[2]

The New Diaspora and the Soviet Armenian Homeland

The federal structure of the Soviet Union enabled Armenians to build a "typical" national state in many respects. Yerevan became the cultural center for the nation. Armenian was the official language of the republic and almost universally used. There were national institutions of research and learning, and by the 1970s history had been "nationalized" in its interpretation. Government and party structures were run by Armenians. It was clear by the 1970s that communist ideology was mostly a veneer covering the patriotic identity and nationalist impulses of the majority of the population, both at the elite and mass levels. The very strong sense of national identity was first and foremost rooted in the territory of the republic and then projected onto the lost lands in Turkey. Of course, all this was within the confines of communist rule and its limits on political power. There were Russian cultural and linguistic influences as well, but they were minimal compared to most other republics. According to Claire Mouradian, "Armenia acquired the demeanor [*l'allure*] of a quasi-perfect nation state."[3] By 1979, 66 percent of Armenians in the Soviet Union lived in their titular republic (with a further 11 percent in Georgia and 11.5 percent in Azerbaijan). Armenia had become the most homogenous of all the Soviet republics; 90 percent of its inhabitants were Armenian.[4] The Armenian SSR not only became the national center demographically, but it also claimed to be the homeland for all Armenians wherever they lived. However, its claim to be the "genuine" homeland was not easily accepted in large segments of the diaspora; the kin-state was, after all, a small fragment of historic Armenia and was, moreover, under communist rule.

Paralleling the "nationalization" of Soviet Armenia, the post-Genocide diaspora went through a similar process. Under the leadership of competing organizations (the ARF and others who had now become the political parties of the community), a heterogeneous group of people with fundamental differences in terms of regional identity, religion (Apostolic, Catholic, and Protestant), language (Armenian, Turkish, dialects), occupation and class, social status (refugees, assimilated elites, intellectuals), political loyalties, and cultural influences from host-states, were molded into a relatively homogenous community with a collective consciousness as a diasporic nation. In short, "Armenianness" as the most important identity category was either created or reinforced in the diaspora, superseding the differences within and among the communities. The key element of unity was the Armenian language, education being the means by which this was to be achieved, while the politics of the community evolved around the "Armenian cause." Social services were provided as well—from neighborhood policing in some Middle Eastern communities, to employment opportunities for Armenians newly arrived in the United States.[5] The bulk of this work was done during the inter-war period, mostly in the Middle East where Armenians had concentrated (especially in Lebanon and Syria) after the Genocide, and where the roots of much of the modern western diaspora lay.[6] A similar process took place in other newly created (or enlarged) diaspora communities in Europe and America.

Despite the emergence of a national–*cum*–diasporic identity, the diaspora was organizationally divided into two over-all blocs centered on the Dashnak and non-Dashnak (Ramkavar and Hnchak) parties. By the 1950s, after thirty years of bitter conflict, each segment had devel-. oped its own sphere of influence and its own institutional, psychological, and sometimes even physical "territory." There were two sets of umbrella organizations with global networks linking the various branches of each bloc scattered in many countries. There existed two parallel Armenian Apostolic church institutions, two sets of cultural organizations, philanthropic societies, sports clubs, school systems, and media outlets.[7] Socialization and intermarriage between the blocs were rare or non-existent. This entrenched system remained the operative dynamic within all major Armenian diaspora communities outside the Soviet Union. Since the 1920s there has been either open conflict (sometimes even leading to bloodshed) or low-intensity opposition between the two sides, ebbing only in the 1970s and 1980s.[8]

The essential cause of this divide was each side's relationship with Soviet Armenia. Indeed, during the Cold War an iron curtain separated not only the diaspora from the "homeland," but also the two major camps within the diaspora itself. The two blocs had contesting visions of the homeland, different approaches to it, and disputed roles for it in national life. Who was the legitimate representative and leader of the nation and of the diaspora? This entailed a two-pronged battle: for legitimacy and for control of diaspora communities. The politically more significant Dashnak bloc, in alliance with the west, was staunchly opposed to Armenia because of its Soviet regime, while the Ramkavar–Hnchak bloc supported the kin-state. Ironically, the party which started as the organization representing bourgeois–liberal interests was the main ally of Soviet Armenia; its logic was that the "homeland" must be supported whatever its regime. This relationship was the main link between the kin-state and the diaspora, or with one segment of it, up to 1988. The alliance between the Ramkavars and the Armenian SSR became a small hole in the global iron curtain.

In 1964 the Soviet Armenian government established the Committee for Cultural Relations with Diaspora Armenians in order to augment the republic's influence on the diaspora outside the Soviet Union.[9] Its approach was to promote contacts and cultural exchanges. It provided language textbooks and newspapers, invited intellectuals to visit Armenia, sent dance troupes and choirs abroad to perform in Armenian communities, and sponsored diaspora youth to study for university degrees in Armenia.[10] Its contacts were made explicitly on the terrain of culture and education, with no overt political agenda or agitation. It was a subtle form of propaganda which portrayed the Armenian SSR as the homeland, the exclusive source of national identity where the nation was being conserved and advanced. In contrast to the 1920s, the roles of donor and recipient were reversed. Armenia was viewed as a concerned homeland providing cultural nourishment for the diaspora so that it could survive by preserving its weakening "Armenianness" in foreign lands. Hence, the diaspora came to be viewed as a mere annex of the Soviet Armenian kin-state, with no purpose or identity of its own. While the republic's security and prosperity were emphasized, there was no mention of liberty and independence, and no anti-Russian sentiment was expressed.[11] It was argued that being part of the Soviet Union—that is, under Russian hegemony—was vital for the nation's physical survival.

This new mentality eventually took root in the diaspora, including among the Dashnaks,[12] and became the dominant paradigm of the diaspora's relations with the Armenian SSR. A stable pattern of coexistence between Armenia and the diaspora was the norm in the 1970s and 1980s. From this point on, it was generally possible to use the terms "kin-state" and "homeland" interchangeably when referring to (Soviet) Armenia. But the Armenian SSR did not replace the Dashnak ideal of a greater Armenian homeland, including the "lost lands" in Turkey and elsewhere.

However, all was not well in the republic for some. There was discontent about conditions, particularly among the immigrants to Armenia who had arrived after the Second World War and who had difficulty assimilating to mainstream Soviet society. The last wave of emigrants to leave Armenia for the diaspora before the 1990s was overwhelmingly made up of these "repatriates"—those who had moved to Soviet Armenia after the war—and their descendants.[13] Almost all moved to the United States. Between 1971 and 1989, some 60,000 entered the United States, with 90–95 percent of them settling in the Los Angeles area.[14] This exodus from the republic was frowned upon by both homeland and diaspora nationalists, but for many ordinary people in Armenia emigrating to the west was a dream come true.

There was also another, less visible, movement of Armenians away from the republic and into the "internal" diaspora within the Soviet Union, mostly for professional and employment reasons (although there was still a positive in-flow of immigrants into Armenia until the early 1980s).[15] More importantly, however, there were already established Armenian communities in Georgia (448,000) and in Azerbaijan (475,000). The total number of Armenians in the Soviet Union living outside their titular republic in 1979 was 1.4 million.[16] Co-ethnics living in Moscow, Crimea, or Tashkent were no doubt seen by Armenians within the Armenian SSR as a diaspora—albeit qualified as "internal" and somehow less diasporic than the "real" diaspora outside the Soviet Union; this was particularly true of Armenians in Tbilisi and Baku because of their long history of residency. However, Armenians did not perceive the adjacent (contiguous) kin communities as diasporic. Namely, Armenians in Nagorno-Karabakh (Gharabagh) in Azerbaijan and in the Javakheti area of Georgia were not at all conceived as a diaspora.[17] It was thought that they lived on their ancestral lands which happened to be in a neighboring republic. These areas fell under the rubric of land claims (especially Gharabagh) and not under homeland–diaspora relations. This thinking continued after independence even though the regions suddenly fell on the other side of international boundaries. In 1996 it was said that 1.5 million to 2 million Armenians lived in the "internal" diaspora, i.e., within other former Soviet republics.

By the early 1990s, the size of the "external" diaspora was estimated to be anywhere from 1.5 million to 2.5 million, with communities in approximately fifty countries.[18] The predominant dynamic in this population since the 1950s—particularly in the 1970s and 1980s—has been one of migration and relocation, but within the diaspora and not between the homeland and diaspora. There has been a substantial east-to-west shift, a movement from Middle Eastern communities to the west, particularly to the Los Angeles area and other parts of the United States. In the last twenty-five years, the size of the American Armenian community has doubled from approximately 400,000 to 800,000 people.[19] This is one-seventh of all Armenians, or about one-third to one half of the entire diaspora outside the former Soviet Union.

"Armenianness" has acquired a particular meaning in the western diaspora; it has become an identity far removed from the homeland and from the idea of return. The actual homeland is believed to be not only geographically distant, but also culturally foreign and emotionally remote. Conversely, the "host" society has become "home" as the boundaries around the community are eroding, making Armenians more and more susceptible to assimilation (which is not a real problem in the Middle East). But the community as a whole is not simply withering away; rather, it is developing into a unique diasporic entity based on dual loyalties and a hybrid, hyphenated identity.[20] In her masterful study of Armenian-Americans, Anny Bakalian analyzes this identity as that of "symbolic Armenians."[21] The western diaspora is evolving into a conscious body in its own right, not so much based on "objective" features such as language, religion, and other "traditional" cultural markers, but simply based on a feeling of being Armenian—and American, French, etc. This diaspora is no longer connected in any meaningful way to a specific kin-state (least of all to one that was sovietized). It is not the diaspora of a concrete or "existing" homeland but of an idealized homeland—a "spiritual" diaspora of a "spiritual" kin-state. Its hybrid identity emerges from a *double* imagination: a diaspora which is imagining an "imagined community" found somewhere between the hostland and the homeland. Moreover, this diaspora's idea of the homeland is not fixed on one spot. It could be the ancestral village in the Ottoman empire, the city of birth in the Middle East, present-day Armenia, or the ideal of an Armenia to be—and probably a combination of all these. Nevertheless, there is an active commitment to the Armenian nation (however defined or wherever located), to its national cause, and to mobilization on behalf of other Armenian communities and on behalf of the kin-state.

By 1988, despite closer links between the kin-state and the diaspora, including the Dashnak bloc, there remained a deep divide between the two parts of the nation. This was based on cultural as well as political differences, and above all, on a profound ignorance of each other. The predominant view of the kin-state regarding the diaspora was that Armenians abroad were somehow incomplete in their national identity, especially those who had lost the language, because they lived outside their homeland. The diaspora's ideal of the homeland was, in turn, far removed from the realities of Soviet Armenia. Both sides claimed to belong to the same nation, but each was a different "sort" of Armenian. Onto this scene burst the Gharabagh movement, and homeland–diaspora relations entered a new stage of turmoil.

After 1988:
A Reluctant Embrace, a Honeymoon, and a Separation

It was for a while fashionable to refer to the homeland and the diaspora as two wings of the same bird. One no longer hears this phrase among Armenian intellectuals and political leaders; it became clear in the 1990s that the metaphoric bird was a flightless one. Armenia's independence from Soviet rule brought unprecedented contact and opportunities for cooperation between the diaspora and the kin-state. But it also shattered the myth of return and brought homeland–diaspora relations full circle. The Dashnaks came to oppose the post-Soviet Armenian government, while the non-Dashnaks supported it. The diaspora was both a useful resource for the republic and an additional source of problems.

When the Gharabagh movement exploded in February 1988, with Armenians demanding the Nagorno-Karabakh autonomous *oblast'* from Azerbaijan, the diaspora was caught completely off guard. Diaspora leaders were consistently a few steps behind developments in the republic, both in understanding and action. Meanwhile, the homeland had great expectations of the diaspora, especially of the Dashnaks with their nationalist rhetoric of liberating historically Armenian territory. As a forbidden organization they had a mystic (and a mythic) reputation as anti-Soviet freedom fighters. For the mass of Armenians in the nationalist movement, the ARF was the embodiment of their ideals. As one commentator put it, "The feelings of the people [toward the Dashnaks] in 1988–89 had reached the level of religious reverence."[22] And, by extension, the diaspora was revered—at least the Dashnak side—for its nationalist ideals. The line between the ARF and the diaspora was blurred in the minds of many Armenians. But with great expectations came great disappointment. In October 1988 the ARF, the Ramkavars, and the Hnchaks, in a rare move, issued a joint communiqué on the Gharabagh movement. While they supported the joining of Nagorno-Karabakh to Soviet Armenia, they called for moderation and calm, and the ending of the strikes and disruptive protests that would harm the "good standing" of Armenians in the eyes of "higher Soviet bodies," on whom they called to settle the dispute. This was a complete misreading of the prevalent mood in Yerevan, and it was interpreted by the movement there as condemnation of its activities and support for the Soviet regime.[23] This joint statement, nine months after the beginning of the nationalist movement, was the first step in delegitimizing the ARF in Armenia (the other two parties were already delegitimized for their traditional support of the Soviet government). Notwithstanding their conservatism, neither the Dashnaks nor any of the other diaspora organizations had the material resources, the ideological basis, or the knowledge and connections to have any significant impact in Armenia.

The security argument put forth with such force and conviction by the authorities of the Armenian SSR for decades was so ingrained in the mentality of Dashnak (and Ramkavar and Hnchak) leaders that for them, no matter what, Armenia needed a protector against pan-Turkism. It also needed an outside force to solve its problems. And this had to be Russia (be it Soviet or not). Whereas intellectuals and leaders at the forefront of the nationalist movement in Armenia had begun to conceive of Soviet rule in terms of imperial repression, based on their experience of the center's manipulation of the Gharabagh issue,[24] Dashnaks were declaring that the Russian empire "is the most acceptable, the most bearable" of all empires and Armenia should definitely stay under its suzerainty for its own benefit, if not survival.[25] Such a policy was implemented by lending (indirect) support to the communist leaders of Armenia against the nationalists, and even entertaining thoughts of an alliance with the Communist party in 1990.[26] This was more than irony; it was an outright contradiction of the traditional Dashnak position. Just as the Soviet regime in the homeland and the ARF were coming to terms with each other, the former was dissolving, leaving the Dashnaks with a skeleton it could not—and would not—get rid of. At this point the homeland was opening up to the diaspora, based on the ideals espoused by the latter, but it was the diaspora which could not accept the independence-minded nationalism of homeland intellectuals, counter-elites, and the masses. The initial contact between the two parts of the nation was indeed a reluctant embrace.

Organizationally, all three diaspora parties established themselves with much fanfare in Armenia during the summer and autumn of 1990. They began to publish newspapers, hold meetings, and establish various local bodies linked with the diaspora organizations. Once it became obvious that the communists were doomed, the Ramkavars and Hnchaks came to the staunch support of the nationalist leadership (based on their traditional belief that they should be on the side of any government in Armenia). But they failed to build a mass base for their parties. In the minds of most Armenians in the kin-state, they were tainted by their collaboration with the communist regime. The Dashnaks, in turn, set their sights on obtaining power and began to organize for that purpose. A familiar pattern was re-emerging.

There was, however, a brief "honeymoon" period between the homeland and the diaspora. Starting with Armenia's declaration of independence and the popular election of Levon Ter-Petrossian as president (September 21, 1991), and throughout the following months, Armenians everywhere (except some Dashnak leaders) were in a euphoric mood; there was a tremendous sense of national solidarity. The most visible manifestation of the close relationship between the two parts of the nation was a series of high-level appointments of government officials from the diaspora. Three of the most notable were U.S. citizens: Jirair (Gerard) Libaridian was the first to be appointed (January 1991); he became director of the Department of Research and Analysis attached to the president's office. From November 1995 to September 1997, he was senior advisor to President Ter-Petrossian. In January 1992 Sebouh Tashjian of California was chosen as minister of energy. But the most popular and high-profile appointment was that of Raffi Hovannisian; the 32-year-old, U.S.-born lawyer became independent Armenia's first foreign minister in October 1991. The selective use of a few diaspora experts in government continued throughout the 1990s. These appointments were seen as a clear attempt by the kin-state to reach out to the diaspora, to bridge the gap by extending a hand of cooperation to the diaspora and, more broadly, to the west.[27]

The period 1991–92 was also a time when some diaspora Armenians went to the homeland either to settle there (a minute number),[28] or to help with the nation building process by providing their skills to the country. Some were involved in the military effort in Gharabagh (probably fewer than two hundred), while others helped with civilian activities in the fields of medical care, education, and construction. It was seen as a matter of "duty" for diaspora Armenians from all sectors to go help the homeland in any way they could. Many of these direct contacts—whether through private initiatives or through work with non-governmental organizations or government agencies—have persisted through to the late 1990s, even though the earlier enthusiasm has subsided considerably. Although going to Armenia for at least a couple of weeks is seen as a rite of passage for many members of the diaspora, it remains a passage that only a few undertake. Difficult economic conditions in Armenia are partly to blame, but there is also an implicit realization that the homeland feels too different, too "foreign," for the diaspora—and, of course, vice versa.

Direct contact by both sides meant more knowledge of each other, and this in turn meant increased tensions and antagonism as the two bodies did not necessarily like what they saw on the "other" side. Armenians in the republic came to view the diaspora as more talk than assistance, as condescending and arrogant, eager to dispense advice despite being culturally "corrupted." Their limitations did not at all correspond to the high expectations the homeland had of its kin abroad. The diaspora, on the other hand, came to perceive Armenians in the homeland as lazy, opportunist, corrupted by Soviet rule—not at all the "pure" Armenians they were expecting to find. Both sides soon realized how culturally different they were from each other in terms of values, beliefs, and outlook. There was—and still is—much disappointment and even resentment, although many personal relationships transcend this popular view.[29]

The symbolic end of the honeymoon period was Raffi Hovannisian's resignation as foreign minister in October 1992, a year after his appointment. There were tensions between the kin-state and the diaspora much earlier, but Hovannisian's departure confirmed the obvious, especially since he left over policy differences regarding relations with Turkey. Once again the diaspora clearly split over the issue of how to relate to the republic. In addition to popular perceptions, acute political differences emerged between the Armenian government and the Dashnak side of the diaspora. The antagonism became more serious than simple political opposition because Dashnaks confused the kin-state with the kin-government. For the Dashnaks, opposing Ter-Petrossian also meant lack of assistance for the Armenian state; henceforth, they not only limited their support to the ARF network within Armenia, but they also tried to undermine activities outside the Dashnak realm, be it in the republic or elsewhere. This is not to say that the diaspora as a whole opposed the government, but one significant bloc of it came to work against the leadership of the kin-state, and by extension against the republic itself.[30] The ARF–government tension has become the most important dynamic in relations between the homeland and the diaspora.

The disputes which led to the chasm between the ARF and Ter-Petrossian were based on fundamental issues relating to the Armenian nation. They began over demands for independence from 1990 onward and relations with Moscow. The ARF has consistently advocated even closer ties with Russia. Turkey is another source of disagreement. The republic is willing to establish relations with Turkey without any conditions while the ARF puts Turkish recognition of the 1915 Genocide as a precondition. Diaspora Armenians on the whole tend to be more anti-Turkish than their kin in the republic. There are differences on the solution of the Gharabagh conflict as well. The ARF is more hardline than the government in its pronouncements, criticizing any solution short of complete independence for the region. On domestic issues, Dashnaks do not favor the mass privatization of the economy, maintaining that large industries and the country's infrastructure should remain under state control. They also opposed the 1995 constitution since it created a powerful presidential position. Accusations of lack of democracy, human rights abuses, and corruption in Armenia are recurrent themes in the Dashnak discourse as well.[31]

On the issue of citizenship, the ARF opposed the law forbidding dual citizenship, a provision which effectively prevented anyone in the diaspora from becoming a citizen of both the kin-state and a host-state. The Armenian government, on the other hand, objected to dual citizenship on the grounds that it would be a loophole through which Armenian citizens could avoid military service. More significantly, it would give members of the diaspora too much political clout within the republic while their long-term commitment and responsibility to it could not be guaranteed. It was reasoned that diaspora Armenians, living abroad, should not be on an equal footing with the locals, as dual citizenship would imply. Dual citizenship is specifically forbidden under Article 14 of the Armenian constitution, adopted in July 1995; however, according to the Law on the Legal Status of Foreign Citizens (adopted in June 1994), a foreign citizen of Armenian origin—or others with interests in Armenia—can obtain a ten-year, renewable residency permit (Article 21) at the cost of one thousand dollars. There are also other exceptions to the ban on dual citizenship; special "citizenships" can be granted by presidential decree, for example, to government advisors and ministers from abroad.

The citizenship issue underscored the basic difference between President Ter-Petrossian and the ARF on the role of the diaspora in the internal affairs of the republic. The Dashnaks, using the slogan "one nation, one homeland," blurred the line between the diaspora and the homeland. Their mentality is based on the belief that the nation is indivisible and therefore its politics should represent a symbiosis between the homeland and the diaspora. It is legitimate, in their view, for diaspora-based "pan-national" parties such as the ARF to have a direct say in the affairs of the kin-state. As Apo Boghigian, a Dashnak leader, says, "imposing distinctions between native Armenians and Diasporans when it comes to involvement in Armenia's politics is insulting."[32] Ter-Petrossian's approach was quite different. For the president, Armenia and the diaspora are two different political communities, and they should not meddle in each other's internal affairs. In his words, "the concept of national political parties which exist and function outside their country is unnatural. There will always be a mutual lack of understanding and trust, so long as the Diaspora leadership does not come to terms with the reality that policy is determined here, on this land."[33] For Ter-Petrossian the ARF is a "foreign" party which should not have the right to function in the homeland as long as it maintains organizational links with the worldwide party abroad. The ARF was banned in Armenia on December 28, 1994. The president issued a decree accusing the Dashnaks of harboring a secret paramilitary organization called Dro which, he said, was responsible for assassinations, drug trafficking, and activities designed to undermine the government. However, the legal basis of the ban (on which the Supreme Court later upheld the president's decree) was that the ARF was a "foreign" organization controlled from abroad. As of December 1997, the party remained outlawed, although it continued to operate semi-legally.

The Ter-Petrossian–ARF enmity was fiercely fought on the pages of the Armenian media, especially in the diaspora. The Dashnaks presented the ban not only as a sign of the dictatorial nature of the homeland's regime, but also as a wholesale rejection of the diaspora. Some of their attacks were directed personally against the president and were so vicious that even rank–and–file party members resented them. For example, the Montreal-based *Horizon Armenian Weekly* published a cartoon on January 23, 1995, which likened Ter-Petrossian to Stalin and Talaat Pasha (the architect of the 1915 Genocide and the ultimate symbol of evil for Armenians). Much of the diaspora Dashnak press degenerated to this level while covering political news from Armenia.[34] Even the "independent" press took sides, especially in North America. Supporting the homeland meant being sympathetic to Ter-Petrossian and his government and publishing anti-Dashnak opinion pieces. Once again, how to relate to Armenia divided rather than united the diaspora.

The Politics of Aid

Besides the Gharabagh movement, the December 1988 earthquake also had profound ramifications for homeland–diaspora relations. It caused massive devastation and took the lives of approximately 25,000 people. The diaspora mobilized on an unprecedented scale to collect and send much-needed aid to the homeland. The earthquake prompted an important change of attitude on the part of the diaspora. Roles were reversed, and once again the homeland was the one in need. This relationship intensified as conditions in Armenia became worse due to the war with Azerbaijan and economic collapse. Since 1988 sending aid to Armenia has become the operative paradigm of homeland–diaspora relations.

Diaspora organizations and individuals, a labor force abroad (mostly in the CIS),[35] as well as united efforts at fundraising[36] have been crucial in sending aid to the kin-state. But the organization that merits the longest discussion is the "Hayastan All–Armenian Fund" (the Armenia Fund) because of its potential significance in reformulating homeland–diaspora relations. It was established by the Armenian government in May 1992 as the main fundraising organization that would coordinate (and centralize) the efforts of the diaspora. It was representative of all important Armenian organizations. Its board of trustees by 1995 included Ter-Petrossian (as chair), the president of Gharabagh, the prime minister of Armenia, other government officials, both catholici of the Armenian Apostolic church, leaders of the three diaspora political parties, as well as major organizations and prominent Armenian individuals. The Armenia Fund is meant to be a strictly apolitical fundraising body. Its major projects include rebuilding the road that connects Armenia to Ghara-bagh, the Iran–Armenia gas pipeline, irrigation systems, and residential units damaged in the earthquake, as well as providing more day–to–day assistance. Money spent on its projects as of mid-1995 totaled $40 million. Its funds are distributed through state agencies, and the government has primary say on where the money goes.[37] But despite its attempts to keep politics out, the Armenia Fund is susceptible to homeland–diaspora tensions, as well as intra-community competition and infighting. For example, in 1995 the ARF withdrew its support because of the party's opposition to Ter-Petrossian. A year later, however, it agreed to participate in some of its fundraising activities.

Regardless of such tensions, it seems that the homeland government has decided to make the Armenia Fund the principal mechanism for its relations with the diaspora. Using the Fund as the main—if not the only—mediating body between the two, it seeks to take politics out of the relationship.[38] The president has concluded that using the established diaspora organizations as the republic's links to Armenians abroad is at best inefficient and at worse counterproductive. He has therefore emphasized the republic's own efforts to tap the resources of the diaspora directly and to control them through the Armenia Fund. Moreover, the Fund provides an opportunity to undermine traditional political parties by eroding their monopoly on community fundraising and on connections to the homeland. This approach could have important ramifications in the future. If it succeeds, it would push aside the diaspora parties by linking the kin-state with a "depoliticized" diaspora, connected to the homeland only on matters of aid and culture and through an organization controlled by the government of Armenia. Such a policy is a classic example of a kin-state using its "own" organization, including its allies abroad, to side-step opposition diaspora parties.[39]

The Politics of Lobbying

If financial aid is one element of the diaspora's contribution to the homeland, the other is lobbying and related political activities in relation to the kin-state. Ethnic lobbies play a significant role because they can support the kin-state by presenting its interests in the style and context of the political culture and foreign relations of the host-state—a particularly important task if the latter is a major power such as the United States. In some ways lobbies act like a political fifth column, but they "must justify their actions in terms of American national interests and values, answer to their US compatriots, and prove their loyalty to their home country."[40] The Armenian lobby in the United States has managed to do this reasonably well since 1991. Its most important accomplishments, in addition to presenting Armenia in a positive light to the U.S. government and facilitating links between the two states, have been the Humanitarian Aid Corridor Act and Section 907 of the Freedom Support Act. The latter, passed by Congress in 1992 and renewed every year since, bars direct U.S. government assistance to Azerbaijan because of its blockade of Armenia and Gharabagh. The former, which came into effect in 1996, prevents U.S. aid being sent to countries (such as Turkey) that blockade another recipient country.[41] The lobby is also active in ensuring that Armenia receives large amounts of foreign aid (in the range of $120 million to $150 million per year). It mobilizes against developments that favor Azerbaijan, such as the visit to the United States by Azerbaijan's president, Haidar Aliev, in July 1997. However, after late 1996 the work of the Armenian lobby became increasingly difficult. Armenians found that they were being pushed toward the "wrong" end of U.S. foreign policy in the region. The $8 billion in oil deals concluded between Azerbaijani and American companies since 1991 tilted the Clinton administration's policies more toward Azerbaijan than Armenia, a realignment that the Armenian lobby has found difficult to counter.

The activities of the main lobbying organizations—the Armenian Assembly of America and the Armenian National Committee of America (ANC)—are usually in full congruence with the policies of the Armenian government on most issues. The Assembly has been particularly supportive of the kin-state's agenda, acting almost like a second embassy. In addition, many diaspora individuals and community organizations materially support Armenian embassies and visiting delegations, helping the kin-state to maintain a wide network of consular and ambassadorial representatives from Washington to London to Beijing. But this is one side of the equation. The other is that diaspora groups can pursue policies independent of the kin-state's agenda, and even lobby against the homeland's government. The ANC, which is affiliated with the ARF, has been doing this as well since 1995. It has criticized the government for human rights abuses, it has taken a harder line on the Gharabagh issue and on relations with Turkey, and it has lobbied for lifting the ban on the ARF. In so doing it has been accused by many Armenians of undermining the work of the Assembly and the image of the Ter-Petrossian government. But the ANC, as with any other lobby organization unsupportive of the kin-state's leadership, must tread a fine line between criticizing the government and being labeled "anti-homeland." It is a difficult balancing act: how to lobby for the homeland while in opposition to its government.

Two additional issues have been important in relations between the diaspora and the kin-state. The first was the election of Karekin I as the All Armenian Catholicos of Ejmiatzin in April 1995. This was significant because Karekin was already the catholicos of the diaspora-based Holy See of Cilicia (under ARF hegemony in Lebanon). His election was "encouraged" by President Ter-Petrossian in a move which, on the one hand, seemed to facilitate national unity via church unity, and on the other, undermined Dashnak influence over the Cilician church, a development which led to resentment in that side of the diaspora. There was also displeasure in the non-Dashnak bloc since they now had a catholicos in Armenia whose legitimacy they had questioned while he was the head of the "rival" side of the church in Lebanon. Far from being seen as a move to reach out to the diaspora, Karekin's election led to further discontent among many Armenians in the republic. As far as they were concerned, both heads of the nation—the president and the catholicos—were now "outsiders."

The second issue is the relative lack of importance in Armenian politics of the "internal" diaspora, i.e., Armenians living in other former Soviet republics. The status of these communities was an election issue in 1996, in the context of the brain and labor drain in the country. But it has not been a source of tension or debate between Armenia and other post-Soviet countries (the refugee issue with Azerbaijan notwithstanding). Armenians in Georgia are mentioned occasionally, but only to emphasize that Armenia does not have any territorial claims against its neighbor, and that Yerevan does not wish to use the kin population there for any political purpose. The CIS diaspora (outside of Georgia and some other established communities, e.g., in Moscow) is a relatively new creation. It is predominantly a labor diaspora and is not politically organized. It is possible that in the future it could become more significant, but at this point when Armenians speak of homeland–diaspora relations, they still have in mind communities in the Middle East and in the west.

Conclusion

Since 1988 the fundamental transformations in Armenia have affected homeland–diaspora relations. But the essential question remains: How should the diaspora and the homeland relate to each other? On one side of this perennial issue is the post-Soviet leadership of the republic of Armenia, which sees itself as the government only of the three million Armenians who constitute the core of the national state. In the government's view, the diaspora could support Armenia materially, but there should be no formal political ties between the diaspora and the Armenian state. Others want to see the leader of the republic take more responsibility for the entire nation—both within and outside the state— by being more responsive to the homeland–diaspora duality. Vazgen Manukian, the opposition candidate during the 1996 presidential elections, criticized Ter-Petrossian on these grounds. Commenting on the differences between himself and the president, he remarked that there were "radical differences [in our] characterization of the Armenian people as a nation." According to Manukian, Ter-Petrossian "always insisted on ignoring the Diaspora as a 'dying presence,'" and instead focused only on the Armenians who live in the homeland as the people who would build statehood. "The president simply has written off the Diaspora as a vibrant and supportive entity and appears to be more interested in their financial input in Armenia."[42] The ARF argument is an extension of this logic: The Armenian state is the most significant element of the Armenian polity, but by no means the only one. The first of these two approaches, that of the government, is state-centric. The second, that of the opposition, is more pan-national. The diaspora itself is divided along these lines.

At the base of these divisions lies a subtext that Armenians rarely discuss: that there are simply different entities, with different interests and identities, which make up the nation. On the diaspora side, Genocide-related issues, the fear of assimilation (which Armenians powerfully call the "white genocide"), religious and cultural practices, and anti-Turkishness are of primary importance. For the homeland, the issues are different. Peace and regional security are of paramount concern; the Gharabagh conflict and economic difficulties dictate political priorities. The homeland's concerns have more to do with the physical survival of the kin-state than with cultural survival and the wider "Armenian cause." This is not to say that one side is not concerned, or does not empathize, with the problems of the other. But their historical experiences differ and hence their political mentalities, cultures, and priorities—their appreciation of the problems facing the nation—are not necessarily congruent. The answer to the question "Where is my homeland?" thus shifts among, or exists simultaneously as, the host-state, the kin-state, and the "multi-local" diaspora itself.

Despite such profound divisions, differences, and competing identities, a sense of belonging to the same nation—of being, or feeling, Armenian—prevails. There is a thread that ties the diaspora to the Armenian state and vice versa, that makes it possible to discuss homeland–diaspora relations, that connects all the diaspora Armenians together, in short, that makes it possible to speak of "Armenianness" in the context of one nation. This thread is the subjectivity of national identity, the idea of belonging to one particular nation despite real differences. Perhaps the power of the thread comes from the fact that Armenians have very deep historical roots as a (persecuted) collective deprived of their homeland, of a state, and hence constantly feeling the insecurities of a diaspora existence. Being on the threshold of disappearance is a powerful incentive not to disappear. Still, Armenians are divided between two sets of institutions, polities, imaginations, and cultures—with each set itself fragmented along political lines. But they all maintain they are one nation, bound by a subjective sense of belonging. The irony is that the notion of "homeland" is the core of their identity, of being Armenian, but it is also the source of many divisions. How to relate to their existing homeland is what keeps Armenians separate, while the imperative of relating to a homeland itself keeps them united as a nation.

Notes

The author would like to thank Dr. Ara Sanjian for his insightful and detailed comments on earlier drafts of this chapter. This chapter was written before the departure from office of Levon Ter-Petrossian.

1. There were periodic local rebellions in Armenia proper against the Ottoman state/army and Kurdish overlords (Zeitun and Van, 1862; Erzerum, 1863). Military activity acquired an explicitly national character in the 1890s with the establishment of revolutionary parties. The rebellions, however, did provide an extremely important precedent of resistance.

2. These figures are from Khachig Tölölyan, "Exile Governments in Armenian Polity," in Yossi Shain, ed., *Governments–in–Exile in Contemporary World Politics* (New York: Routledge, 1991), 170, 180. No sources are cited. According to primary sources, there were approximately two million Armenians in the Ottoman empire in 1914; half lived in the six villayets of Armenia, the other half in other parts of the empire. See Levon Marashlian, *Politics and Demography: Armenians, Turks, and Kurds in the Ottoman Empire* (Cambridge: Zoryan Institute, 1991), 30–38.

3. Claire Mouradian, "L'Arménie soviétique et la diaspora," *Les temps modernes*, nos. 504–505–506 (July–August–September 1988): 286. See also Ronald Suny, "The Revenge of the Past: Socialism and Ethnic Conflict in Transcaucasia," *New Left Review*, no. 184 (November–December 1990): 5–34.

4. This trend was part of the larger homogenization process within each of the Transcaucasian republics. In 1926 Armenians made up 47 percent of the republic's population; in 1959 the figure had increased to 56 percent. According to the 1979 census, 2.7 million out of the 3 million inhabitants were Armenian. The general trend was for Armenians to migrate from other Soviet republics (especially Georgia and Azerbaijan) to their "own" republic where they could easily get education, services, and jobs in their language. The largest minority in Armenia, 5.2 percent or 161,000 people, were the Azeris (who were expelled after 1988, making the republic more than 95 percent homogenous). Figures are based on the 1979 Soviet census; Mouradian, "L'Arménie," 286; and Claire Mouradian, "L'immigration des Arméniens de la diaspora vers la RSS d'Arménie, 1946–1962," *Cahiers du monde russe et soviétique* 20, no.1 (1979): 100.

5. Tölölyan refers to these activities using the concept "governments–of–exile." See his "Exile Governments," 167.

6. My account here is generalized from Nikola B. Schahgaldian, *The Political Integration of an Immigrant Community into a Composite Society: The Armenians in Lebanon, 1920–1974* (Ph.D. diss., Columbia University, 1979), particularly chapter 3. Suny develops the same argument in Ronald Suny, *Looking Toward Ararat: Armenia in Modern History* (Bloomington: Indiana University Press, 1993), 218–19.

7. The Armenian "national" church is divided along political lines. Since the 1950s it has had two competing heads, both with the title of "catholicos." One is based in Lebanon and is the head of the Holy See of Cilicia (under Dashnak

hegemony); the other is based in Ejmiatzin, Armenia, with the title of Catholicos of All Armenians. The latter, until 1991, was subject to Soviet authority. Since 1991 the two sides of the church have been cooperating, but they have not united. The schism in the 1950s was purely political in nature (Dashnaks versus Soviet Armenia) and not at all theological. It led to the institutional division of the church in the diaspora as a whole and within specific diaspora communities, as various parish churches pledged their allegiance to one or the other of the catholici.

8. This, of course, is a generalization of a complex dynamic. First, there were also "neutral" (*chezok*) elements, especially large in North America by the 1980s, but they usually dovetailed with the prevailing blocs. Second, the diaspora was not just one homogenous entity. There were marked differences in terms of habits and outlook between communities in the west and the Middle East. Third, within each bloc there were divisions, but not deep enough to undermine the bloc system. Finally, there were no blocs in the Armenian community in Turkey and in some very small communities, such as in India.

9. The first instrument on the Soviet Armenian side to deal with the diaspora (to generate aid, disseminate propaganda, and control parts of it against Dashnak influence) was the Aid Committee for Armenia (HOK). It was founded in 1921 and dissolved in 1937. See Mouradian, "L'Arménie," 260–67; Ulf Björklund, "Armenia Remembered and Remade: Evolving Issues in a Diaspora," *Ethnos* 58, nos. 3–4 (1993): 341.

10. Diaspora Armenian students were first admitted to institutions of higher learning (vocational schools and universities) in Soviet Armenia in 1959. Between 1963 and 1985, out of the 1,590 admitted, 1,244 graduated. Approximately 80 percent were from the Middle East. In 1985–86 there were 108 diaspora Armenian students registered in Armenia. Ludwig Gharibjanian, "Grtagan-Mshagoutayin gyanke hayasdani metch," *Ararat* [Beirut], January 1, 1986, pp. 56–57.

11. Mouradian, "L'Arménie," 287–90, 292; Björklund, "Armenia Remembered," 343.

12. One explanation of the party's change of attitude—becoming "pro-Soviet" and less concerned about independence despite its official position against Soviet rule—is attributed to KGB infiltration of its top leadership. See Oleg Kalugin, *Spy Master: My 32 Years in Intelligence and Espionage Against the West* (London: Smith Gryphon Publishers, 1994), 193; S. Melik-Hakobian, "Establishment of the Second Republic of Armenia and the Dashnaktsutiun (ARF)," *Nor Gyank*, November 28, 1996, p. 54.

13. In 1945 a "repatriation" drive was launched by the Soviet authorities, ostensibly to populate the historic Armenian regions of Kars and Ardahan to be acquired in the future from Turkey. The land claims, made in the context of superpower geopolitical maneuvering, came to naught, but between 1946 and 1948 some 100,000 Armenians immigrated to Soviet Armenia (67 percent from the Middle East and the rest from Europe.) About 90–95 percent were originally from western Armenia and were Genocide survivors. They represented 9

percent of the 1946 Soviet Armenian population of 1.2 million. None of these immigrants, however, was a returnee *per se*, and the official term "repatriation" is therefore a misnomer. Importantly, the "repatriates" introduced a new cleavage in Armenian society. In addition to existing regional divides, there was now a divide between locals and *aghpars* (meaning "brother" but used as a derogatory term). This divide remains, albeit in milder form, today. Already in the 1920s and 1930s, approximately 40,000 had migrated to Armenia, and a further 32,000 moved there between 1962 and the mid-1980s. See Mouradian, "L'immigration," 79–88, 99–100; Mouradian, "L'Arménie," 284, 286; Suny, *Looking Toward Ararat*, 163–69; and from the Soviet Armenian perspective, H. Yu. Meliksetian, *Hayrenik-spiurk arnchutiunnere ev hayrenadardzutiune (1920–1980)* (Yerevan: Yerevan University Publications, 1985).

14. The numbers are based on Anny Bakalian, *Armenian-Americans: From Being to Feeling Armenian* (New Brunswick: Transaction Publishers, 1993), 12–13, 80 (note 13). Note that Armenians from the Soviet republic do not comprise more than 5–10 percent of the total diaspora population in the United States (p. 25).

15. Between 1970 and 1982, 352,000 people moved to Armenia from other Soviet republics. The outflow was 208,000. *Sovetakan Hayastan* (Yerevan: Armenian Soviet Encyclopedia, 1987), 24.

16. There were 365,000 Armenians in the RSFSR. These figures are based on the 1979 census. The 1979 census is more reliable than the 1989 census; sudden population shifts among Armenians as a result of the December 1988 earthquake, the growing refugee problem, and the confusion of early 1989 made the census figures relating to Armenians questionable.

17. In the Javakheti area, which includes the Akhalkalaki and Ninitsminda *raions*, Armenians make up 90 percent (approximately 100,000 people) of the population. In Akhaltsikhe they are 50 percent and in Tbilisi 12 percent (150,000). There were also some 76,000 Armenians in Abkhazia, comprising 14.6 percent of that region's population. These figures are from 1989 and are based on Revaz Gachechiladze, *The New Georgia: Space, Society, Politics* (London: UCL Press, 1995), especially pp. 74, 89–90. The Armenian population in the Nagorno-Karabakh autonomous *oblast'* was 130,000 in 1988.

18. The estimated world population of Armenians by the mid-1990s was six to seven million. These figures are no more than "guesstimates" in the absence of any reliable data about Armenians living outside the kin-state. Of the diaspora, approximately 25 percent live in the west (Europe, the Americas, and Australia—this figure was one percent in 1914), 8 percent in the Middle East, and 20 percent in CIS countries, excluding Armenia. Slightly less than half the world's Armenians live in the homeland. For various estimates see Bakalian, *Armenian-Americans*, 145–56; George Bournoutian, *A History of the Armenian People*, vol. 2 (Costa Mesa: Mazda Publishers, 1994), 177–89; *Sovetakan Hayastan*, 27; Khachig Tölölyan, "Cultural Narrative and the Motivation of the Terrorist," *Journal of Strategic Studies* 10, no. 4 (1987): 222; Claire Mouradian, *L'Arménie* (Paris: Presses universitaires de France, Que sais–je Series, 1995), 111.

19. Based on figures cited by Bakalian, *Armenian-Americans*, 14. See also pp. 11–18.

20. For an analysis of the literary manifestation of this hybrid culture see, Lorne Shirinian, "Transculturation and Armenian Diaspora Writing: Literature on the Edge," *Armenian Review* 45, no. 4 (1992): 39–46.

21. For a concise statement of her argument, see Bakalian, *Armenian-Americans*, 5–6, 44. For a critique, see Susan Pattie, "At Home in Diaspora: Armenians in America," *Diaspora* 3, no. 2 (1994): 185–98.

22. Melik-Hakobian, "Establishment," 51.

23. Both the communiqué and a particularly virulent response to it from Armenia (by Paruir Hayrikian's National Self-Determination Group) are published in Gerard J. Libaridian, ed., *Armenia at the Crossroads: Democracy and Nationhood in the Post-Soviet Era* (Watertown: Blue Crane Books, 1991), 127–29, 130–34.

24. For two of the most influential statements which advocated a "separate path" away from the Soviet Union, see Rafael Ishkhanian, "The Law of Excluding the Third Force" (1989) and Vazgen Manukian, "It is Time to Jump off the Train" (1990). They are both reprinted in Libaridian, ed., *Armenia at the Crossroads*, 9–38, 51–86. It should, however, be emphasized that the Gharabagh movement did not begin as an anti-Soviet independence movement. It sought, on the whole, to address problems facing Armenians within the context of the reforming Soviet Union. Only after it became clear that the central authorities were not going to solve the issue in favor of the Armenians did the movement put forth demands for autonomy and independence.

25. Interview with Edik Hovhannisian, *Horizon Armenian Weekly*, July 3, 1989, pp. 7, 14. Hovhannisian, who had fled the Soviet Union some seventeen years earlier, had joined the ARF and become one of its most prominent representatives. In the 1980s he was accused by some Armenians of being a CIA operative and in the 1990s of being a KGB agent and playing an instrumental role in making the ARF a pro-Soviet organization. See Melik-Hakobian, "Establishment," 54. See also "Nshmarner," *Yeraguin Droshak*, October 1996, pp. 18–21.

26. Melik-Hakobian, "Establishment," 53, and private discussions with party "insiders."

27. The president himself is difficult to include in the category of diaspora Armenian despite the fact that he was born in Syria. His family moved to Armenia in 1946 as part of the post-war repatriation drive when Levon Ter-Petrossian was one year old. For all intents and purposes he is a "native" Armenian, although there is some antagonism against him for being a "repatriate" *aghpar*. On a number of occasions during the 1996 elections, the author heard tirades against Ter-Petrossian that emphasized his "foreignness:" He was sometimes described, in profane language, as the "son" of Arabs and the "groom" of Jews!

28. Reliable numbers are scarce, but probably fewer than one thousand have moved from the diaspora to Armenia since independence—not taking into

account refugees from Azerbaijan and other returnees from the CIS. Despite the insignificant numbers, the topic of "return" was prevalent in the diaspora. See, for example, the special issue of *Armenian International Magazine (AIM)* devoted to the subject, February 1993, pp. 10–17.

29. See Björklund, "Armenia Remembered," 356–57; William Safran, "Diasporas in Modern Societies: Myths of Homeland and Return," *Diaspora* 1, no. 1 (1991): 93–94.

30. It is difficult for the ARF to distinguish between government and state because it simply does not have any experience of being a political party within an Armenian state. In only two years in their 100–year history (1918–1920) have Dashnaks operated within the confines of a specific state. At all other times, they have been a party (or a "government") of Armenians in many countries.

31. This summary is based on the Dashnak press in the diaspora since 1992, the opposition press in Armenia in 1996, as well as interviews with ARF leaders in Yerevan, August–September 1996. For a brief summary of the ARF platform in English, see *Armenia and Karabagh Factbook* (Washington: Armenian Assembly of America, 1996), 24–26.

32. *AIM*, November–December 1994, p. 39.

33. Interview in *AIM*, March 1994, p. 32. See also interview in *AIM*, January–February 1997, p. 31.

34. One commentator went to the extreme of writing, "At this stage, it is possible to assert with a clear conscience that the situation would have been preferable if Armenia was directly occupied by Turkey." *Horizon Armenian Weekly*, March 13, 1995, p. 16.

35. According to the chairman of the Armenian Central Bank, personal transfers to Armenia totaled $100 million in 1995 alone. Noyan Tapan News Agency, Yerevan, November 16, 1996. This seems like a fantastically high amount given the fact that the government's total budget revenue for 1996 was estimated at $237 million. In addition to the $100 million, another $120 million entered the country as humanitarian aid and $30 million as investment, bringing the total to $250 million, according to the chairman.

36. The main example of this has been the "United Armenian Fund" (which includes six other organizations from all major sectors of the U.S. diaspora). It has sent $150 million worth of aid to Armenia in the past seven years—from heating fuel to medicine. Its financial core has been the American Armenian billionaire Kirk Kerkorian and his Lincy Foundation. *AIM*, December 1993, pp. 16–21; *Factbook*, 46. The Armenian General Benevolent Union, the most important and established philanthropic institution of the (non-Dashnak) diaspora, should also be mentioned as it has reoriented its efforts toward Armenia. Its assistance stretches from soup kitchens to the American University of Armenia.

37. *AIM*, February 1993, pp. 21–24; April 1996, pp. 16–20; *Factbook*, 47; *Nor Gyank*, September 21, 1995; Armenia Fund brochures.

38. See, for example, Ter-Petrossian's election manifesto, *Entrakan tzragir* (Yerevan, 1996), 14–15.

39. Besides the Armenia Fund, Ter-Petrossian's government does not have a clear or coherent policy toward the diaspora. However, on May 7, 1997, the president did sign a decree creating the State Council for Relations with the Diaspora to handle relations with Armenians abroad. It remains to be seen what will come of it.

40. Yossi Shain, "Ethnic Diasporas and U.S. Foreign Policy," *Political Science Quarterly* 109, no. 5 (1994–95): 813.

41. The U.S. president can waive this provision for reasons of national security; Bill Clinton has done so. For more information on the Armenian lobby in the United States, see *AIM*, February 1996, pp. 16–21.

42. *Armenian Reporter International*, November 11, 1995, p. 25.

5

The Ukrainians:
Engaging the "Eastern Diaspora"

Andrew Wilson

The better-known half of the Ukrainian diaspora lives in the west, above all in North America.[1] In Canada, the United States, and elsewhere, Ukrainians have been quite successful in maintaining a sense of identity, developing social and political networks, and organizing themselves for collective action and lobby politics.[2] This chapter, however, will concentrate on what Ukrainians refer to as the "eastern diaspora," ethnic Ukrainian communities living in the states of the former Soviet Union and in Poland, Slovakia, and Romania.[3] This half-forgotten "other" diaspora has a much weaker sense of Ukrainian identity and has to date been relatively quiescent politically. Ukrainians living in the mainly border regions of former communist Europe have historically been subject to a variety of cross-cutting pressures on their identity. Ukraine never really had fixed state boundaries until 1991, and the complex forms of engagement between the Ukrainian and Russian peoples that developed during the Romanov and Soviet periods created a complex environment in which the fluid boundaries of ethnic identity mirrored the flexible boundaries of Ukraine itself. Likewise, there is no clear-cut identity boundary on Ukraine's western borders between Ukrainians and Belarusians, Slovaks, and others. Indeed, the founder of Ukrainian political geography, Stepan Rudnyts'kyi (1877–1937), argued that the first task of the discipline was to define who actually was a Ukrainian.[4]

The Ukrainian case therefore points to the relative importance of the kin-state and its ability to "diasporize" the identity of its co-ethnics abroad. Processes of identity definition are always relational, and the kin-state rather than the diaspora itself is often the key force in defining diaspora politics. If the new Ukrainian state adopts an aggressive policy toward the diaspora, it may therefore help to firm up identities that have been amorphous and fluid in the past.

Other relational factors are also likely to affect identities among Ukraine's eastern diaspora. If host-states adopt and pursue powerful nationalizing agendas, they may ironically help to consolidate a diasporic identity (unless they are strong enough to generate overriding assimilative pressures). However, there are other relationships beyond Rogers Brubaker's famous "triadic nexus" of national minorities, nationalizing states, and national homelands.[5] Links with other ethnic groups, both majorities and minorities, are likely to be particularly important in the Ukrainian case. First, Ukrainians abroad are also bound up in Russia's process of defining its post-Soviet identity. In the Russian Federation, Ukrainians must therefore relate to a Russian nationalizing state, but in third-party host-states like Latvia and Moldova, Ukrainians and Russians—as representatives of a broad "East Slavic" minority group—may jointly be the object of nationalizing policies. Ukrainians further abroad must develop their identities in relation to still other diasporic groups. Finally, international organizations will also have a role in interacting with the various parties and influencing processes of identity formation.

Of course, given the tendency of Soviet census practice to reify ethnicity and ignore phenomena of mixed, situational, or blurred identity, it cannot be assumed that all those nominally labeled as Ukrainian (or Russian) necessarily possess a Ukrainian (or Russian) identity. Nor will they automatically identify with the modern Ukrainian state as their "homeland." A diasporic group will always contain rival ethnic (and non-ethnic) entrepreneurs, with different discourses and political agendas.

Two extreme points of view exist about Ukraine's eastern diaspora. On the one hand, Ukrainian nationalists argue that "denationalization" or "russification" (and analogous processes in other states) has masked the presence of some ten to twelve million, or even fifteen to twenty million, ethnic Ukrainians in the east, and that the modern Ukrainian state should act as their patron and protector. On the other hand, many commentators in both east and west have argued that Ukrainians abroad are more likely to make common cause with their fellow Slavs as part of a general "Russian-speaking" (*russkoiazychne*) or "post-Soviet" diaspora.

This chapter will analyze both these views, but will also seek to look beyond them and use different categories of analysis. The chapter first briefly addresses the issue of the actual number of Ukrainians in the eastern diaspora, before examining the different relational configurations and geographical and sociological contexts of the diaspora. Finally, the chapter explores the development of Ukraine's policy toward the eastern diaspora, seeking to explain why Kyiv has been relatively restrained in its efforts to reach out to co-ethnic communities since 1991.

How Many Ukrainians?

There is little agreement on the size of the eastern diaspora. The first column in Table 5.1 shows figures from the last official Soviet census taken in 1989, which recorded 6.8 million Ukrainians as resident in the Soviet Union outside Ukraine, along with the number of Ukrainians officially recorded in neighboring states to the west. The figures for Slovakia are derived from the 1991 Czechoslovak census and those for Romania from the census conducted in 1992. Polish censuses, however, never asked direct questions concerning ethnic minority affiliation, so the figure is a more general estimate. The number of Ukrainians in Hungary is negligible.[6]

However, many Ukrainians argue that official figures are a vast underestimate, because they have been distorted by deliberate under-reporting and by the legacy of decades of forcible "russification," "romanianization," "belarusianization," and their equivalents elsewhere.[7] Most ostensibly scientific estimates place the number of Ukrainians resident in the non-Ukrainian Soviet republics in 1989 as in fact closer to 10–12 million,[8] although some can go as high as 16 million or even 20 million.[9] Soviet census figures for the Baltic, Transcaucasian, and Central Asian republics are accepted as reasonably accurate; controversy has centered on former republics where "denationalization" was supposedly more prevalent. In Moldova population estimates have risen to 800,000; in Belarus to between 500,000 and 1 million; in Russia to 6.5 million; and in Kazakhstan sharply higher to 2.4 million. The second column in Table 5.1 shows the most frequent upper estimates given by Ukrainians (still higher figures are mentioned in the sections on individual countries below where relevant). There is no third column for lower estimates. If Ukrainians continue to assimilate, it is possible that their reported numbers could actually fall below the official 1989 Soviet figures as the post-Soviet states begin to hold their own censuses, but no precise projections for this scenario exist.

Types of Diasporic Community

Although Ukrainian nationalist political entrepreneurs often try to project a homogenous identity onto the eastern Ukrainian diaspora, this chapter will seek to analyze several different ways of living as a diasporic group. Ukrainians in Russia have been subject to the nationalizing pressure of a powerful host-state (the Romanov empire, the

TABLE 5.1   Ukrainians in the Former Soviet Union and Eastern Europe

	Officially Recorded	Upper Estimates
Russian Federation	4,362,872	6,500,000
Belarus	291,008	1,000,000
Moldova	600,366	800,000
Central Asia		
Kazakhstan	896,240	2,400,000
Uzbekistan	153,197	——
Kyrgyzstan	108,027	——
Tajikistan	41,375	——
Turkmenistan	35,578	——
Baltic states		
Latvia	92,101	——
Estonia	48,271	——
Lithuania	44,789	——
Transcaucasia		
Georgia	52,445	——
Azerbaijan	32,345	——
Armenia	8,341	——
Total for former		10,000,000–
Soviet Union	6,766,953	12,000,000
Poland	180,000	500,000
Slovakia	30,478[a]	203,000
Romania	65,764	300,000

[a]Includes Ruthenians.

Sources: First column, former Soviet Union: 1989 census and Ann Lencyk Pawliczko, ed., *Ukraine and Ukrainians Throughout the World: A Demographic and Sociological Guide to the Homeland and its Diaspora* (Toronto: University of Toronto Press, 1994), 127. First column, Poland: B. Kravtsiv et al., "Poland," in Danylo Husar Struk, ed., *Encyclopaedia of Ukraine*, vol. 4 (Toronto: University of Toronto Press, 1993), 82. First column, Slovakia: Robert J. Kaiser, "Czechoslovakia: The Disintegration of a Binational State," in Graham Smith, ed., *Federalism: The Multiethnic Challenge* (London: Longman, 1995), 215. First column, Romania: Pawliczko, *Ukraine and Ukrainians*, 189. Second column, areas outside Russia: Volodymyr Patrushev et al., *Ukraïns'ka diaspora u sviti* (Kyiv: Znannia, 1993), 18–20. Second column, Russia: Oleksandr Rudenko-Desniak, ed., *My—grazhdane Rossii: materialy I kongressa ukraintsev Rossiiskoi Federatsii* (Moscow: Slavianskii dialog, 1994), 85, based on materials from the Union of Ukrainians in Russia.

Soviet Union, and now independent Russia) for centuries. Moreover, they still exist in a Russian-language environment. Second, there are Ukrainians who live alongside Russians in third-party host-states where both are minorities, creating a different type of dynamic in the Ukrainian–Russian relationship. Third, there are Ukrainians in western host-states, such as Poland and Slovakia, where there are virtually no Russians but there are other historical obstacles to developing a Ukrainian diasporic identity.

Overlaying these distinctions are differences in the geography and sociology of diasporic communities. Some Ukrainians live in potential ethno-regional units, mostly contiguous to the Ukrainian border. Others live as a non-territorial cultural community or as isolated individuals. Finally, there are those nominal Ukrainians who live as members of other diasporic communities. Ethnic entrepreneurs are likely to find it easiest to mobilize individuals in the first type of community, especially if: first, the region in which they live is perceived to be an irredenta of the broader homeland; second, the diasporic community is still ethnically dominant in the region; and third, powerful symbols of past statehood or administrative status are attached to the ethno-region or there is some myth of attachment to the original "homeland," as with Albanians in Kosovo, Russians in Crimea, or Armenians in Nagorno-Karabakh.

In the case of the eastern Ukrainian diaspora, such myths and symbols do exist, but their contemporary resonance is limited. As different Ukrainian territories have only rarely enjoyed the benefits of statehood, in their efforts to mobilize diasporic communities, nationalist political entrepreneurs cannot always refer to concrete historical entities, such as the historical region of Slobids'ka (or "free") Ukraine that straddled the current Ukrainian–Russian border, and the early medieval "city-state" of Tmutorokan in the Kuban. Instead, Ukrainian political geography has relied on migration myths to delineate diasporic territories, and on the definition of Ukrainian "ethno-linguistic territory" as those areas in which ethnic Ukrainians make up, or once made up, an ethnic majority or plurality in the countryside (rather than in the "cosmopolitan" cities).[10]

Ukrainians in Russia

The majority of the Ukrainian eastern diaspora, 4.4 million out of the official 6.8 million, lives in Russia. Most were originally Orthodox peasants who left Ukraine when their sense of "homeland" was limited and in essence parochial, and when no Ukrainian state was in existence. Many barely understood themselves as migrants, since they were simply spreading across the steppe in search of land and security. The eastern borders of the Ukrainian "ethnographic territory," therefore, gradually merged with those of southern Russia, without clear boundary markers ever having been established. Local Ukrainian and Russian dialects are close and contain many mutual borrowings.[11] For those who traveled further afield, apart from a brief period in the 1920s and early 1930s when some Ukrainian educational and cultural institutions were created outside the Ukrainian Soviet republic, "national" loyalties were shaped in a Soviet/Russian context. Because the consolidation of the east Slavic peoples was the cornerstone of "Soviet" identity, the only officially recognized Ukrainian diaspora under the Soviet Union was outside the Soviet federation, in western Europe and North America.

The Kuban

Of all potential *Ukraïna irredenta* , the Kuban region (the western part of the Caucasian steppe, between the Sea of Azov, the Straits of Kerch, and Stavropol—now the Krasnodar *krai* within the Russian Federation) has historically had the closest connection with the Ukrainian heartland. It is also known as *Malynovyi Klyn* (the painted wedge).[12]

The local myth of origin/arrival holds that the region was first populated in the modern era by Ukrainian Cossacks from Zaporozhia (Zaporizhzhia), after the destruction of their headquarters on the river Dnieper (Dnipro) in 1775 forced them to seek a new home further afield (they first settled on the river Danube and arrived in the Kuban in 1792).[13] Some historians, however, go even further back and date the origins of Ukrainian settlement to the 1630s, or even to the "kingdom of Tmutorokan," established as an outpost of Kievan Rus' on the eastern shore of the Straits of Kerch in A.D. 965.[14] Ukrainian historians also stress the importance of the tradition of military service under the tsars in maintaining a sense of identity in the region, despite the abolition of its administrative unity in 1924. On the other hand, the Kuban was also settled by Russian peasants from the north, particularly after the emancipation in 1861, and by Cossacks from the Don and Volga regions.

During the Ukrainian "national revival" in the quarter century before 1917, a small but growing local intelligentsia, including the historians Ivan Popko and Fedir Shcherbyna, had considerable success in propagating the Zaporozhian and other myths.[15] Consequently, a small but significant local Ukrainian movement already existed in 1917, and in the turmoil after the revolution was able to set up a Kuban Popular Republic in February 1918. These ukrainophiles established diplomatic relations with the Ukrainian Popular Republic in Kyiv and even developed plans for a political union between the two republics. Significantly, however, the ukrainophile republic was only one of several forces in the region, including the Bolsheviks and a rival "Cossack" republic.[16] The arrival of Denikin's White armies meant that the ukrainophiles' plans came to naught, and many local Ukrainian activists were shot or forced to flee.

Ukrainians have argued that the policy of "nativization" (*korenizatsiia*)—adopted in the 1920s as politicians from the Ukrainian SSR, such as Mykola Skrypnyk, sought to extend their influence in the region—would have achieved significant results in the Kuban had the policy been allowed to run its course. Some 2.3 million Ukrainians lived in the Kuban in 1926, making up 67 percent of the population of Kuban *okrug*, and by the end of the decade there were over 2,000 Ukrainian-language schools with just under 300,000 pupils.[17] However, the Kuban was one of the first regions to suffer from Moscow's crackdown on Ukrainian activism, beginning with the uncovering in 1929 of a supposed organization for the "Union of Kuban with Ukraine." A decree of December 1932 ordered the wholesale conversion of local schools and media to Russian,[18] and the population suffered particularly in the 1932–33 famine.[19] Only 196,000 Ukrainians were recorded in the 1989 Soviet census in Krasnodar *krai*.[20]

The Ukrainian version of history is that the Kuban was singled out for harsh treatment precisely because of the strong local Ukrainian movement. The Russian version argues that ukrainophilism was only one identity option among many and that its decline was due to the natural victory of the Russian/Soviet option. The early "diasporizing project" of Skrypnyk and others in the 1920s was therefore, on this view, more artificial than its termination in the 1930s. In the 1990s, activists from Ukraine helped set up a ukrainophile movement and publish a newspaper, *Kozats'kyi krai* (Cossack Land). Significantly, however, as in the 1917–21 period, the ukrainophiles must compete with a rival russophile Cossack movement with its own myths and symbols.[21]

East Slobozhanshchyna

A second possible ethno-region is the historical territory of Slobozhanshchyna, or Slobids'ka Ukraine.[22] The five Cossack *polky* (regimental districts) that defined the region in the seventeenth and eighteenth centuries covered an area stretching from Sumy and Kharkiv to Ostrogorsk and the banks of the Don, straddling what is now the Ukrainian–Russian border.[23] "East Slobozhanshchyna" (the title of a ukrainophile newspaper published in the region since 1993) is therefore the southeastern half of the modern Russian *oblast'* of Voronezh and parts of the Kursk and Belgorod *oblasts*.[24] "West Slobozhanshchyna" lies inside Ukraine. The 1989 Soviet census recorded 122,622 Ukrainians in Voronezh, 22,728 in Kursk, and 78,931 in Belgorod,[25] but Ukrainian activists claim the true figure is up to "a million" in Voronezh alone.[26]

Ukrainians claim that the territory was first settled by the Siveriany (a proto-Ukrainian tribe) at the time of Kievan Rus'.[27] Although largely emptied by the Tatar incursion, it was re-populated by migrants from central Ukraine from the 1630s onward. The region achieved a special administrative status linked to the Hetmanate (the Cossack quasi-state established in 1648) until 1765, and it survived as a separate province (*guberniia*) until 1835, when it was divided between Kharkiv, Voronezh, and Kursk. Religious and cultural links to the Hetmanate were strong. Originally, only the Ostrogors'k *polk* belonged to the Russian Orthodox church (via the Voronezh eparchy); the rest of Slobids'ka Ukraine had strong links with the Hetmanate church (via the Belgorod, or Bilhorod, eparchy).

As in the Kuban, in the period before 1917 the local Ukrainian intelligentsia was active in promoting national "revival" (Kharkiv was the original center of the national movement in the early nineteenth century). Two congresses of local Ukrainians in Ostrogorsk in May and August 1917 demanded that the region come under the jurisdiction of the Central Rada in Kyiv,[28] and the Soviet Ukrainian government regularly repeated the demand (in 1920, 1922, 1924–25, and 1927) so as to incorporate the 1.7 million Ukrainians who were then recorded in the region.[29] Although unsuccessful, the government was able to promote a limited ukrainianization of the region in the late 1920s, but after 1932 all Ukrainian schools and media were closed.

Also, as in the Kuban, East Slobozhanshchyna was in reality populated from both the west and the north. Although the stream from the west may initially have been stronger, in practice East Slobozhanshchyna could be regarded as a paradigm case of the transitional identity of the border region. Ukrainians have always shared the area with Russians. Had the region been granted to the Ukrainian SSR, the inhabitants might have been turned into Ukrainians, with a strong residual Russian influence. The reality, however, was the other way around.

Povolzhia and Donshchyna

Migrants leaving left-bank Ukraine from the middle of the sixteenth century onward also reached marginal Ukrainian "ethnolinguistic territory" in the areas of the Don and Lower Volga rivers. In the Lower Volga region, known in Ukrainian as "Povolzhia," they were relatively dispersed,[30] but near the mouth of the Don river (the "Donshchyna" region), Ukrainians claim three separate areas of ethnolinguistic territory: around the town of Taganrog (Tahanrih); the area between the rivers Don and Donets', east of the border between what is now Luhansk *oblast'* in Ukraine and Rostov *oblast'* in Russia; and the area to the south of the Don river toward the Caucasian foothills.

The Ukrainian claim is that the region was settled simultaneously by Zaporozhian (i.e., Ukrainian) and Don Cossacks.[31] The Tahanrih region (recorded as 71 percent Ukrainian in the 1920s) was part of the Ukrainian SSR between 1921 and 1925, but the effects of ukrainianization were limited.[32] The Don Cossack tradition in the region is clearly the stronger.

Non-Contiguous Territories

Siryi Klyn. Between 1880 and 1914 some two million peasants from the Ukrainian *guberniias* in the Russian empire migrated to what was then the steppe *krais* of southwest Siberia and northern Turkestan, spurred by land hunger after the 1861 emancipation, the growth of the railways, and Stolypin's reforms. To Ukrainians, the area they settled (today the wedge of territory straddling the Russia–Kazakhstan border, and stretching from Omsk in the north to Karaganda in the south, and from Kustanai in the west to Ust-Kamenogorsk in the east) is known as *Siryi Klyn* (the gray wedge). However, it was never a clearly delineated historic territory as such.[33]

Significantly, Ukrainians in the area have been particularly vulnerable to assimilation. Many Ukrainians saw themselves as part of a general wave of European (later Soviet) settlement, continuing up to the Virgin Lands campaign in the 1950s. Moreover, the agricultural ideal of "Siryi Klyn" has been overtaken by the twentieth-century realities of urbanization and industrialization, and Ukrainians have moved from the land into the melting pot of the multi-ethnic cities. A ukrainophile movement struggled to get off the ground after 1917, despite the establishment of a Supreme Ukrainian Council of Siberia at two conferences in Omsk in August 1917 and August 1918. Moreover, compared to East Slobozhanshchyna and the Kuban, and even the Far East (see below), ukrainianization made little impact in the 1920s and early 1930s (there were 40 Ukrainian schools in 1927),[34] although a Ukrainian autonomous *oblast'* existed at Kustanai until 1934.

Consequently, the 830,000 Ukrainians recorded in west Siberia in 1926 (9.8 percent of the local population) had shrunk to only 584,000 in 1989.[35]

Numbers in Kazakhstan apparently stagnated, with 896,000 in 1989 compared to 860,000 in 1926.[36] Only in residual areas of compact rural settlement is use of the Ukrainian language still significant. There is evidence that Ukrainians in northern Kazakhstan, faced with the pressure of a nationalizing host-state, are more likely to see themselves as part of a general "Russian-speaking" diaspora and make common cause with fellow Slavs.[37]

Considerable numbers of Ukrainians also live in Tiumen *oblast'* (260,000 in 1989, although some have claimed 600,000 or 700,000), where many work in the local oil and gas industries.[38] Some Ukrainian nationalists have come to regard the local Ukrainians as a potential strategic asset with which to restrain Russian ambition, but there is little evidence of any significant Ukrainian movement on the ground.[39]

Zelenyi Klyn. In the late tsarist era, Ukrainians also settled in large numbers in the Far East, in the area known as *Zelenyi Klyn* (the green wedge), that is, the Amur and Primor'e districts of the Russian Federation. After China ceded its claims in the region to Russia in the period 1858–60, the area was at first mainly populated by a trickle of migrants from neighboring Siberia. But from 1882 onward, sea voyages from Odessa began a mass resettlement program of peasants from Ukraine and created a powerful migration myth (railway journeys became more common in the 1900s).[40] Most of the migrants came from the left-bank *guberniias*. Between 1883 and 1905, 109,510 out of 172,876 of those resettled (63 percent) were from Ukraine. Between 1906 and 1917, a further 64,169 arrived in Amur and 102,600 in Primor'e.[41] One Ukrainian estimate is that, in Primor'e, Ukrainians made up 75–80 percent of the population, and in Amur 60–65 percent.[42] By 1926 there were 315,000 Ukrainians recorded in the region.[43]

Local Ukrainian activists took advantage of the political vacuum in the region after 1917 to hold four Far Eastern Ukrainian Congresses, but as in the Kuban it proved difficult to establish meaningful local autonomy in competition with Kolchak's White armies and the "Far Eastern Republic." Bolshevik power was firmly established by 1922, and most of the leaders of the Ukrainian movement were purged in the years 1923–24 for "attempting to separate the Far East from Russia."[44]

However, in the 1920s considerable progress was made in establishing local Ukrainian schools, newspapers, and journals until, as elsewhere, the experiment was snuffed out in the mid-1930s (in 1932 some 1,076 Ukrainian primary and 219 secondary schools taught 60,000 pupils).[45] By the time of the 1989 census only 185,000 Ukrainians were recorded in Primor'e (8.2 percent of the local population) and 70,800 in Amur (6.7 percent), although this was still one of the highest concentrations of Ukrainians in Russia. The region has always possessed a certain natural territorial identity, and Ukrainian activists were able to arrange a fifth congress of local Ukrainians (after the four held in 1917 and 1918) in March 1993.[46] Nevertheless, in the late 1990s the Ukrainian movement was still only a side-show to politically more salient demands for general Siberian autonomy.

Non-Territorial Communities

Ukrainians elsewhere in the former Soviet Union live mainly as scattered individuals, for example, the 253,000 Ukrainians living in Moscow in 1989 or the 151,000 in St. Petersburg.[47] In most of Russia, as well as in the Baltic states, Transcaucasia, and Central Asia, and in certain areas of Belarus or Moldova (such as in Minsk or Chisinau), Ukrainians lack even the limited symbolic capital of historical "ethno-regions" such as the Kuban; they are consequently much more vulnerable to assimilation. Despite the existence of scattered enclaves, where a group of Ukrainian migrants has remained settled in a particular area and preserved Ukrainian language and culture,[48] most Ukrainians in Russia have only a weak sense of national identity.

According to a survey undertaken by Oleksandr Hrushevs'kyi in Moscow in the early 1990s, only 36 percent of Ukrainians in Russia could speak Ukrainian freely (a further 26 percent could understand but not use it). Only 10 percent wanted to acquire Ukrainian citizenship, although 48 percent "did not want to lose links with either Ukraine or Russia" and hoped for a system of dual citizenship.[49] In research conducted among their membership by the Union of Ukrainians in Russia (see below), 87.1 percent supported "national–cultural autonomy" and the "establishment of national–cultural centers, groups and associations," but only a minuscule 2.2 percent favored the creation of "national [administrative] regions."[50]

Significantly, the Union of Ukrainians in Russia, created in Moscow in October 1993, largely reflects the interests of the "non-territorial" diaspora. Its maximum demand was only for "extra-territorial cultural–national autonomy,"[51] and the Union defined its primary tasks somewhat defensively as "defending the national and spiritual needs of Ukrainian society in the Russian Federation, the rebirth and preservation of its national identity, opposition to assimilation, the nursing and transmission to [our] descendants of the language, culture and traditions of the Ukrainian people."[52] In its appeal to Kyiv, the Union declared plaintively that "without state support from Ukraine our attempts at self-preservation as a part of the Ukrainian ethnos have no future."[53]

The Union has had a pragmatic agenda, calling on Ukraine to ease citizenship requirements and provide greater practical support for Ukrainian-language media.[54] It has also supported the Ukrainian line in disputes with Russia, criticizing the Russian Duma for its stance on Crimea and condemning the demands of the Russian diaspora in Ukraine.[55] But there is little evidence that it has had any effect on official Russian policy. It has not become a major player in Russian domestic politics, despite helping to found the broader Congress of National (that is, ethnic minority) Associations of Russia in April 1994.

The weakness of Ukrainian identity among non-territorial Ukrainians in Russia (and elsewhere) is a fact that is not actually contested by Ukrainian nationalists. The World Forum of Ukrainians, convened in Kyiv in 1992, declared that "it is especially important to take care of our brothers and sisters of the eastern diaspora, because they themselves have sustained the biggest losses, because it was most difficult for them to defend their ethnic and spiritual birthright in those expanses [of the Soviet Union] dominated by the ideology of a single community of russified *mankurty* [a pejorative term for the 'denationalized']."[56]

Ukrainians and Russians in Third-Party Host-States

In many cases, assimilation may be an ongoing process. Moreover, where Ukrainians and Russians both live as minorities in nationalizing host-states, there will be natural pressures for them to make common cause in defense of their rights. The Ukrainian state is unlikely to be a more powerful patron than Russia. Ukrainians may therefore be more likely to perceive themselves as, and act as part of, a general "Russian-speaking" diaspora, as David Laitin and others have argued.[57] Ukrainians in Latvia and in Moldova may provide two such examples, in addition to that of Kazakhstan already referred to above.

Ukrainians in Latvia

According to the 1989 census, there were 92,101 Ukrainians in Latvia, but official statistics recorded only 69,334 in February 1995. A total of 13,827 Ukrainians left for Ukraine in the period 1992–94, but that still leaves another 9,000 or so who disappeared from the figures. Research in Latvia suggests that 2,600 were assimilated (to a "Russian" identity) from 1989 to 1992 alone.[58]

Ukrainians in Latvia provide an instructive example of a group particularly vulnerable to assimilation. First, the vast majority are post-war migrants without much of a historical tradition in the region; there were only 1,800 Ukrainians in Latvia in 1935. Second, they are largely urban residents prone to intermarriage; 71.4 percent of Ukrainians in 1989 lived in Latvia's seven largest cities, and a massive 85.5 percent of Ukrainian men and 84 percent of Ukrainian women married spouses of other nationalities in 1988. Third, their children, if they do not study in Latvian, study at Russian-language schools; 126 students were enrolled at the Ukrainian secondary school in Riga in the 1994–95 school year, while 6,222 Ukrainian children were studying at Russian-language schools.[59] Half of all Ukrainians speak Russian, even at home "with their families."[60] Ukrainians who live compactly in the countryside (in Lithuania) have been better able to preserve their language, although their level of political activity is low.[61]

Many Ukrainians in Latvia participated in the anti-independence Interfront movement of the early 1990s. Significantly, diasporic political entrepreneurs in parties representing the minority community, such as Ravnopravie (Equal Rights) in Latvia or the Estonian United People's Party, have preferred to target Russian-speakers as a whole rather than ethnic Russians only. A similar situation exists in the Transdniester region of Moldova and in northern Kazakhstan, where specifically Ukrainian cultural organizations have taken second place to Russian-speaking lobbies.

Most remaining Ukrainians in Latvia have expressed a desire to remain, in which case, since both the Russian and Ukrainian states have only limited resources with which to protect their interests, it makes sense for these communities to join forces with their fellow non-citizens to fight against the political exclusion which is the most serious threat to their identity and interests (only 4,151 Ukrainians, 6 percent of the remaining total, were Latvian citizens at the end of 1994).[62]

Moldova: Khotynshchyna (Hotin) and Transdniester (Prydnistrov"ia, Pridnestrov'e)

Moldova presents a more ambiguous case. Many of its Ukrainian communities have lived there for centuries, while others are part of the general "Soviet settler" influx. According to Ukrainian historians, "Bessarabia—the territory between the Dniester and the Prut [rivers]—is an eternal [Ukrainian] land, on which the ancestors of Ukrainians and Moldovans, East Slavs and Wallachians, have lived together" since

Roman times. Many other Ukrainians arrived in the region before the Soviet period as refugees from slavery or as political exiles, in particular some of the Zaporozhian Cossacks after the destruction of their headquarters in 1775.[63] The lands east of the river Dniester (Transdniester, or in Ukrainian Prydnistrov"ia, the site of the so-called Dniester Republic) belonged to Kievan Rus' and the kingdom of Galicia–Volhynia from the ninth to fourteenth centuries and were also part of the Ukrainian SSR until 1940.[64] Khotynshchyna (Hotin, in Romanian) in the north was also part of the Rus' and Volhynian states. Galicia retained a powerful influence on church life in the region until the late Middle Ages.

The 1989 Soviet census recorded 600,000 Ukrainians in Moldova. Like the Russian population, many are post-war migrants, living alongside their fellow Slavs in the key towns of the "Dniester Republic," such as Bendery/Tighina (18 percent Ukrainian, 52 percent Russian) or Tiraspol (33 percent Ukrainian, 41 percent Russian).[65] There were 100,000 Ukrainians in the Moldovan capital of Chisinau in 1989 (15 percent).[66] Elsewhere, Ukrainians have lived in rural areas for centuries; 380,000 "Little Russian-speakers" were recorded in Bessarabia in 1897, and 420,000 out of the 600,000 Ukrainians in 1989 were rural inhabitants.[67] The more northerly districts of Transdniester and the Moldovan *raions* of Camenca and Rîbniţa are mainly ethnic Ukrainian, as are the 300 or so villages in northeastern Moldova which form part of the historical Ukrainian region of Khotynshchyna (most of which is now part of the Chernivtsi *oblast'* in Ukraine); in these areas Ukrainians live compactly and continue to speak Ukrainian.[68] In Moldovan *raions* such as Ocniţa, Briceni, and Edineţ, Ukrainians make up 33–40 percent of the population.

In Transdniester as a whole, 28.3 percent of the population of 601,100 are Ukrainian (170,000), though Ukrainians have claimed "more than 250,000"[69] or even 400,000.[70] Estimates of the total Ukrainian population in Moldova center around 800,000 but go as high as one million. Radical Ukrainian nationalist groups have claimed Transdniester at least as "Ukrainian ethnic territory" and have called for it to be incorporated into the Ukrainian state.[71] However, without schools, media, and other cultural institutions, many Ukrainians, especially in urban areas, have been vulnerable to assimilation to the Russian population. In the 1989 census, only 52,000 out of 600,000 Ukrainians said they were fully proficient in Ukrainian; 220,000 admitted no knowledge of the language.[72] The leadership of the "Dniester Republic" is proudly "multinational." On the other hand, since 1991 Ukrainians in Moldova have benefited from the desire of the authorities in Chisinau to prevent the consolidation of a single "Russian-speaking" minority, and schools, libraries, and cultural centers have been opened.[73] Ukrainians in Moldova may therefore be somewhat less vulnerable to assimilation than those in Latvia, although there is little sign of mass "revival," despite the formation of Ukrainian societies in both Transdniester and Moldova as a whole.[74]

Ukrainians in the Western Host-States

In the western host-states (Slovakia, Romania, and Poland) there are hardly any Russians. This is also true of Belarus, although titular national identity is of course much weaker. Moreover, most Ukrainians live in historic rather than "Soviet settler" communities. Ukrainians are therefore more likely to act as a minority on their own. However, in all four states, as in Russia, Ukrainians have historically been subject to a variety of cross-cutting pressures on their identity. Linguistic boundaries, except between Ukrainians and Romanians, have never been sharp. The main bulwark of Ukrainian identity has been the Uniate (eastern-rite Catholic) church, although at times its existence has provided a bridge to the assimilation of Ukrainians to Roman Catholic cultures, as in Poland and Slovakia. Ukrainians have therefore been vulnerable to local divide–and–rule tactics that have attempted to prevent the East Slavic population from acting as a consolidated minority.

(Czecho)Slovakia

In Czechoslovakia and its successor states there have traditionally been three rival orientations: ukrainophile, russophile, and "ruthenophile," with the last claiming that the local East Slavs in Slovakia are in fact a distinct ethnic group.[75] In the 1920s the new Czechoslovak state favored the ukrainophile option since the Ruthenians (or Rusyns) were seen as pro-Hungarian and the russophiles as a Bolshevik front. But the post-war Czechoslovak state was more even-handed, allowing local East Slavs, historically concentrated in the northeastern corner of Slovakia north of the town of Prešov, to classify themselves as either Ukrainian or Ruthenian/Rusyn. Official figures for the numbers of Ukrainians and Ruthenians, derived from the 1991 Czechoslovak census, are given in Table 5.2.

TABLE 5.2   Ukrainians and Ruthenians in the Former Czechoslovakia

	Czech Republic	Slovakia	Total
Ukrainians	8,220	13,281	21,501
Ruthenians	1,926	17,197	19,123
Total	10,146	30,478	40,624

Source: Adapted from Robert J. Kaiser, "Czechoslovakia: The Disintegration of a Binational State," in Graham Smith, ed., *Federalism: The Multiethnic Challenge* (London: Longman, 1995), 215.

Ukrainians claim that the number of their kin has been artificially reduced by the promotion of the imaginary "Ruthenian" identity and its separate branch of the Uniate faith. The locals' traditional Uniate faith and the Slovaks' desire for a numerically more equal relationship with the Czechs and Hungarians has also meant gradual assimilation to Roman Catholic, Slovak culture. Significantly, Ruthenians outnumber Ukrainians in Slovakia, but the situation is reversed in the Czech Republic. In 1857 there were 199,506 "Rusyn–Ukrainians" recorded in what is now Slovakia, and still 95,783 in 1930. It is claimed that 34,000 "re-identified" as Slovaks after the Second World War (between 1950 and 1980).[76] Ruthenian leaders, however, argue their separation from Ukrainians is perfectly natural. In any case, it has shown no sign of disappearing in the 1990s.[77]

Romania

The official Ukrainian population in Romania according to the 1992 census was 66,000, but Ukrainians have claimed the real figure is nearer 250,000 or 300,000. There are two historic enclaves of Ukrainian "ethnolinguistic territory" in Romania. Southern Bucovina (Bukovyna, in Ukrainian), located in the northeastern corner of the Romanian county of Suceava, is the remnant of the historical Habsburg province of Bukowina, most of which was transferred to the modern-day Ukrainian *oblast'* of Chernivtsi in 1945. There are still 72 mainly Ukrainian villages in the region, but local Ukrainians are Orthodox and services are conducted in Romanian, so many have adopted a Romanian identity (especially after most Ukrainian schools were closed by Nicolae Ceauşescu in the 1960s).

To the west, adjoining Ukrainian Transcarpathia, is the tiny region of Maramureş (Marmaroshchyna, in Ukrainian). Ukrainians live more compactly in Maramureş, and their Uniate religion has left them less vulnerable to assimilation to a Romanian identity. On the other hand, it makes some Ukrainians identify themselves as Ruthenians.[78] Nationalists in Kyiv have claimed a total Ukrainian population of 110,000 in southern Bucovina and 100,000 in Maramureş, plus scattered groups in the southeast (the Dobrogea region) and the west (the Banat).[79] However, the rural character of all these regions has made it extremely difficult to mobilize Ukrainians politically.[80]

Poland

Although post-war Polish censuses have not directly established the size of the Ukrainian minority, the official figure is some 180,000; unofficial claims congregate between 250,000 and 300,000, and some go as high as 500,000.[81] A precise ethnographic boundary between Poles and Ukrainians has always been difficult to draw. In the southeastern corner of present-day Poland, the regions of Lemkivshchyna (the area centered on the Low Beskyd hills), Przemyśl, Chełm, and Podlasie (Podlachia) have contained sizable "Ukrainian" populations since the early Middle Ages. But populations have always intermingled, and identities, at least in rural areas, have remained blurred; in the last century, many rural Poles were classed as "Ruthenians [Ukrainians] of the Catholic rite." Most of the border area came under Romanov control after the partitions of Poland (1772–95).

A separate *guberniia* of Chełm/Kholm was established by the Russian empire in 1912 (ironically, because of pressure from Russian nationalists) in order to protect the local Orthodox Christians (i.e., "Ukrainians") from "polonization." Had it been created earlier, and enjoyed a longer life, clearer local boundary markers might well have emerged. However, in the inter-war period the region reverted to Poland, and identities were once again blurred by the Polish authorities' attempts to divide and rule, particularly in the Carpathian foothills. There, in a process similar to "ruthenianization" in Czechoslovakia, the local population was classified not as Ukrainians but as "Lemkos," "Hutsuls," or plain "tuteishi" ("locals").

The establishment of the modern state borders in 1945 left an estimated 700,000 Ukrainians in the eastern Polish regions of Lemkivshchyna, Przemyśl, and Chełm,[82] but most were forcibly dispersed in the period 1944–47,[83] first over the new border to Ukraine and then in *Operation Vistula* in 1947 to former German territories in the west. The Uniate church was subject to harsh repression. One author has argued that this early attempt at "ethnic cleansing" (hundreds of thousands of Poles were expelled from Ukraine at the same time) did not succeed in extirpating the Ukrainian tradition in southeastern Poland. If anything, it provides a potent identity marker and mobilizing symbol for modern-day ethnic entrepreneurs.[84] However, it is also possible that the dispersion tactics were successful and that, without an institutional, regional, or religious base, local Ukrainian identities are likely to remain diffuse.

Belarus

Until the Second World War, the area around Brest in what is now southwest Belarus (known in Ukrainian as Beresteishchyna, the land between the Bug, Pripet, and Yaselda rivers) was considered by most Ukrainians to be a natural part of Ukrainian ethno-linguistic territory and its inhabitants referred to as "Pynchuks."[85] It belonged to Kievan Rus' (when Ukrainians claim it was settled by proto-Ukrainian tribes such as the Volyniany and Drevliany rather than by the proto-Belarusian Dryhavichy), then to the Volhynian kingdom until 1341, and remained a separate administrative region (*voievodstvo*) under first Lithuanian and then Polish rule until 1795. According to the 1897 census, there were some 407,000 speakers of "Little Russian" in the region, who made up 81 percent of the rural population in Brest *povit* (county) and 83 percent in neighboring Kobrin.[86] The 1918 Treaty of Brest-Litovsk awarded the region to the Ukrainian Popular Republic.

When the region became part of inter-war Poland, however, as with the "Lemkos" and "Ruthenians" in the Carpathians, the local population was reclassified as "Polissians." Moreover, as (most of) the region was separated from Soviet Ukraine, there was no ukrainianization campaign in the 1920s. Small Ukrainian parties were unable to make much of an impact under the limited opportunities provided by Polish rule. In 1945 the region was absorbed into the Belarusian SSR and the local population reclassified as "Belarusian." Alternatively, as with the relatively plastic and transitional identities elsewhere around Ukraine's borders, it was claimed that the local population was a specific sub-ethnos, the "Yatviahy." The traditional Ukrainian name for Brest—Berestia—disappeared (to Belarusians the region was simply "West Polissia"),[87] and only 31,626 Ukrainians were recorded in Brest *oblast'* in the 1989 census (2.4 percent of the total population).[88] Therefore, when a local "civic–cultural union" was founded in February 1990, it claimed to represent hundreds of thousands of "vanished" Ukrainians (some claims going as high as one million),[89] but it was unable to establish a solid foundation for its activity.[90] The region has remained a rural backwater where any form of political mobilization is difficult.

Ukraine and Diaspora Politics

Nationalist groups in Ukraine have consistently called for Kyiv to cultivate links with the diaspora in both east and west. The "denationalization" that Ukrainians have supposedly suffered elsewhere in the former Soviet Union is held to be simply a stronger version of what they suffered at home. "National revival" at home and abroad are therefore thought to be mutually dependent processes. Moreover, given the size of the diaspora, political mobilization would add significantly to the strength of the national movement at home, which often feels like a minority in its own state.[91] Finally, by focusing on the manner in which Russia treats the Ukrainian diaspora, nationalists argue that it would be possible to deflect Russia's attempts to act as kin-state and patron for its own diaspora within Ukraine.

A Congress of Ukrainians of the former Soviet Union was held as early as January 1992,[92] and a World Forum of Ukrainians the following August.[93] The two assemblies called on the Ukrainian state to sponsor a program of organized return to the homeland, to negotiate a series of agreements with host-states on the treatment of the diaspora, to assist in the formation of cultural centers abroad (with the ministry of education providing books and teachers), and to encourage an interchange of contacts and ideas between the western and eastern diasporas.[94] As in Kazakhstan, nationalists also argued that "in-gathering" the diaspora could be a means of counterbalancing the strength of the Russian diaspora at home, particularly in the armed forces.[95] Members of the diaspora, it was argued, should therefore be granted a fast track for obtaining Ukrainian citizenship.

The one concrete result of the August 1992 congress was the creation of a Ukrainian World Coordinating Council in January 1993. The council has equal representation of the eastern and western diasporas and is headed by the poet and politician Ivan Drach, a former leader of Rukh, the main nationalist opposition movement. The council is a state-sponsored body, unlike the much older World Congress of Ukrainians, which was established largely by North American Ukrainians in 1967 as the World Congress of Free Ukrainians and which now groups approximately fifty member organizations from eighteen countries. The Ukraine Society, a state-sponsored organization established in 1960, has also been encouraged to transform itself from a Soviet front organization to a channel for broadening cultural contacts, and to pay as much attention to the eastern as to the western diaspora (the latter having been its only remit in the Soviet era).[96]

Relations between the various diaspora organizations have not always been smooth.[97] The World Congress, and the western diaspora in general, considers the World Council and the Ukrainian state to have been too timid in their approach to the eastern diaspora. The World Council and the authorities in Kyiv, on the other hand, think that the western diaspora does not understand the situation on the ground. As in Poland, since 1991 money has flowed from the west, through Kyiv, to the east, and the western diaspora has served as a model of organization for eastern Ukrainians. But the role of the western diaspora has been more problematic in Ukraine than elsewhere. Most members of the western diaspora left west Ukraine when it was under the Habsburgs or inter-war Poland, Czechoslovakia, and Romania. The eastern diaspora, by contrast, was populated by migrants from central, southern, and eastern Ukraine during the Romanov and Soviet periods. The cultural gap between the two diasporas is considerable and was reinforced by the westerners' long sojourn in the west. Ukrainians from Canada or the United States bemoan the "russification" of Kyiv, while Ukrainians who experienced Soviet rule resent their proselytizing approach.

The western diaspora is therefore not necessarily a model to be emulated. West Ukrainian nationalists might empathize with the western diaspora, but the authorities in Kyiv consider their approach too radical for Ukraine's ethnic Russian and Russian-speaking populations. Returnees from the west have occupied middle-ranking and advisory positions in Kyiv, but have not risen as high as in independent Estonia or Armenia. Significantly, the main political organization of the western returnees, the Congress of Ukrainian Nationalists, has remained on the political fringes, electing only eight deputies in the 1994 parliamentary elections. It has been criticized by many for re-introducing the disputes of the 1940s back into Ukraine.[98] The congress is a pale shadow of the Armenian Dashnaks.

In 1992 the Soviet-era Ukrainian constitution was amended to oblige the president of Ukraine "to assist in [*spryiaie*] the satisfaction of the national–cultural, spiritual and linguistic needs of Ukrainians who live in other states."[99] A ministry for nationalities and migration was duly established by President Leonid Kravchuk in April 1993, but it has had only a limited remit for helping Ukrainians abroad (its primary responsibility being for minorities within Ukraine). In August 1996 it was downgraded to the status of a "state commission." Often, representation is made on an informal level or by Ukrainian delegations in Moscow and other capitals.[100]

The Ukrainian state has been reluctant to adopt a more aggressive diaspora policy for several reasons. First and foremost, it is afraid of justifying similar interference by the Russian state in Ukraine. Second, as in Tatarstan, Ukraine's declared intention of building a multi-ethnic "civic" state at home makes the adoption of an explicitly ethnic diaspora policy difficult (although the ethnic undercurrents in Ukrainian policy demonstrate that domestic politics is not entirely "civic"). Third, successive Ukrainian governments in Kyiv have always included large numbers of ethnic Russians and Russian-speakers. Ukrainian nationalists do not have the political strength to impose their agenda in Kyiv. Fourth, Ukrainian restraint is undoubtedly also based on a realistic assessment of the diaspora's political potential and an awareness that nationalists seriously underestimate the real complexities of Ukrainian identity abroad. The eastern diaspora can therefore hardly be expected to exert the kind of pressure on the Russian host-state that the Russian diaspora is able to exert on Kyiv. Moreover, the Ukrainian state is well aware of its own limited resources. Finally, Kyiv's main priority is managing its general relationship with Russia. It would be unlikely to risk worsening an already unequal relationship to pursue a diasporizing policy with such uncertain returns.

Significantly, when Ukraine finally adopted a post-Soviet constitution in June 1996, no mention was made of any specific responsibilities of the president, parliament, or cabinet of ministers with regard to the diaspora. Article 12 of the constitution declared loftily that "Ukraine provides for [*dbaie pro*] the satisfaction of the national–cultural and linguistic needs of Ukrainians who live beyond the borders of the state," but did not identify how this might be achieved.[101] The interstate treaty finally signed between Ukraine and Russia in May 1997 confined itself to vague commitments concerning "defending the ethnic, cultural, linguistic and religious uniqueness [*samobutnist'*] of national minorities" on each other's territory, and potentially more significantly, "creating equal possibilities and bases for the study of the Ukrainian language in the Russian Federation and the Russian language in Ukraine."[102] No mention was made of dual citizenship arrangements—in practice a victory for the Ukrainian side given the size of the Russian diaspora in Ukraine. In 1997 Ukraine introduced minor amendments to its 1991 citizenship law, but without opening the doors to the diaspora.[103]

Engagement with other neighboring host-states has proceeded on a similarly cautious basis. Ukraine's diaspora policy has largely consisted of negotiating a series of bilateral treaties that promise, as in the case of the June 1997 treaty with Romania, "to defend the ethnic, cultural, linguistic and religious identity of the Ukrainian minority in Romania and the Romanian minority in Ukraine" by adherence to the international norms of the UN, the OSCE, and the Council of Europe. Ukraine has usually been happy to accept the bias of these organizations toward individual rights over collective rights, and state interests over the interests of broader culturally defined nations. The treaty with Romania explicitly states that mutual oversight does not imply any move toward asserting "collective rights" or "territorial autonomy on ethnic criteria."[104]

Ukrainian nationalists have therefore continued to complain that the authorities in Kyiv have no formal program for dealing with the diaspora,[105] and have consistently called for Ukraine to pay more attention to "developing and implementing a plan of economic and cultural–educational support for Ukrainians abroad, especially in Russia,"[106] so that the rights and privileges of Ukrainians in Russia can be raised to the level enjoyed by Russians in Ukraine. However, the second World Forum of Ukrainians held in Kyiv in August 1997—which produced little in the way of new initiatives—demonstrated that they were still struggling to make their influence felt.

Conclusion

The nationalist Ukrainian political geographer Iurii Lypa argued in the 1940s that Ukraine should seek to use the eastern diaspora in the Kuban and elsewhere to undermine Russia via its soft southern underbelly.[107] Modern-day nationalists have expressed the hope that the diaspora will be both a geopolitical lever and a factor helping to "raise Ukraine's authority as a state."[108] However, the potential for the political mobilization of the Ukrainian diaspora, even in "historically Ukrainian" ethno-regions remains limited.

In areas such as the Kuban or east Slobozhanshchyna, local activists have a certain amount of mythic and symbolic capital with which to promote ethnic mobilization, such as the celebrations of the two hundredth anniversary of the arrival of the Zaporozhian Cossacks in Kuban, held in Taman in 1992. Typically, however, the ukrainophile orientation is only one among several. The extent of ukrainianization in the 1920s has also proved of some importance in determining prospects for mobilization, both for its actual effect and for its symbolic importance in designating a particular land as "Ukrainian." It had most effect in the Kuban and the least in Siryi Klyn. Significantly, there was no comparable process in areas such as Beresteishchyna, which was a part of Poland in the inter-war years. In all cases, however, a decade of ukrainianization in the 1920s has had to compete with generations of russification or sovietization before and after that period.

The creation of a Ukrainian state in 1991 may in time help to solidify a sense of identification with the kin-state as a "homeland," but Kyiv currently has only limited resources with which to promote an active diaspora policy and only a limited desire to do so. The "diasporizing agenda" is still largely the preserve of opposition nationalists. Moreover, Ukrainians abroad also live in a world where the nature of Russian diasporic identity is still being defined. Where it is plastic enough to include nominally ethnic Ukrainians (and millions of "former" Ukrainians), Ukrainians may add significantly to the strength of the "Russian-speaking" or "Soviet settler" diaspora. In turn, this makes it less likely that ethnic considerations will predominate in Russia's diaspora policy, but the very size of this Russian-speaking diaspora will make it an unwieldy instrument.

Notes

1. The main work in English on the Ukrainian diaspora is Ann Lencyk Pawliczko, ed., *Ukraine and Ukrainians Throughout the World: A Demographic and Sociological Guide to the Homeland and its Diaspora* (Toronto: University of Toronto Press, 1994). On the eastern diaspora, see Serge Cipko, *Ukrainians in Russia: A Bibliographic and Statistical Guide* (Edmonton: CIUS, 1994), and idem, "The Second Revival: Russia's Ukrainian Minority as an Emerging Factor in Eurasian Politics," *Harriman Institute Review* (March 1996): 70–80. Works in Ukrainian include Ihor Vynnychenko, *Ukraïntsi v derzhavakh kolyshn'oho SRSR: istoryko-heohrafichnyi narys* (Zhytomyr: L'onok, 1992); three books by Fedir Zastavnyi, *Skhidna ukraïns'ka diaspora* (Lviv: Svit, 1992), *Ukraïns'ki etnichni zemli* (Lviv: Svit, 1993), and *Heohrafiia Ukraïny* (Lviv: Svit, 1994), 192–254. See also Volodymyr Serhiichuk, *Ukraïntsi v imperiï* (Kyiv: Biblioteka Ukraïntsia, no. 3, 1992); and the detailed historical atlas produced by Rostyslav Sossa, *Ukraïntsi: skhidna diaspora* (Kyiv: Mapa, 1993). The regular journal *Ukraïns'ka diaspora* (Institute of Sociology/Encyclopaedia of the Ukrainian Diaspora) contains much interesting material.

2. Orest Subtelny, *Ukrainians in North America: An Illustrated History* (Toronto: University of Toronto Press, 1991); Myron B. Kuropas, *The Ukrainian Americans: Roots and Aspirations, 1884–1954* (Toronto: University of Toronto Press, 1991);

and Lubomyr Luciuk and Stella Hryniuk, *Canada's Ukrainians: Negotiating an Identity* (Toronto: University of Toronto Press, 1991).

3. Ukrainian practice is to use the term "eastern diaspora" solely to refer to the former Soviet Union, but I have also included Ukrainians resident in the neighboring ex-communist states of east central Europe, as their situation is in many respects similar.

4. Rudnyts'kyi's main works are reprinted in *Chomu my khochemo samostiinoï Ukraïny* (Lviv: Svit, 1994). See especially p. 94.

5. Rogers Brubaker, *Nationalism Reframed: Nationhood and the National Question in the New Europe* (Cambridge: Cambridge University Press, 1996).

6. See Vasyl Markus', "Ukrainians in Hungary," in Pawliczko, ed., *Ukraine and Ukrainians*, 167, which cites a figure of 11,000.

7. "5 mil'ioniv za statystykoiu. A naspravdi?," *Visti z Ukraïny*, no. 14 (1992); "Skil'ky nas? Ukraïntsi v Rosiï," *Krynytsia*, nos. 3–4 (1993); V. Baklanov, "Skil'ky zh bulo ukraïntsiv? Storinky istoriï," *Sil's'ki visti*, August 13, 1992.

8. Volodymyr Patrushev et al., *Ukraïns'ka diaspora u sviti* (Kyiv: Znannia, 1993), 16. Anatolii Ponomar'ov, *Ukraïns'ka etnohrafiia* (Kyiv: Lybid', 1994), 183, gives a figure of 11 million.

9. *Holos Ukraïny*, December 3, 1994; Ivan Drach, "Ukraïntsi v Rosiï: obiideni doleiu chy zabuti Ukraïnoiu?," *Literaturna Ukraïna*, July 22, 1993.

10. See Rudnyts'yi's essay "Ohliad natsional'noï terytoriï Ukraïny," in his *Chomu my khochemo*, originally published in 1923. This "potato principle," although methodologically questionable, was common practice among populist nationalists of Rudnyts'kyi's era.

11. Ludmila Chizhikova, *Russko-ukrainskoe pranich'e: istoriia i sud'by traditsionno-bytovoi kul'tury (XIX–XX vv.)* (Moscow: Nauka, 1988). See also N. V. Chernaia, "Ukrainskoe naselenie Rossii i SSSR za predelami Ukrainy (XVIII–XX vv.). Dinamika chislennosti i razmeshcheniia," *Rasy i narody*, no. 21 (1991). The latter work has been harshly criticized by Ukrainians, for example Zastavnyi, *Skhidna*, 63.

12. N. Bei, "Malynovyi Klyn," *Visti z Ukraïny*, no. 15 (1994).

13. V. Vilets'kyi, "Iak my na Kuban' khodyly;" O. Borhardt, "Zvidky pishlo ukraïns'ke kozatstvo;" and "Vytoky kozats'koho rodovodu," *Kozats'kyi krai*, nos. 2, 4, and 5 (1994). See also I. I. Vynnychenko, "Ukraïntsi na Kubani ta Stavropol'shchyni (kinets' XVIII–pochatok XX st.)," in V. S. Trubenko and V. I. Horbyk, eds., *Istorychno-heohrafichni doslidzhennia v Ukraïni* (Kyiv: Naukova dumka, 1994), 64–73.

14. Dmytro Bilyi, *Malynovyi Klyn. Narysy z istoriï ukraïntsiv Kubani* (Kyiv: Ukraïna, 1994), 5–11. A 1745 decree of Tsarina Elizabeth sought to keep the Zaporozhian Cossacks out of the Kuban.

15. Bilyi, *Malynovyi Klyn*, 62–74; V. Olifirenko, "Vidrodzhennia na Kubani: iakym vono bulo?," *Kozats'kyi krai*, no. 1 (1994).

16. Petro Lavriv, "Kubans'ka narodna respublika," *Visti z Ukraïny*, no. 27 (1994); Bilyi, *Malynovyi Klyn*, 79–83.

17. Bilyi, *Malynovyi Klyn*, 89, 103.

18. Bilyi, *Malynovyi Klyn*, 102.

19. Bilyi, *Malynovyi Klyn*, 94–104. See also the reprint from Robert Conquest, "Holodomor na Kubani," *Kozats'kyi krai*, no. 2 (1994).

20. Vynnychenko, *Ukraïntsi*, 156.

21. Georgi M. Derluguian and Serge Cipko, "The Politics of Identity in a Russian Borderland Province: The Kuban Neo-Cossack Movement, 1989–1996," *Europe–Asia Studies* 49, no. 8 (1997): 1485–1500.

22. Some Ukrainians also live in Starodub, north of Chernihiv, but the region has been a part of Russia since (initially) 1522.

23. Dmytro Bahalii, *Istoriia Slobids'koï Ukraïny* (1918; reprint, Kharkiv: Del'ta, 1993).

24. M. Ieremenko, "Teslia chy teslev? Rosiis'ka federatsiia—Kurs'ka oblast'. Stanovyshche ukraïntsiv," *Visti z Ukraïny*, no. 26 (1991).

25. Vynnychenko, *Ukraïntsi*, 141.

26. Mykola Biriuk, "Na pivnichnii Slobozhanshchyni (u Voronez'kii oblasti ukraïntsiv blyz'ko mil'iona)," *Visti z Ukraïny*, no. 51 (1991).

27. V. Svystunov, "Z nashoï istoriï," *Skhidna Slobozhanshchyna*, no. 1 (1994); Vynnychenko, *Ukraïntsi*, 29; S. M. Kudelko and S. I. Posokhov, *Kharkiv: nauka, osvita, kul'tura* (Kharkiv: Oko, 1996), 4–5.

28. Vynnychenko, *Ukraïntsi*, 33.

29. Vasyl' Boiechko, Oksana Hanzha, and Borys Zakharchuk, *Kordony Ukraïny: istorychna retrospektyva ta suchasnyi stan* (Kyiv: Osnovy, 1994), 20–28, 50–62; Vynnychenko, *Ukraïntsi*, 34; Zastavnyi, *Skhidna*, 59.

30. Oleksandra Sever'ianova, "Z istoriï avtokhtonnoho ukraïns'koho naselennia nyzovoho Nadvolzhia," *Ukraïns'ka diaspora* 3, no. 6 (1994): 32–38.

31. Petro Lavriv, *Istoriia pivdenno-skhidnoï Ukraïny* (Lviv: Slovo, 1992), 45–55; Andrew Wilson, "The Donbas between Ukraine and Russia: The Use of History in Political Disputes," *Journal of Contemporary History* 30, no. 2 (1995): 265–89.

32. See Ivan Zakharchenko, "Tahanrozhchyna, abo Mius'ka Ukraïna," *Rozbudova derzhavy*, nos. 7–8 (July–August 1995): 14–17.

33. B. Kozarenko, "Siryi Klyn—moia storona," *Ukraïns'ka diaspora*, no. 2 (1992): 39–52.

34. Vynnychenko, *Ukraïntsi*, 72. See also Serhii Klymenko, "Ukraïnizatsiia v Kazakhstani (1930–1933 rr.)," *Ukraïns'ka diaspora* 1, no. 2 (1992): 91–97.

35. Zastavnyi, *Skhidna*, 86; Vynnychenko, *Ukraïntsi*, 72. See also V. Kubijovyc, O. Ohloblyn, and I. Svit, "Siberia," in Danylo Husar Struk, ed., *Encyclopedia of Ukraine*, vol. 4 (Toronto: University of Toronto Press, 1993), 700.

36. Vynnychenko, *Ukraïntsi*, 101.

37. "Z diaspory: Kazakhstan ta inshi," *Ukraïns'kyi svit*, January 26, 1995.

38. Vynnychenko, *Ukraïntsi*, 142. The figure of 600,000 was quoted at the 1992 World Forum of Ukrainians. S. S. Zinchuk et al., eds., *Rode nash prekrasnyi: materialy Vsesvitn'oho forumu ukraïnstiv, 21–24 serpnia 1992 roku* (Ternopil': Dialoh, 1993), 126. For the higher figure, see "Ukrainskii iazyk vveden v Tiumenskom universitete," *Kievskie vedomosti*, September 4, 1996.

39. "Tiumentsi pro nas poturbuiut'sia," *Visiti z Ukraïny*, no. 48 (1992); P. Klymenko, "Vidstoiaty interesy ukraïntsiv u Tiumeni," *Uriadovyi kur"ier*, March 27, 1994.

40. Mykhailo Traf"iak, "Zelenyi Klyn," *Suchasnist'*, nos. 3–4 (March–April 1996): 74–86; *Literaturna Ukraïna*, no. 25 (1992).

41. Traf"iak, "Zelenyi," 76; Vynnychenko, *Ukraïntsi*, 75

42. Traf"iak, "Zelenyi," 77. On p. 80, Traf"iak quotes slightly higher figures (80–85 percent and 62–75 percent).

43. Zastavnyi, *Skhidna*, 94.

44. *Literaturna Ukraïna*, January 30, 1992.

45. Traf"iak, "Zelenyi," 81.

46. A. Popok, "Z"ïzd vidbuvsia, ale problem ne vyrishyv (v dalekoskhidnyi z"ïzd ukraïntsiv)," *Visti z Ukraïny*, no. 26 (1993).

47. See the tables in Zastavnyi, *Skhidna*, 99, 103.

48. "Rezoliutsiia pershoho konhresu ukraïntsiv u Komi," *Ukraïns'kyi visnyk*, no. 3 (1993); "I vsesvitnyi z"ïzd ukraïntsiv Iaroslavshchyny," *Zoloti vorota*, no. 3 (1993).

49. Oleksandr Hrushevs'kyi and Tetiana Kutkovets', "Ukraïntsi v Rosiï," *Ukraïns'kyi ohliadach*, no. 12 (1992).

50. "Ukraintsi Rossii: mneniia, orientatsii, zhiznennye problemy: po materialam ekspertnogo oprosa na I Kongresse ukraintsev Rossii," in Oleksandr Rudenko-Desniak, ed., *My—grazhdane Rossii: materialy I kongressa ukraintsev Rossiiskoi Federatsii* (Moscow: Slavianskii dialog, 1994), 88.

51. Oleksandr Rudenko-Desniak, "Pro stanovyshche ukraïntsiv ta rozvytok ukraïns'koï kul'tury v Rosiis'kii Federatsiï," in Rudenko-Desniak, ed., *My—grazhdane*, 19.

52. "Prohramni tezy Ob"iednannia ukraïntsiv Rosiï," in Rudenko-Desniak, ed., *My—grazhdane*, 67.

53. "Zvernennia I Kongresu ukraïntsiv Rosiis'koï Federatsiï do Prezydenta Ukraïny p. L. Kravchuka, Verkhovnoï Rady ta Kabinet Ministriv Ukraïny," in Rudenko-Desniak, ed., *My—grazhdane*, 71.

54. "Pro stanovyshche ukraïntsiv ta rozvytok ukraïns'koï kul'tury v Rosiis'kii Federatsiï," in Rudenko-Desniak, *My—grazhdane*, 65–67.

55. Oksen Onopenko, "Dva diaspory—dva svitohliady," *Vechirnii Kyïv*, March 23, 1996.

56. "Rezoliutsiia Vsesvitn'oho forumu ukraïntsiv," in Zinchuk et al., eds., *Rode nash prekrasnyi*, 182.

57. The possible development of a single "Russian-speaking diaspora" is the subject of a forthcoming book by David Laitin. See also his articles "Language and Nationalism in the Post-Soviet Republics" and "National Renewal and Competitive Assimilation in Estonia," *Post-Soviet Affairs* 12, no. 1 (1996), pp. 4–39.

58. Leo Dribins, *Ukraini Latvija* (Riga: Latvian Institute of Philosophy and Sociology, 1995), 65–66.

59. Dribins, *Ukraini*, 62–63, 67.

60. "Ukrainians," in *National and Ethnic Groups in Latvia* (Riga: Ministry of Justice, 1996), 51.

61. Oleksandr Nel'ha, "Ukraïntsi v Lytvi," *Viche* (August 1994): 104–11.

62. Dribins, *Ukraini*, 66.

63. V. Boiko, "Zaporozhtsi za Dunaiem," *Pam'iatky Ukraïny*, no. 6 (1991).

64. Vasyl' Boiechko, "Kordony Ukraïny: Moldova," *Vechirnii Kyïv*, July 24, 1992. See also Hannes Hofbauer, *Bukowina, Bessarabien, Moldawien: vergessenes Land zwischen Westeuropa, Russland und der Türkei* (Vienna: Promedia, 1993).

65. Bohdan Nahaylo, "Ukraine and Moldova: The View from Kiev" and "Moldovan Conflict Creates New Dilemmas for Ukraine," *RFE/RL Research Report*, May 1 and 15, 1992.

66. Kost' Chavaha, "Terny u vynohradnyku," *Za vil'nu Ukraïnu*, February 1, 1992.

67. Vynnychenko, *Ukraïnsti*, 80, 115.

68. N. Bai, "My ne rosiis'komovni, my ukraïntsi (6 bereznia v m Dubosarakh vidbuvsia I z"ïzd ukraïntsiv v Prydnistrov"ia)," *Visti z Ukraïny*, no. 11 (1993).

69. Interview with Oleksandr But, head of the Union of Ukrainians of Transdniester and then member of the Moldovan parliament, *Holos Ukraïny*, May 13, 1992.

70. See the appeal of local Ukrainians in *Za vil'nu Ukraïnu*, October 29, 1991.

71. "Prohrama Ukraïns'koï natsional'noï asambleï," *Ukraïns'ki obriï*, no. 1 (1994).

72. Nahaylo, "Ukraine and Moldova," 42.

73. *Za vil'nu Ukraïnu*, March 22, 1991.

74. S. Shandar, "Edynokrovni braty prosiat' pidtrymky: notatky z pershoho z"ïzdu ukraïntsiv Prydnistrov"ia," *Sil's'ki visti*, March 11, 1993; I. Babenko, "Nova ukraïns'ka hromada (u Moldovi)," *Visti z Ukraïny*, no. 48 (1993).

75. On the Rusyn question in Slovakia and elsewhere, see Paul Robert Magosci, *The Shaping of a National Identity: Subcarpathian Rus', 1848–1948* (London: Harvard University Press, 1978).

76. Mykola Mushynka, "Sotsiolohichna doslidzhennia pro ukraïntsiv u Slovachchyni," *Ukraïns'ka diaspora* 2, no. 4 (1993): 115–18; Kaiser, "Czechoslovakia," 223.

77. Iurii Bacha et al., *Chomu, koly i iak? Zapytannia i vidpovidi z istoriï i kul'tury rusyniv–ukraïntsiv Chekho-Slovachchyny* (Prešov–Kyiv: INTEL, 1992).

78. Taras Boichuk, "Ukraïntsi v Rumuniï," *Post-postup*, no. 23 (1992); A. Zhukovsky, "Rumania," in Struk, ed., *Encyclopedia*, vol. 4, 434.

79. Patrushev, *Ukraïns'ka diaspora*, 13.

80. I. Kovach, "Nelehka vesna vidrodzhennia: ukraïntsi v Rumuniï," *Polityka i chas*, no. 2 (1993): 95–96.

81. Andrzej Saladiak, ed., *Pamiatki i zabutki kultury ukrainskiej w Polsce* (Warsaw: Burhard, 1993), 15; B. Kravtsiv et al., "Poland," in Struk, ed., *Encyclopedia*, vol. 4, 82; "Ukraïntsi v Pol'shchi: problemy i spodivannia," *Holos Ukraïny*, June 10, 1992.

82. Halyna Shcherba, "Deportatsiï naselennia z pol's'ko-ukraïns'koho pohranychchia 40-kh rokiv," in S. Holovko et al., eds., *Ukraïna–Pol'shcha: istorychna spadshchyna i suspil'na svidomist'* (Kyiv: Lybid', 1993), 249.

83. Vitalii Protsiuk, *1944–1994: Knyha pam'iati* (Lviv: Vil'na Ukraïna, 1994).

84. Chris Hann, "Ethnic Cleansing in Eastern Europe: Poles and Ukrainians beside the Curzon Line," *Nations and Nationalism* 2, no. 3 (1996): 389–406, and idem, "Ethnicity in the New Civil Society: Lemko-Ukrainians in Poland," in László Kürti and Juliet Langman, eds., *Beyond Borders: Remaking Cultural Identities in the New Central and Eastern Europe* (Boulder: Westview, 1997), 17–38.

85. M. Kozlovs'kyi, "To khto zh my taki naspravdi?," *Holos Beresteishchyny*, no. 1 (1991); Oleksandr Skopnenko, "Beresteishchyna," *Rozbudova derzhavy*, no. 11 (1995): 10–16.

86. Vynnychenko, *Ukraïntsi*, 84; Zastavnyi, *Skhidna*, 111.

87. "Zakhadniae Palesse," *Etnahrafiia Belarusi: Entsyklapedyia* (Minsk: Belaruskaia savetskaia entsyklapedyia, 1989), 208–9.

88. Vynnychenko, *Ukraïntsi*, 134.

89. *Za vil'nu Ukraïnu*, January 21, 1992. See also the speech by the delegate from Belarus, Arsentii Teteruk, at the 1992 World Forum of Ukrainians. Zinchuk et al., eds., *Rode nash prekrasnyi*, 106.

90. Ihor Vynnychenko, "Budyteli bilorus'koho polissia: hromads'ko-kul't. ob'iednannia brests'koï oblasti," *Visti z Ukraïny*, no. 5 (1995); O. Redchenko, "Ukraïntsi na beresteishchyni," *Narodna hazeta*, nos. 43 and 44 (1992).

91. Andrew Wilson, *Ukrainian Nationalism in the 1990s: A Minority Faith* (Cambridge: Cambridge University Press, 1997).

92. P. V. Babych, A. P. Ieropunova et al., eds., *My dity tvoï, Ukraïno: materialy I konhresu ukraïntsiv nezalezhnykh derzhav kolyshn'oho SRSR, 22–23 sichnia 1992 roku* (Kyiv: Ukraïna, 1992); *Literaturna Ukraïna*, January 30 and February 20, 1992; *Visti z Ukraïny*, no. 6 (1992).

93. Zinchuk et al., eds., *Rode nash prekrasnyi*; *Suchasnist'*, no. 12 (December 1992).

94. "Rezoliutsiia Vsesvitn'oho forumu ukraïntsiv," in Zinchuk et al., eds., *Rode nash prekrasnyi*, 183–84.

95. For example, "Posytsiia URP shchodo rozbudovy Zbroinykh Syl Ukraïny," *Samostiina Ukraïna*, no. 25 (1992).

96. *Visti z Ukraïny*, no. 15 (1991), no. 6 (1993), no. 149 (1994).

97. *The Ukrainian Weekly*, July 16, 1995; Kateryna Chernova, "Evoliutsiia form spivpratsi ukraïns'koï diaspory z Ukraïnoiu," *Ukraïns'ka diaspora* 4, no. 7 (1995): 5–18.

98. The main backer of the Congress of Ukrainian Nationalists (KUN) is the Organization of Ukrainian Nationalists (OUN), founded in Vienna in 1929. The OUN split in 1938 and again in 1955; KUN was established by the heirs of the more radical faction that resulted from the 1938 split.

99. "Pro vnesennia zmin i dopovnen' do konstytutsiï (osnovnoho zakonu) Ukraïny," *Holos Ukraïny*, April 7, 1992, article 114, paragraph 7, section 7.

100. See the interview with Ivan Kuras in *Ukraïns'ka hazeta*, March 2, 1995.

101. *Konstytutsiia Ukraïny* (Kyiv: Secretariat of the Supreme Council of Ukraine, 1996), 7.

102. "Dohovir pro druzhbu, spivrobitnytstvo, i partnerstvo mizh Ukraïnoiu i Rosiis'koiu Federatsiieiu," *Uriadovyi kur"ier*, June 3, 1997. Possibilities are hardly equal at the moment.

103. "Pravo na hromadianstvo," *Uriadovyi kur"ier*, June 10, 1997.

104. "Dohovir pro vidnosyny dobrosusidstva i spivrobitnytstva mizh Ukraïnoiu ta Rumuniieiu," *Uriadovyi kur"ier*, June 5, 1997.

105. Author's interview with then minister for migration and nationalities, Volodymyr Yevtukh, February 9, 1996.

106. "Postanova Konhresu ukraïns'koï intelihentsiï," *Literaturna Ukraïna*, November 16, 1995. See also "Zaiva Ukraïns'koï respublikans'koï partiï pro neobkhidnist' zakhystu etnichnykh ukraïntsiv na terytoriï Rosiis'koï Federatsiï," *V z"ïzd Ukraïns'koï respublikans'koï partiï*, party document, Kyiv, 1994, pp. 165–66; and the Rukh program, *A Concept of State-Building in Ukraine* (Kyiv: Taki spravy, 1993), 38. See also V. Klym, "Chy bude derzhavna prohrama povernennia ukraïntsiv v Ukraïnu?" *Rozbudova derzhavy*, no. 4 (1994).

107. Iurii Lypa, *Rozpodil Rossiï* (New York: Hoverlia, 1954).

108. "Rezoliutsiia Vsesvitn'oho forumu ukraïntsiv," in Zinchuk et al., eds., *Rode nash prekrasnyi*, 184.

6

The Kazakhs: Demographics, Diasporas, and "Return"

Sally N. Cummings

Boranbaia Beisembaiuly, depicted in 1996 in the Kazakhstani regional newspaper *Panorama Shimkenta*, is typical of an important class of ethnic Kazakhs. Along with his two wives and eight children, Beisembaiuly had decided to uproot from his "host-state," Turkey, in order to return to his newly independent "kin-state," the Republic of Kazakhstan.[1] Beisembaiuly's decision, though, was not made unilaterally. Since Kazakhstan became independent almost by accident in December 1991, its leadership has actively sponsored the return of ethnic Kazakhs living beyond the frontiers of the new state. Unlike all other Soviet successor states, Kazakhstan adopted a wide-ranging policy designed to encourage the repatriation of selected ethnic Kazakh populations living abroad.

This chapter aims to demonstrate how the policy of selective repatriation has reflected the peculiar tensions inherent in recent Kazakhstani history: Kazakhs are at the same time an ethnic population that has only recently emerged from a status of ethnic minority within its own state, and a newly empowered ethnic group that must rule within a manifestly multiethnic society. This tension expresses the dichotomy between a civic state identity and a more ethnic, organic one—discourses that are both to be found in recent Kazakhstani politics.[2] President Nursultan Abishevich Nazarbaev has publicly reiterated that the multicultural and municonfessional nature of the republic demands an inclusive conception of citizenship. The state's task, he stresses, is to create an inclusive, state-centered "Kazakhstani" identity, rather than an exclusive, narrowly defined, ethnic "Kazakh" identity. The emphasis on political over cultural identity has, however, proven problematic, and state policy toward the Kazakh diaspora is a prime example of the tension between these two conceptions of the state. As the fortunes of various societal and governmental groups with a stake in the diaspora issue have waxed and waned, the inclusive vision of state identity has gradually given way to the organic.

The analysis of this chapter is state-centric. While giving some consideration to the culture, values, and opinions of the diaspora communities in host-states, this chapter focuses on kin-state policy.[3] The chapter will therefore not consider the varied nature of ethnic Kazakh identities abroad, which like all other identities are complex, multiple, and always undergoing transformation.[4] Instead, the analysis will concentrate on the origins and outcomes of Kazakhstan's policy toward the diaspora, particularly the stress on the "return" of co-ethnic populations to the homeland. The chapter is divided into three sections. The first provides a historical account of the creation of a Kazakh diaspora and outlines the communities' situation at the time of Kazakhstani independence; the second analyzes the genesis and structure of the state policy of repatriation; and the third section considers the difficulties of the repatriation policy and assesses the policy's impact on Kazakhstan's domestic politics.

Routes to Diaspora:
The Formation of a Kazakh Diaspora Before 1991

The ethnic mosaic of Central Asia is intricate. The region's complex cultures are products of its geographic location at the crossroads of civilizations, the effects of nomadic migration, and the impact of a succession of conquests and empires in antiquity. The Kazakhs are a prime example of the complicated and overlapping origins and histories of Central Asia's ethnic groups. Most sources date the emergence of the Kazakhs as a distinct group to the fifteenth century, but the nature of their origins remains unclear. Scholars are divided about whether their nomadic ancestors were essentially Mongol or Turkic. Ethnographically, the Kazakhs are normally classified as South Siberian Mongoloid, but the Kazakh language belongs to the Kipchak division of Turkic languages. Historically, the Kazakhs have been nomads of the steppe, practicing a pastoral economy, and as such their conversion to Islam was relatively recent; Islamic belief was grafted onto traditional beliefs.[5] Traditionally, Kazakh allegiances are first to the family, then the tribe, and then to the horde (*zhuz*), the largest social sub-grouping within the Kazakh ethnic group.[6]

The origins of the *zhuz* groupings remain speculative, but they are generally seen as early military formations whose boundaries were determined largely by topography and by the existence of three "economic units" on the Central Asian steppe. The three areas were termed the Great Horde (*Ulu zhuz*, in the south), the Middle Horde (*Orta zhuz*, in the center), and the Small Horde (*Kishi zhuz*, in the west).[7] The hordes did not unite to develop a national identity, nor did they develop broader territorial units that might have formed lasting political entities. The region traversed by these hordes and which traditionally formed the "Kazakh lands" was somewhat larger than that of present-day Kazakhstan. For centuries, though, the boundaries were fluid, imposed not by natural constraints on migration but by inter-nomadic rivalry. From the eighteenth century onward, however, the Russian and Chinese empires steadily extended their respective frontiers into the steppe lands.[8]

Colonial expansion, the primary agent of modernization for Kazakh nomads, provided the first catalyst for the emigration of Kazakhs beyond their (mutable) borders. Movement into the steppe from three sides reduced the area of pasturage available to the Kazakhs and forced the nomads to search for new pasturelands. As nomadic warriors with expert horsemanship and martial skills at the "pivot of Asia," Kazakhs were one of the many tribes absorbed from the east by imperial China when the empire established Xinjiang (literally, the "New Territory" located today in the far western People's Republic of China) in 1896.[9] In the east the constriction of traditional Kazakh lands was also accentuated in the eighteenth century by the rise of the powerful Jungar (Oirat) people and the push of one Oirat group, the Kalmyks, westward across the Kazakh domain to the Volga river. Russian traders, soldiers, and administrators arrived from the north; they were followed by Russian and Ukrainian peasants who settled in the fertile steppe, and by railroad workers who immigrated to the region with the construction of the Turkestan–Siberian railroad in the late nineteenth century. Between 1896 and 1916, more than 1.4 million new settlers poured into the steppe lands.[10] The revolt that resulted from the 1916 Russian imperial edict conscripting Kazakhs to fight in the First World War, as well as the period of civil war following the Bolshevik revolution, led to many Kazakh deaths and the further dispersal of Kazakh populations. Territorial–administrative changes also left Kazakhs outside their lands; in 1914 the traditionally Kazakh territories around Omsk and Orenburg became part of the Russian state. There were also pressures from the south; in the early nineteenth century, the expansion of Khiva, a powerful khanate south of the Aral Sea, drove Kazakhs out of their traditional pasture lands near the Amu Darya river.[11]

The onset of the Bolshevik revolution and the subsequent consolidation of Soviet power in Central Asia was the second force behind the creation of a Kazakh diaspora. Soviet policy aimed to modernize traditional indigenous society through industrialization and collectivization. For the nomads collectivization was accompanied by brutal policies of forced sedentarization and the cessation of a whole way of life. Some two million people, totaling 42 percent of the ethnic Kazakh population, died in the early years of Soviet power. One-third of the remaining Kazakhs fled abroad, mainly to China, Afghanistan, Iran, and Turkey. Saulesh Esenova cites total losses of Kazakhs for the period 1916–1939 at 3,635,000.[12] The notion of a diaspora was also strengthened by the Soviet creation of the Kazakh Soviet Socialist Republic (KSSR). Initially an autonomous republic within the Russian Federation, the KSSR was the largest of the new entities created by the Soviets in Central Asia and encompassed the traditional Kazakh steppe area. At the same time, the ethnic Kazakh population within the KSSR was progressively diminished by the immigration of non-Kazakhs to the republic, as many as 6 million during the entire Soviet period.[13]

In short, these two eras—the period of colonization and imperial expansion in the nineteenth and early twentieth centuries, and the period of sedentarization, immigration, and modernization under the Soviets—combined to create a Kazakh diaspora; at the same time, through immigration of non-Kazakhs to the KSSR and deportation of Kazakhs from the republic, a "titular minority" arose within the Kazakh republic itself. By the time of the 1979 census, the Kazakhs were outnumbered by ethnic Russians. Although this demographic disadvantage had begun to change in the Kazakhs' favor by the time of the 1989 census, in the late Soviet period Kazakhs were nevertheless still a minority in their own republic. By 1991, though, eight principal diasporic populations had developed in China, Russia, Uzbekistan, Kyrgyzstan, Mongolia, Afghanistan, Iran, and Turkey. This diaspora is almost equally divided between the republics of the former Soviet Union (1,665,000) and the rest of the world (1,535,000).[14]

China

The largest and most politically sensitive of these diasporic communities developed in the Xinjiang–Uighur autonomous region of the People's Republic of China (hereafter referred to as Xinjiang).[15] Although Kazakh groups have at various times ventured farther east, entering the Chinese provinces of Gansu, Qinghai, and Tibet, they eventually settled in three main areas of northwestern Xinjiang: Ili, Tacheng, and Tarbatai.[16] The most common contemporary estimate of Kazakhs in China is around one

TABLE 6.1   Principal Settlements of the Kazakh Diaspora in the 1990s

Area	Population (year)	Specific Location (towns, cities, regions)
China	907,582 (1982) 1 million-plus (1990)	Gansu, Qinghai, northern Xinjiang regions
Russia	700,000 (1996)	Lower Volga, southern Urals, western Siberia, southern Altai regions
Uzbekistan	808,000 (1989)	——
Mongolia	177,000 (1989)	Hovd, Selenge, Ulan Bator cities; Bayan-Olgiy, Hentiy, Dornot regions
Kyrgyzstan	37,000 (1989)	——
Afghanistan	3,000–21,000 (1970s)	Baghlan and Takhar regions
Turkey	5,000 (mid-1980s)	Istanbul, Adana, Aksakal, Konya, Urfa cities
Iran	3,000–5,000 (1993)	Gorgan and Behshar cities in northern Iran

Sources: For China: Most figures for the 1990s vary between 1 million and 1.5 million; see Linda Benson and Ingvar Svanberg, eds., *The Kazaks of China: Essays on an Ethnic Minority*, Studia Multiethnica Upsaliensia 5 (Uppsala: Almquist and Wiksell International, 1988). For Russia: 1996 figures from Gulnara M. Mendikulova, "Istoriia vozniknoveniia kazakhskoi irredenty v Kitae i ego sovremennoe razvitie," unpublished article, Almaty, 1997. For Uzbekistan and Kyrgyzstan: 1989 Soviet census. For Mongolia: 1989 Mongolian census figures supplied by Ingvar Svanberg in communication with the author, September 1997; see also Ingvar Svanberg, "In Search of a Kazakhstani Identity," *Journal of Area Studies* 12, no. 4 (1994): 113–23. For Afghanistan: A 1978 estimate in Ingvar Svanberg, "Contemporary Changes among the Kazaks," in Ingvar Svanberg, ed., *Ethnicity, Minorities and Cultural Encounters* (Uppsala: Centre for Multiethnic Research, 1991), 83–101. For Turkey: Estimates from Ingvar Svanberg, *Kazak Refugees in Turkey: A Study of Cultural Persistence and Social Change*, Studia Multiethnica Upsaliensia 8 (Uppsala: Almquist and Wiksell International, 1989). For Iran: Various news reports and other information at http://netiran.com /news/ IRNA/html/, and Svanberg, "Contemporary Changes."

million.[17] Kazakhs, arriving in the 1930s, settled principally in rural areas; in the 1980s, 85 percent were engaged in livestock breeding and agriculture. They have remained fairly compact and isolated, preserving their Kazakh language and many of their traditions. However, there is little natural affinity between Kazakh communities in China and those in Kazakhstan. More than 80 percent of ethnic Kazakh children in China were born, and therefore also socialized, after the formation of the people's republic, more than 70 percent after 1962, and more than 50 percent after the Cultural Revolution.[18] For all the ties of culture and custom that might bind them to Kazakh communities in other states, their separate experience over the last half-century has created important divisions between the diaspora and the homeland.

Xinjiang was a major issue in interstate relations between the Soviet Union and China. Sino-Soviet tensions mounted and relations deteriorated after 1955; the Soviet–Chinese frontier became the most militarized of the Soviet empire. Some of the main sources of discord involved China's longstanding border grievances against the Soviet Union. Under treaties imposed on imperial China by tsarist Russia in 1858, 1860, and 1881, China was forced to cede almost one million square miles of territory in the maritime provinces of Siberia and in Central Asia, an area that incorporated present-day Almaty and much of its environs. Even though the Bolsheviks abrogated these treaties, they failed to return the land to China. Moscow has refused to renegotiate the agreements, which Beijing still refers to as the "unequal treaties."

The KSSR became a center for Soviet anti-Chinese propaganda in the 1960s and 1970s.[19] Kazakh infiltrators were dispatched to Xinjiang to spread propaganda among the Chinese Kazakhs, and sympathetic Soviet agents provided leaders of dissident ethnic groups with financial aid and advice. Major rebellions of Uighurs, Kazakhs, and Kyrgyz in China broke out in 1959, 1962, and 1974. During the 1962 rebellion, the border with the Soviet Union was opened, and 120,000 refugees from Xinjiang fled to settle in the eastern regions of the KSSR.[20] In China the Turkic minorities briefly established their own independent state, the so-called East Turkestan Republic, whose capital, Ining, was situated in an area of Xinjiang still today dominated by ethnic Kazakhs. These Kazakhs provided cavalry to the East Turkestan Republic until the Soviet Union withdrew its support. With the exception of this period, however, the status of the Kazakhs in China was rarely discussed; when the issue arose, it was only "as a means of favourably comparing what the Soviets had done and what the Chinese were doing" for ethnic Kazakhs.[21]

Russia, Turkey, and Other Host-States

The second largest community of Kazakhs beyond contemporary Kazakhstan lives along Russia's southern borders. In 1991 Kazakhs in

Russia numbered approximately 700,000.[22] They live in the border regions of southern Altai, Orenburg, and western Siberia—more precisely, the Astrakhan, Volgograd, Orenburg, Omsk, and Tiumen *oblasts*, and the Gorno-Altai autonomous *oblast'*.[23] Other significant Kazakh groups in the former Soviet Union are found in Uzbekistan and Kyrgyzstan (808,000 and 37,000 respectively, according to the 1989 census).[24] Compared with Kazakhs in China, these communities are less traditional and more assimilated to local cultures.

Significant numbers of Kazakhs also live in Mongolia, where like their co-ethnics in China they continue to be engaged primarily in livestock breeding. As many as 70,000 Kazakhs may have resided in the Mongolian People's Republic in the 1970s,[25] a number that had risen to approximately 100,000–150,000 by the mid-1980s. In 1991 their number reportedly stood at approximately 120,000.[26] As mainly stockbreeders, they live principally in the agricultural areas of Bayan-Olgiy and Kobdo. About a hundred Kazakh families live in the capital, Ulan Bator.[27]

Other Kazakh diasporas were created in the 1950s. In response to Chinese repression, several thousand Kazakh refugees, many of whom had participated in a rebellion against communist China, fled to Pakistan, Kashmir, Afghanistan, and Iran.[28] Some 5,000 are said presently to live in Iran.[29] Although they left their livestock behind, Kazakhs were gradually able to establish themselves in their new host-states. By virtue of their fewer numbers and greater dispersion, they were more powerfully influenced by their environment than Kazakhs in China, Russia, or Mongolia, and became far more assimilated to local cultures. Most visibly, they adopted the Muslim faith of each of these host-states.

Many of the Kazakhs in Pakistan and Iran accepted a 1952 invitation by Turkey to settle in refugee settlements in Anatolia. Kazakhs from Afghanistan followed in the 1970s. By the mid-1970s, most of these resettled Kazakhs in Turkey were urbanized and employed as small-scale hide manufacturers or managers of plastics factories.[30] By virtue of having been exposed to what now amounted to some three different host-states, these urbanized Kazakhs lacked any strong affiliation with Kazakhstan. Indeed, since their ancestors originated from eastern Turkestan, they often considered their homeland Xinjiang rather than Kazakhstan. In Turkey the young urban elite formed a movement in the 1970s to resist acculturation, but the backlash against assimilation to Turkish language and culture lasted only briefly.[31] Nevertheless, "Kazakhs have never doubted their loyalties vis-à-vis the Turkish state."[32] Already by the close of the 1970s, however, some ethnic Kazakhs had left Turkey for the Arabian peninsula or, more frequently, for France, West Germany, and Sweden, and in smaller numbers for Austria, Belgium, the Netherlands, and Norway.[33]

Origins and Implementation
of Kazakhstan's Repatriation Policy

Although Kazakhstan was the penultimate Soviet republic to declare independence, ethnic Kazakh groups had already, under Gorbachev, placed their demands for ethnic regeneration on the political agenda. Several important informal opposition and cultural groups arose in the late 1980s, including *Azat* (Freedom), *Alash* (named for the mythical progenitor of the Kazakh nation), and *Zheltoksan* (December). The leadership of these movements changed frequently, and they were able to canvass only scant popular support. But they did give voice to a growing undercurrent of anti-Russian sentiment in the republic, a sentiment that was most forcefully expressed in the Almaty riots of December 1986, sparked by the appointment of an ethnic Russian as first secretary of the Communist Party of Kazakhstan.[34] In addition to these early groups, the *Qazaq Tili* (Kazakh Language) association was formed in 1989. Financed and sponsored by the state, its primary aim was to ensure that the Kazakh language would be designated the state language of the republic, a status that it received in new language laws adopted in September 1989.

All four groups were united by their unmitigated antipathy toward Russian hegemony and by their determination to have their own nation-state. They all also incorporated the plight of co-ethnics abroad into their platforms and programs; they called for Kazakhs abroad to return to what they defined as the ethnic homeland of all Kazakhs. The nationalist weekly *Zaman–Qazaqstan* summarized the feelings expressed by movements calling for a Kazakh national renaissance: "Kazakhs, who on their own territory have only just been delivered from their minority status, need to flourish."[35] *Qazaq Tili* in particular regarded the diaspora as a powerful weapon in its armory, since Kazakh communities abroad, who had been spared the experience of state-led russification under the Soviets, had managed to preserve their knowledge of both written and spoken Kazakh. Paradoxically, then, repatriated Kazakhs would be able to teach sovietized local Kazakhs their own language and inculcate traditions long lost by their modernized brethren in the homeland.

The collapse of the Soviet Union in 1991 destroyed the context within which modern Kazakh identity had been shaped and prompted the official adoption by the Kazakhstani state of a policy of ethnic repatriation a year later. The repatriation policy was couched in terms of two interlinked policy imperatives: first, legitimating the territorial boundaries of the new state and overcoming the disadvantageous demographic position of ethnic Kazakhs within Kazakhstan; and second, addressing the legacies of the past, especially the history of Soviet developmental policies that had led to the extermination of over half the Kazakh population.

The repatriation of Kazakhs rested on the premise that an ethnos can only flourish within the borders of its own nation-state. Merely establishing links with a diaspora would not ensure the survival of a nation that had emerged upon independence as a "titular minority." Thus, as the Kazakhstani official demographer, Makash Tatimov, stated, the government "must work out its conception for the republic's demographic evolution, and ensure that population changes best serve the interests of internal and domestic policies."[36] Repatriated Kazakhs would boost the ethnic Kazakh share of the republic's population and would be settled in those areas where Kazakhs were in the minority. Hence, Kazakh "returnees" from Mongolia were settled principally in the Russian-majority oblasts of northern Kazakhstan and in some Uighur- and Uzbek-dominated areas in the south.[37] The relocation of repatriated Kazakhs would dovetail with a separate policy of internal migration, initiated in 1992 and designed to encourage ethnic Kazakhs already residing within the republic to move to regions dominated by non-Kazakhs.

Moreover, repatriation was viewed as one visible way of addressing the checkered history of Kazakhstan. The "return" of Kazakhs provided a convenient occasion for the hitherto suppressed discussion of how many had perished or fled during the Soviet era. Addressing Kazakhstan's Assembly of Nationalities in March 1995, President Nazarbaev emphasized the richness of Kazakh diasporic communities, who "even if not exerting a direct impact on politics, have been successful in the most diverse fields."[38] One of these fields was the use of repatriated Kazakhs in the official rewriting of history, portraying the establishment of the independent Republic of Kazakhstan as the culmination of a tortuous history of national dispersion and struggle.

The repatriation policy was officially launched by the November 1992 World Congress of Kazakhs. This reunion of Kazakhs from around the world was the first such government-sponsored event. The congress aimed to encourage diverse Kazakhs to exchange experiences of language and culture. Significantly, the congress was given the name *qurultai*, the ancient Kazakh term for a tribal gathering. As a celebration of the Kazakh ethnos, it provided the ideal forum for the tracing of genealogy, witnessed by the large number of genealogical charts displayed on various walls around the capital city of Almaty.[39]

The congress was only the beginning, however. To ensure a smooth progression from drawing board to policy, appropriate bilateral agreements, legislation, and institutional mechanisms were prepared. President Nazarbaev signed state agreements on the repatriation of ethnic Kazakhs with Afghanistan, Iran, Mongolia, and Turkey. During Nazarbaev's visit to Tehran in 1992, an agreement was signed with the Iranian president on the repatriation of Iranian Kazakhs. During the trip to Almaty by Mongolian Premier Puntsagiyn Jasray in November 1994, Nazarbaev and the Mongolian premier signed a series of agreements which included the regulation of "voluntary migration." At the same time, the Kazakhstani ministry of foreign affairs was charged with advertising the state's willingness to finance the repatriation of ethnic Kazakhs abroad.

The legal basis for repatriation was codified in several important decrees and laws issued from 1992 through 1995: the law on immigration (June 26, 1992); the presidential decree (no. 1184) "On Immigration Quotas and the Organization of Immigration of Co-ethnics from Iran and Other States" (April 15, 1993); and a governmental decree (no. 2366) on the implementation of presidential directives on repatriation (July 18, 1995). Furthermore, every year new presidential edicts establish immigration quotas, including quotas for repatriated Kazakhs.

These and other laws established three major principles according to which the repatriation policy would be implemented. The first required a repatriate to be an ethnic Kazakh, literally "a person of indigenous nationality" (*litso korennoi natsional'nosti*). Article 17 of the 1992 immigration law grants repatriate status to all refugees who fled in the 1930s and their descendants, but in practice ethnic distinctions are made among these former refugee groups; for example, ethnic Uighurs, many of whom fled along with Kazakhs in the 1930s, are not automatically entitled to return to Kazakhstan.[40]

Second, although Kazakhstan prohibited dual citizenship, ethnic Kazakhs abroad were initially exempted from this provision. Third, even though this right to dual citizenship was withdrawn in October 1995, the five-year residency requirement for citizenship was waived for repatriated Kazakhs. Throughout this legislation, the laws' vague wording often allows public authorities to avoid charges of ethnic discrimination; hence, according to one official at the visa and immigration department within the foreign ministry, repatriates "are faced with the same procedure required of all citizens. We do not adopt the favoritist approach, say, of Germany or Israel."[41]

An elaborate network of political institutions has been responsible for the details of repatriation: the customs committee, subordinated to the Kazakhstani council of ministers; the ministry of labor and social protection (which succeeded the former ministry of labor in 1996); the ministry of foreign affairs; the ministry of transport and communications; the ministry of interior; the ministry of health; the ministry of education;

regional administration heads (*akims*); and the city of Almaty. The ministry of labor and social protection is the institutional coordinator, organizing quotas, allocating money to the repatriated from the state repatriation fund, and supervising housing, employment, and training programs for the newly arrived Kazakhs. The ministry of foreign affairs assists with diplomatic problems and oversees the Kazakhs' initial departure from their host-states. The ministry of transport and communications, specifically the Kazakhstan state airline, Kazakhstan Aue Zholy, provides free flights and transport to the repatriates' final destinations. In association with the customs committee, the transport ministry also ensures that the repatriates and their property—of which the most important element is often livestock—gain smooth passage. Once the repatriates arrive in Kazakhstan, the ministry of interior promises initial protection of people and property moving across the republic's territory and the expedited processing of residency and passport documentation. Free medical examinations and (often unnecessary) language courses are provided by the ministries of health and education.[42]

The most common estimate cited for the number of individuals repatriated since 1992 is 150,000 to 200,000 (these figures are difficult to assess, however, since data are often given in terms of repatriated families rather than individuals). During a cabinet meeting on December 30, 1997, the minister of labor and social protection, Natalia Korzhova, stated that 35,000 Kazakh families had been repatriated since 1992. This figure is equivalent to over 160,000 individuals.[43] *Express khronika* of December 11, 1997, confirmed that as of 1991 "36,839 Kazakh families, or more than 160,000 individuals, have moved permanently to Kazakhstan from Mongolia, Iran, Turkey, China, Saudi Arabia, and the CIS."[44]

The Problems of Repatriation

Despite the government's active engagement and its well-orchestrated publicity drive, even by the highest estimates of "returnees" the initial results of repatriation have been unimpressive—especially considering that Kazakhstan could conceivably claim a worldwide ethnic diaspora of over three million. Three main difficulties with the repatriation policy are evident. First, the Kazakhstani government did not honor its financial, material, or legal obligations to the returnees. The repatriation policy put considerable strain on the state budget. Without providing the necessary finances, central authorities in practice devolved responsibility for the payment of repatriate allowances onto cash-strapped regional administrations. Returnees complained about not receiving allowances from these regional authorities. Returnees said that, while they had been offered land, there was frequently no housing to go with it. In 1997 in the Southern Kazakhstan *oblast'*, about 14,000 repatriates remained without adequate housing; the regional administration, instead of its projected expenditure on resettlement of 15 million *tenge*, had spent only 2.5 million *tenge* ($32,000).[45]

According to the newspaper *Express khronika*, "certain regions, such as Almaty, Jambul, Kustanai, and Northern Kazakhstan, have not allocated any money toward the support of repatriates."[46] Often accustomed to warmer climates, returnees suffered particularly during Kazakhstan's harsh winter of 1994–95, when even Southern Kazakhstan's regional government was forced to organize a collection of goods and warm clothes for them. Frustrations encountered by the newly arrived were summarized in a letter published in the weekly *Turkestan*. Written by a woman, Nasilina Shaidaiuly, who had recently been resettled in Za-rechnyi village of the Taldi-Kurgan region, the letter recounted that:

> Six families arrived in Zarechnyi village in 1995. Of them, four sons and six daughters are jobless. Upon our arrival here, a presidential decree unexpectedly placed the responsibility for finding homes onto regional authorities. However, my son and his children are forced to live on the street, a fact of which both the town mayor and regional *akim* are aware. . . . When mass privatization began, all livestock was given to established inhabitants, and not even a bone was thrown to the newly arrived. This is really unfair.[47]

The legal and bureaucratic hurdles faced by returnees, although supposedly reduced by the array of legislation to encourage repatriation, remained formidable. While the Mongolian ambassador to Kazakhstan in 1996 maintained that "more than eighty percent of those Kazakhs who have returned will stay," he acknowledged that to "change citizenship, you need to complete fifteen different documents. . . . Many of the returnees live in remote places, and some cannot even read."[48] Even Kazakhs who emigrated from China at the beginning of the repatriation drive had still not managed to obtain Kazakhstani citizenship some four years after their arrival.

A second problem concerns the stark cultural differences between "locals" (*starozhili* or *mestnye*, in Russian) and the repatriates (often loosely termed "those from abroad," or persons *iz-za rubezha*, in Russian). In contrast to returnees in some other successor states, Kazakh repatriates are not perceived as less genuinely Kazakh; if anything, they are considered too Kazakh. Local Kazakhs—modern, sovietized, secular, and

Russian-speaking—often regard the newly arrived as anachronistic Muslim, Kazakh-speaking traditionalists. After all, Kazakhs in Xinjiang still write Kazakh in Arabic script, rather than the Cyrillic script used in Kazakhstan. Locals often distinguish themselves from the newly arrived, as one local Kazakh wrote in the newspaper *Ana tili*: "Ah, those are the people who have just arrived from China, Mongolia, and Turkey. They won't stay here for long. They do not accept us as equals."[49]

Cultural problems exist not only within ethnic lines but across them as well. Non-Kazakhs have complained about a policy that they perceive as favoring the indigenous nationality. Frictions have emerged between ethnic Russian communities in the north and newly arrived Kazakhs from Mongolia who, often arriving with their herds in tow, are striking evidence to non-Kazakh locals of the state's desire to increase the predominance and preponderance of the titular nation. Potentially more serious has been the friction in Uighur-dominated areas of the south, such as in the Panfilovsk *raion* in the Taldi-Kurgan region, where returnees compete for scarce land and water resources with local Uighurs.[50]

For these reasons many newly arrived Kazakhs, especially those from Mongolia, have attempted to move back to their host-states. In an articled entitled "Strangers Among Friends" in the newspaper *Karavan–Blits*, Mongolia's ambassador to Kazakhstan contended that "migration from Mongolia has stopped once and for all."[51] The *Qazaq tili* newspaper stated that "about 600 families returned to Mongolia from Kazakhstan in 1995 and 1996; the expected number of Kazakh Mongolians who will return in 1997 alone is estimated at 750."[52] While some 8,000 ethnic Kazakhs arrived in Kazakhstan between January and September 1997, 9,000 left during that same period.[53] According to Kazakhstan's National Statistics Agency, six times fewer Kazakhs arrived in their kin-state in 1997 than in 1995. Since 1995 approximately one in twenty repatriated Kazakhs has returned to his host-state.[54]

A final constraint on the success of Kazakhstan's repatriation policy has been considerations of geopolitics. In the interests of state security, the Kazakhstani government has been unable and unwilling to extend repatriation to two of the largest communities abroad, those in China and in Russia. In the case of China, the "unequal treaties" of the last century form the basis for the Chinese government's claim to southeastern portions of Kazakhstan.[55] The Kazakhstani government continues to fear Beijing's foreign policy; one unofficial reason for moving the Kazakhstani capital from Almaty to Akmola in 1997 was to increase the physical distance between the state's central institutions and the regions of potential Chinese irredentism.

There are also pragmatic reasons for the reticence of the Nazarbaev administration to speak out on the position of Kazakh co-ethnics in Xinjiang. The border region of Xinjiang and southeastern Kazakhstan is becoming one of the fastest growing border economies and trading zones in the world. A \$9.5 billion oil deal with China's national petroleum company concluded in September 1997 paved the way for the construction of a pipeline from western Kazakhstan through Xinjiang.[56] Politically, Xinjiang is fraught with unrest as the Muslim Uighur minority clamors for the creation of its own state. The most serious incident occurred in February 1997 when, according to official Chinese figures, Uighurs killed ten and wounded 144 others during the February 5–6 riots in Ining.[57] Nazarbaev, acutely aware that the Uighur government–in–exile is based in Almaty, has repeatedly assured Deng Xiaoping's successor, Jiang Zemin, that Kazakhstan is "against national splittism and activities by any organization aimed at dividing China by using Kazakh territories."[58] From mid-1995, official Kazakhstani statements on relations with China routinely condemned both the principle of separatism as well as the recognition of Taiwan and Tibet as independent states.[59]

A similar situation obtains in regard to Kazakhs in Russia. Socialized in Russia and perceived by the Kazakhstani government as inconstant Kazakhstani patriots, russified Kazakhs probably serve the needs of the Kazakhstani state more effectively by remaining across the border. There they offer possibilities for future business contacts or even intelligence gathering. Moreover, few have voluntarily returned over a border that remains, for all intents and purposes, open. Anecdotal evidence suggests that those who return freely from Russia are "'largely USSR-era bureaucrats . . . and students who were waiting to finish their education in Russian cities before returning to Central Asia.'"[60] Central authorities have encouraged northern Kazakhstani regions to conclude inter-regional agreements with southern Russian regions, such as the March 1994 economic agreement signed between the Ekaterinburg, Cheliabinsk, and Omsk regions of Russia and the Pavlodar region of Kazakhstan. Moreover, President Nazarbaev's much-vaunted Eurasian Union initiative, aimed at the elimination of border and customs controls among the former Soviet republics, would also increase cross-border contacts with local Russian Kazakh communities. But beyond these limited initiatives, there has been little effort to reach out to the substantial Kazakh diaspora within the Russian Federation.

In neither the Chinese nor the Russian case has the Kazakh kin-state advocated the rights of co-ethnics in international forums and among non-governmental organizations, nor has it interceded directly with the host-state to ensure that the cultural, linguistic, and political rights of the co-ethnic minority are respected. These issues, though, are increasingly the domain of quasi-governmental organizations such as *Qazaq Tili*, which have provided the financial means for the establishment of Kazakh newspapers abroad in both Russia and Xinjiang.

The Kazakhstani government is proud of the fact that, according to official statistics, by early 1997 ethnic Kazakhs comprised over 50 percent of Kazakhstan's population. However, even if these figures are correct, the repatriation policy was only marginally responsible for the demographic shift. The main reason was the substantial and continuing outmigration of Russians, Ukrainians, and Germans. As a result Kazakhstan witnessed a net drop in its population—from about 17 million in 1993 to just under 16 million in 1997.[61] A demographic study published in Almaty found that population dynamics presaged a continuing increase in the ethnic Kazakh population and a decrease in the Russian population in both absolute and relative terms. The study projected for the year 2015 a ratio of 10 million Kazakhs to 3.6 million Russians.[62]

These dynamics were, moreover, part of a longer trend that predated the collapse of the Soviet Union. While in 1979 ethnic Kazakhs predominated in only five of Kazakhstan's *oblasts*, in 1989 they were already a majority in nine, and in 1995 in twelve.[63] Thus, according to the government, the existential threat of the early years of independence had, by the late 1990s, begun to recede, strengthening the state's confidence in the demographic prospects of the titular nationality. This confidence was reflected in President Nazarbaev's strategic development plan, released in autumn 1997, which predicted a population of 25 million for the republic by the year 2030.[64]

Still, despite this optimism, the jury is out on whether Kazakhs in reality form a majority of the population. In 1995 they constituted 44 percent, and although there has been substantial Slav emigration and some Kazakh immigration, the Kazakh birth rate is declining (even though it is still high relative to that of other Central Asian peoples). Presidential statements and government policies confirm that the demographic situation is far from resolved. Nazarbaev has expressed his concern about the republic's general depopulation, and an agency for immigration and demography was established by presidential decree in December 1997 in order to encourage and regulate immigration.[65] At the same time, the minister for labor and social protection, Natalia Korzhova, reaffirmed the government's special commitment to repatriating ethnic Kazakhs.[66] In early February 1998, President Nazarbaev published a further decree that also reaffirmed state support for the repatriates.

Conclusion

The Kazakhstani state has adopted an instrumental approach to its diaspora. It has avoided making an interstate issue out of the diaspora by differentiating between adjoining and non-contiguous diasporic communities. This distinction has enabled the republic to shy away from entanglement with powerful states while simultaneously realizing its goal of attracting some Kazakhs "home." The government has specifically avoided an aggressive foreign policy and has been committed to post-1991 borders. The active diaspora policy of Kazakhstan in the early years of independence was the sign of a weak state, a policy tool that the government utilized both as a way of correcting the disadvantageous demographic situation of the titular nationality and of legitimating independence, a status into which Kazakhstani elites had stumbled almost unwittingly in 1991.

The policy of repatriation was in line with many of the nation building projects of the late Soviet period that continued to be employed after 1991, such as the rewriting of history, the renaming of public places, and the introduction of new symbols, institutions, and cultural manifestations linked with ostensibly authentic local cultures. The policy, however, reflected a rather simplistic understanding by the state of what constitutes and consolidates a nation, with the emphasis on the quantity of ethnic Kazakhs rather than the particular qualities that the returning co-ethnics might bring to the newly independent state. Although co-ethnic repatriates were hailed as valuable living repositories of half-forgotten national traditions, the reality was rather different. Mostly unskilled and poor, the repatriated Kazakhs found themselves at odds with their urban and largely russified compatriots; it is illustrative of the problems of integration that no representative of the returnees ever occupied an important position in the Nazarbaev administration. Most importantly, the policy reflected the inability of the Kazakhstani leadership to correct the realities of Kazakh ethnohistory, a history marked by the absence of a solidary national community and the presence of loose, divisive kinship affiliations that have impeded mutual understanding within the Kazakh population. Indeed, rather than strengthening the Kazakh ethnos, the policy served largely to deepen the cultural divides within the Kazakh ethnic group itself.

However, there is another, potentially more important element to the Kazakh diaspora. Trans-border linkages are likely to grow in the face of the emergence of what will constitute possibly the first diaspora that is both self-consciously Kazakh and commitedly Kazakhstani. Between 1993 and 1995, over 36,000 Kazakhs emigrated from Kazakhstan, principally to western Europe and North America (the total outflow from the republic, though, is still less than the in-flow of new immigrants). As young, KSSR-born Kazakhs who embrace Kazakhstani independence out of the paradoxical reason that it enabled them to leave, this younger generation are the bearers of memories, symbolic connections, and personal networks that tie them to the Kazakh kin-state. Better educated and wealthier than their nomadic forebears, they are likely to form a new Kazakh diaspora with its own elites and communal structures in the host-states. It is this new, post-Soviet diaspora—rather than the older, traditional communities that were the original targets of the repatriation project—that in the future will enjoy the strongest cultural and economic links with the kin-state.

Notes

The author would like to express particular gratitude for the invaluable information and comments provided by Professor Ingvar Svanberg. Her thanks also go to Igor Savin, Gulnara M. Mendikulova, and Asylbek Bisembiev for their helpful insights. She would also like to thank Professor Dominic Lieven for his comments on an earlier draft of this chapter. Finally, she would like to express her indebtedness to the Leverhulme Trust, under whose aegis she was able to conduct the fieldwork for this chapter.

1. *Panoroma Shimkenta,* September 20, 1996.

2. For more on these distinctions, see Clifford Geertz, "The Integrative Revolution: Primordial Sentiments and Civil Politics in the New States," in Clifford Geertz, ed., *Old Societies and New States: The Quest for Modernity in Asia and Africa* (New York: Free Press, 1963), 107–13.

3. For further information on diaspora(s), see Khachig Tölölyan, "Rethinking Diaspora(s): Stateless Power in the Transnational Moment," *Diaspora* 5, no. 1 (1996): 2–3.

4. See the following excellent works: Ingvar Svanberg, *Kazak Refugees in Turkey: A Study of Cultural Persistence and Social Change,* Studia Multiethnica Upsaliensia 8 (Uppsala: Almquist and Wiksell International, 1989); and Linda Benson and Ingvar Svanberg, eds., *The Kazaks of China: Essays on an Ethnic Minority,* Studia Multiethnica Upsaliensia 5 (Uppsala: Almquist and Wiksell International, 1988).

5. For an overview of these issues, see Elizabeth E. Bacon, *Central Asians Under Russian Rule: A Study in Culture Change* (Ithaca: Cornell University Press, 1980).

6. Lawrence Krader, *Peoples of Central Asia* (Bloomington: Indiana University Press, 1963), 193. See also Alfred E. Hudson, "Kazakh Social Structure," *Yale University Publications in Anthropology,* no. 20 (New Haven: Yale University

Press, 1938). See also Ian Morrison, "Some Notes on the Kazaks of Sinkiang," *Journal of the Royal Central Asian Society* 36, no. 26 (1949): 69–71.

7. See Nurbulat Masanov, *Kochevaia tsivilizatsiia kazakhov* (Almaty: Amarata, 1995), part 2, chapter 6.

8. See Shirin Akiner, *The Formation of Kazakh Identity: From Tribe to Nation-State* (London: Royal Institute of International Affairs, 1995), 1–33.

9. See June Teufel Dreyer, "Ethnic Minorities in the Sino-Soviet Dispute, " in William O. McCagg, Jr., and Brian D. Silver, eds., *Soviet Asian Ethnic Frontiers* (New York: Pergamon Press, 1979), 195–226. See also W. J. Drew, "Sinkiang: The Land and the People," *Central Asian Review* 16, no. 3 (1988): 205–16.

10. George Demko, *The Russian Colonization of Kazakhstan, 1896–1916* (Bloomington: Indiana University Press, 1969), 182.

11. Teresa Rakowska-Harmstone, "Soviet Legacies," *Central Asia Monitor*, no. 3 (1994): 23–35.

12. Saulesh Esenova, "The Outflow of Minorities from the Post-Soviet States: The Case of Kazakhstan," *Nationalities Papers* 24, no. 4 (1996): 691–709.

13. Makash Tatimov, "Immigratsionnaia volna priekhavskikh v Kazakhstan evropeiskogo naseleniia po dannym demograficheskoi i migratsionnykh statistiki (chislennost' vsekh v'ekhavskikh za period XVII, XVIII, XIX i XX vekov)," unpublished article, Almaty, 1994. See also his "Regulirovanie migratsionnykh protsessov," in M. Suzhikov, ed., *Mezhnatsional'nye otnosheniia v Kazakhstane: teoriia i praktika regulirovaniia* (Almaty: Gylym, 1993), 22–53.

14. Information supplied by Igor Savin, Institute of Economics, Southern Kazakhstan Academy of Sciences, January 10, 1998.

15. Ingvar Svanberg, *Kazak Refugees*, chapter 5. For a further introduction to the Kazakhs in China, see Konstantin L. Syroezhkin, "Osobennosti migratsionnykh protsessov v SUAR KNR i RK," *Evraziiskoe soobshchestvo: ekonomika, politika, bezopasnost'*, nos. 6–7 (1995): 144–154. See also Drew, "Sinkiang," 205.

16. Gulnara M. Mendikulova, "Istoriia vozniknoveniia kazakhskoi irredenty v Kitae i ego sovremennoe razvitie," unpublished article, Almaty, 1997.

17. The 1979 census puts the number of Kazakh immigrants in China at 840,000, but more recent statistics seem to level out at the figure of one and half million. According to the 1982 Chinese census, the figure in 1982 was already 907,582. David Nissman estimates 9 million Uighurs, 1 million Kazakhs, more than half a million Kyrgyz, and over 5 million Han Chinese. See Nurbulat E. Masanov, "Introduction," in G. E. Taizhanov, ed., *Kazakhi: istoriko-etnograficheskoe issledovanie* (Almaty: Kazakhstan, 1995), 21; and David Nissman, "Ethnopolitics and Pipeline Security," *Jamestown Foundation Prism*, October 6, 1995.

18. Syroezhkin, "Osobennosti," 20. See also idem, *Kazakhi v KNR: ocherki sotsial'no-ekonomicheskogo i kul'turnogo razvitiia* (Almaty: Kazakhstan, 1994).

19. For a concise history of Chinese communist nationalities policy in Xinjiang, see Lee Fu-Hsiang, *The Turkic–Moslem Problem in Sinkiang: A Case Study of the Chinese Communists' Nationality Policy* (Ph.D. diss., Rutgers University, 1973).

20. Mendikulova, "Istoriia," 24.

21. Nissman, "Ethnopolitics." See also idem, "The Kyrgyz, the Uighurs and Xinjiang," *Jamestown Foundation Prism*, October 22, 1995.

22. Gulnara M. Mendikulova, "Kazakhskaia irredenta v Rossii (istoriia i sovremennost')," *Evraziiskoe soobshchestvo: ekonimika, politika, bezopasnost'*, no. 8 (1995): 70–79.

23. Mendikulova, "Kazakhskaia irredenta," 70–79.

24. Masanov, "Introduction," 21.

25. *Qazaq sovet entsiklopedeiasy*, vol. 2 (Almaty: Kazakhskaia Sovetskaia Entsiklopediia, 1973), 510.

26. Jiger Janabel, citing a conversation with the president of the Kazakh Friendly Society, in "Kazakhstan's Ethnic Relations," *Central Asian Survey* 15, no. 1 (1996): 19.

27. Benson and Svanberg, eds., *The Kazaks of China*, 7–8.

28. See Ravan Farhadi, "Die Sprachen von Afghanistan," *Zentralasiatische Studien*, no. 3 (1969): 413.

29. IRNA News Agency report at http://netiran.com/news/IRNA/html.

30. See Svanberg, *Kazak Refugees*, chapter 4.

31. See Svanberg, *Kazak Refugees*, chapter 4.

32. Svanberg, *Kazak Refugees*, 178.

33. For a brief account of Kazakhs and other Turkestanis in the United States, see Alexandre Bennigsen, "Turkistanis," *Harvard Encyclopedia of American Ethnic Groups* (Cambridge: Harvard University Press, 1980), 991–92.

34. See Akiner, *The Formation of Kazakh Identity*, chapter 5.

35. *Zaman–Qazaqstan*, February 28, 1997.

36. Marat Tatimov, "Vliianie demograficheskikh i migratsionnykh protsessov na vnutrinopoliticheskuiu stabil'nost' v Respublike Kazakhstan," *Saiasat*, no. 5 (October 1995): 18–24.

37. For further information on repatriated Kazakhs in the north, see Ian Bremmer, "State-building and Ethnic Relations in Kazakhstan: Nazarbaev and the North," *Ethnic and Racial Studies* 17, no. 4 (1994): 619–35; Ian Bremmer and Cory Welt, "The Trouble with Democracy in Kazakhstan," *Central Asian Survey* 15, no. 2 (1996): 179–201; and Neil Melvin, *Russians Beyond Russia: The Politics of National Identity* (London: Pinter, 1995), chapter 6.

38. Nursultan Abishevich Nazarbaev, *Za mir i soglasie v nashem obshchem dome* (Almaty: Kazakhstan, 1995), 161.

39. Martha Brill Olcott, "Emerging Political Elites," in Ali Banuazizi and Myron Weiner, eds., *The New Geopolitics of Central Asia and its Borderland* (Bloomington: Indiana University Press, 1994), 51.

40. Martha Brill Olcott, "How New the New Russia: Demographic Upheavals in Central Asia," *Orbis* (Fall 1996): 551.

41. Author's interview, March 13, 1996.

42. Information supplied by Igor Savin, January 15, 1998.

43. *Panorama*, January 9, 1998.

44. See also, "Materialy OON: 'Migratsionnye peredvizheniia,'" *Evraziiskoe soobshchestvo: ekonomika, politika, bezopasnost'*, nos. 6–7 (1995): 4–13.

45. Information supplied by Savin, January 15, 1998.

46. *Ekspress khronika*, March 24, 1997.

47. *Turkestan*, February 28–March 4, 1997.

48. *Russia Today Report*, December 12, 1996.

49. *Ana tili*, March 13, 1997.

50. Information supplied by Savin, January 15, 1998.

51. *Karavan–Blits*, October 24, 1995.

52. *Qazaq tili*, March 21, 1997.

53. In 1996, in an equivalent period, 12,000 reportedly arrived and 7,000 emigrated.

54. *Karavan*, September 12, 1997.

55. For a general overview of China and Central Asia, see Peter Ferdinand, ed., *The New Central Asia and its Neighbours* (London: Pinter, 1994).

56. Nissman, "Ethnopolitics."

57. *SWB–SU*, February 18, 1997, and May 10, 1997.

58. *SWB–SU*, April 29, 1997.

59. The Kazakhstani embassy in Moscow on May 7, 1997, issued a similar statement in response to accusations by the Russian media that Kazakhstan's Uighur separatists had been involved in the February killings.

60. Olcott, "How New the New Russia," 537–55.

61. See *Republic of Kazakstan: Human Development Report 1997* (Almaty: United Nations Development Program, 1997), 61–63.

62. *Ekologicheskii vestnik* (Almaty), reported by Xinhua News Agency, January 7, 1997.

63. *Republic of Kazakhstan*, 62.

64. *Kazakhstan—2030: Prosperity, Security, and Ever Growing Welfare of All the Kazakhstanis: Message of the President of the Country to the People of Kazakhstan* (Almaty: Kazakhstan, 1997).

65. *Express khronika*, December 11, 1997.

66. *Panorama*, January 9, 1998.

7

The Volga Tatars:
Diasporas and
the Politics of Federalism

Katherine E. Graney

The Volga Tatars, a Turkic-speaking, Muslim people sometimes referred to as the Kazan Tatars, constitute the second most numerous population group in the Russian Federation after ethnic Russians. Over 6.5 million Volga Tatars lived on the territory of the Soviet Union at the time of the last Soviet state census in 1989.[1] In addition to their sheer numbers, the Volga Tatars are significant for their geographical distribution—they are perhaps, as one observer put it, "the most widely dispersed people in the former Soviet Union."[2] The nominal Tatar homeland is the former Tatar Autonomous Soviet Socialist Republic (ASSR) in the Russian Federation, known in the post-Soviet period as the Republic of Tatarstan; however, only about 25 percent of Volga Tatars actually live in Tatarstan, with the others being scattered throughout the remainder of the Russian Federation and the other former Soviet republics.

In its relationship with the Tatar diaspora during the perestroika and post-Soviet periods, the Tatarstani government, headed by the republic's first president, Mintimer Shaimiev, has presented Tatarstan as the historical and spiritual homeland for the over five million Volga Tatars that live outside Tatarstan. The adoption of this kin-state identity by Tatarstan when dealing with the diaspora, and the political processes it has engendered, provide unique insights into two issues which are of enduring interest to political scientists: the politics of multi-ethnic federations, and state and nation building in situations of cultural pluralism. Diaspora politics in Tatarstan illustrates that the presence of co-ethnic populations beyond the frontiers of an ostensible homeland can have a double impact on kin-states that are part of larger federations. On the one hand, extra-territorial ethnic groups can inspire homeland governments to seek increased power and autonomy within federations, portraying themselves as the rightful focus of the loyalties of a broader co-ethnic community and demanding greater say in the affairs of the federation at large. On the other hand, co-ethnic populations outside the homeland can also serve to bind the homeland territory more tightly within a federation; the homeland government may press the federal leadership to take a more active role in responding to the political and cultural needs of the homeland's co-ethnic populations outside the federation or within other federal constituents. The Tatar case illustrates how the adoption of a kin-state or homeland identity by constituents of multi-ethnic federations can complicate domestic politics and the search for viable forms of political community; at the same time, however, it also suggests that multiple identities, based both on ethnic and civic ideals, can co-exist harmoniously.

The Historical Evolution of the Diaspora

At the time of the 1989 census, the over 6.5 million Tatars in the Soviet Union made up 2.3 percent of the entire Soviet population. According to these figures, 1,765,000 Tatars lived in the present-day Republic of Tatarstan, 5.5 million lived in the Russian Federation as a whole, and close to one million resided in the other Soviet republics. Thus, only one-quarter of Volga Tatars actually lived in the current Republic of Tatarstan. The territory of the republic, located at the confluence of the Volga and Kama Rivers in central Russia, and its capital, Kazan, are identified with three historical entities that have significance for Volga Tatar ethnic consciousness; the legacies and symbolism of these entities have been embraced by the government of Tatarstan in an effort to portray the republic as the proper kin-state for ethnic Tatars.

The first entity is Volga Bulgaria, or Magna Bulgaria (Greater Bulgaria), an early state formation which conducted trade both with Kievan Rus' and the Far East in the ninth and tenth centuries and which was destroyed by the armies of Batu Khan in 1236. The second is the Kazan Khanate, which arose in the mid-fifteenth century as a successor state to the crumbling Golden Horde.[3] After a prolonged period of conflict, the Kazan Khanate finally fell to the forces of Ivan IV (the Terrible) during the siege of Kazan in 1552. Many mark Ivan's conquest of Kazan as the beginning of Russian imperial expansion.[4] The fall of the Kazan Khanate to Russian forces is a key event in Volga Tatar collective consciousness, interpreted as marking the date when the Tatars lost their historical statehood.[5] The third state entity to exist on this territory is the Republic of Tatarstan, whose contemporary borders were created by the Bolshe-viks in June 1920 when the Tatar ASSR was declared.[6] The Republic of Tatarstan as it exists today was brought into being by a declaration of sovereignty in August 1990, with a new republican constitution being adopted in November 1992.

It has already been noted that only one-quarter of Volga Tatars actu-ally live in the Tatar republic. The biggest settlements outside Tatarstan are in the area immediately surrounding the republic (the Volga–Urals region of Russia), in Siberian Russia, and in Central Asia (see Table 7.1). The single largest concentration of Tatars outside Tatarstan is in the neighboring Republic of Bashkortostan, where the over 1.1 million Volga Tatars constitute 35.1 percent of the population (compared with 21 percent formed by the Bashkirs themselves, a Turkic, Islamic population whose ancestral language is closely related to Tatar). Some Volga Tatar scholars insist that the number of Tatars in Bashkortostan is even higher, but that during the Soviet era many Tatars were forced by local officials to register their ethnicity as Bashkir.[7] It is often argued that the borders of the Soviet republics and other administrative units were drawn with a policy of divide and rule among the non-Russian peoples in mind.[8] Many Volga Tatar scholars share this view and argue that the large percentage of Tatars in Bashkortostan is ample proof of Bolshevik intentions. These beliefs have led a small section of the Volga Tatar intelligentsia to call for unification of the two republics to form a single "Idel-Ural," or Volga–Urals, republic that would reflect more realistically the demographic and historical boundaries of the Tatar homeland.[9]

There are large concentrations of Tatars in all of the republics, *oblasts*, and *krais* of Russia's Volga–Urals region; in the Cheliabinsk, Penza, Perm, Sverdlovsk, Orenburg, and Ulianovsk *oblasts*, and in the Marii-El and Mordvin republics, Volga Tatars constitute from 4.5 percent to 7.5 percent of the population. Some Tatars lived in these regions long before 1552; others settled there following the fall of Kazan and the attendant policies of Russian peasant colonization and discrimination against ethnic Tatars. The city of Orenburg in particular became an important intellectual and religious center when the Spiritual Board of the Muslims of the Russian empire, the official imperial institution for dealing with Muslim affairs, was founded there by Catherine the Great in 1789. The most numerous and well-educated of Russia's Muslim population, the Volga Tatars historically played a leading role in the official administra-tion of Islamic affairs in the empire.[10]

Since 1991 there has been some debate in the Volga Tatar community about the ethnic identification of two other numerous populations of Tatars located in the Russian Federation: those concentrated in and around Astrakhan *oblast'* (known as the Astrakhan Tatars) and those living in western Siberia, especially in Tiumen *oblast'* and in the Yamalo-Nenets and Khanti–Mansi autonomous *okrugs* (known as the Siberian Tatars). Tatars living in both these regions have presented themselves as unique ethnic groups, historically and linguistically distinct from the Volga Tatars. Astrakhan Tatars cite the separate history of the Astrakhan Khanate (also a successor state to the Golden Horde which was formed, like the Kazan Khanate, in the mid-fifteenth century) and linguistic particularities to differentiate themselves from Volga Tatars.[11]

The situation of the Siberian Tatars is even more interesting in this respect. Tatar intellectuals in Siberia differentiate between the older populations of Tatars, who moved to Siberian Russia in the sixteenth and seventeenth centuries to escape the land pressure of increasing Russian colonization, and those Tatars who moved from the Volga–Urals region to Siberian Russia in the 1960s and 1970s to work in the expanding oil and mining industries. The "original" Siberian Tatars consider themselves and their language and culture to be unique and distinct from those of the Volga Tatars who came later, and argue that the "legitimate homeland" of those late arrivals is the Republic of Tatarstan, not Siberia.[12] Both Astrakhan and Siberian Tatars have formed their own cultural and socio-political organizations in the post-Soviet period. Siberian Tatars even assert that the presence of Volga Tatars in Siberia detracts from the "original" Siberian Tatars' quest for increased cultural and political development in post-Soviet Russia.[13]

Many intellectuals in Kazan, however, insist that both Astrakhan and Siberian Tatars must be considered a part of the Volga Tatar ethnic group. They assert that the linguistic differences cited by Astrakhan and Siberian Tatars as proof of their unique ethnicity are too minor to distinguish them from Tatars in and around Kazan. New publications devoted to the history of the Tatar people, including one by the head of Tatarstan's official state body for relations with the diaspora, portray the Astrakhan and Siberian Tatars as members of one united Volga Tatar ethnic group.[14]

There are also large communities of Volga Tatars in Moscow and St. Petersburg. Each of these cities historically had a "Tatar quarter," whose residents settled there from the earliest interactions between Tatars and Russians.[15] The Tatar diaspora in Moscow (officially reported as 187,000 people, although Tatar activists claim there are as many half a million to a million Tatars in the Moscow area) has been particularly active since the late 1980s. By 1997 there were over twenty Tatar cultural, religious, and socio-political organizations in Moscow, including youth, business, and women's organizations.[16]

TABLE 7.1   Major Volga Tatar Populations (1989 and Estimates)

	Population	% of Total Local Population
Russian Federation	5,552,000	3.8
Republic of Tatarstan	1,765,400	48.5
Republic of Bashkortostan	1,120,702	35.1
Tiumen *oblast'*	227,422	7.3
Cheliabinsk *oblast'*	224,605	6.2
Sverdlovsk *oblast'*	183,781	4.0
Ul'ianovsk *oblast'*	159,093	1.1
City of Moscow	157,376	1.7
Orenburg *oblast'*	158,564	7.3
Perm *oblast'*	150,469	4.8
Kuibyshev *oblast'*	115,280	3.5
Republic of Udmurtia	110, 490	6.0
Khanti–Mansi AO	97,689	7.6
Penza *oblast'*	81,307	5.0
Astrakhan *oblast'*	71,655	7.2
Other former Soviet republics		
Uzbekistan	468,000	2.4
Kazakhstan	328,000	2.0
Ukraine	87,000	0.2
Tajikistan	72,000	1.4
Kyrgyzstan	70,000	1.6
Outside former Soviet Union		
China	5,000–10,000	——
Turkey	5,000–10,000	——
Romania, Bulgaria[a]	5,000–10,000	——
Poland	5,000	——
Finland	1,500–2,000	——
United States	1,500–2,000	——

[a]These populations are referred to as "Turco-Tatars." It is unclear what, if any, self-consciousness as Volga Tatars they might have.

Sources: For Russia and other former Soviet republics: 1989 Soviet census. For other locations: *Tatarskii mir* (Kazan: Apparat Prezidenta Tatarstana, 1995), 11; A. G. Karimullin, "Po kontinentam," in *Materialy po istorii tatarskogo naroda* (Kazan: Akademiia Nauk Tatarstana, 1996), 455–67.

Outside the Russian Federation, the largest populations of Tatars are found in the republics of Central Asia. It should be noted that there are significant linguistic and historical differences between Volga Tatar populations in Central Asia and the deported Crimean Tatar populations that were relocated to Central Asia during the Soviet period. The two groups do not consider themselves to be co-ethnics. In Central Asia, Volga Tatars are most numerous in Uzbekistan, where the almost half-million Volga Tatars are 2.4 percent of the population, and in Kazakhstan, where the 328,000 Volga Tatars are 2 percent of the population. Some Tatars migrated to the steppe oases of Central Asia to escape increasing land pressure and religious persecution as the Russian imperial presence strengthened in the Middle Volga region in the seventeenth and eighteenth centuries; others came as traders and merchants.[17] Still other Tatars found their way to Central Asia as "middlemen" minorities between the Russian empire and the Muslims of Central Asia. Being the most educated Muslim population in the expanding Russian empire and having a long history of interaction with and service to the tsarist empire, Tatars were the natural choice to serve as agents of Russian political, economic, and religious interests in the east.[18] Tatars served as translators, diplomats, and educators in Central Asia—an arrangement that served both their own interests as well as those of the empire.[19]

This association with the imperial bureaucracy meant Tatars traditionally played roles of political, cultural, educational, and economic importance in the Central Asian territories. Despite the linguistic and religious affinity between Tatars and Kazakhs, Uzbeks, and Kyrgyz, the historical identification of Tatars with Russian rule—coupled with the feeling among Central Asians that Tatars often consider them to be intellectually and culturally inferior—has led to resentment against local Tatar populations. Since the late 1980s there have been reports of discrimination against Volga Tatars in Central Asia; while these reports may be apocryphal, Volga Tatars from Central Asia have been by far the largest group of immigrants into Tatarstan in the post-Soviet period.[20]

The Tatar diaspora in the rest of the former Soviet Union consists of small communities in Belarus, Lithuania, and Latvia, and a rather large community in Ukraine (mostly centered around Kyiv). The communities in Belarus, Lithuania, and Latvia, and a larger group of about 5,500 Tatars in Poland, settled in these lands at the end of the fourteenth century and beginning of the fifteenth century at the invitation of the Lithuanian prince Vitold (Vytautas), to help in his battles against the Teutonic Knights.[21] While these populations have long since lost any Turkic language ability, many within these communities have retained their self-identifications as Islamic and Tatar to this day.

Outside postcommunist Europe, there are significant communities of Volga Tatars in China (5,000 or more), Turkey (5,000 or more), the United States (2,000), Finland (1,000), Australia, and Canada. Tatars migrated to Turkey and Finland in two distinct phases: first during the Crimean war and later during the 1905–17 revolutionary period.[22] In these two areas, Tatars tended to settle as merchants. The somewhat larger Tatar population in China, centered around the cities of Harbin in Manchuria and Urumqi in Xinjiang province, first arrived there during the building of the China–East railroad by the tsarist empire at the end of the nineteenth century, and continued to flow as revolution and famine struck the Volga–Urals region during the early twentieth century.[23] The Chinese Tatars have had relatively little contact with Tatars in Russia, a result of restrictive Chinese nationalities policies.[24] Finally, Volga Tatars made their way to the United States, Australia, and Canada mostly after the Second World War, via China and Turkey.

Wherever they reside, since the late 1980s Tatars have expressed a renewed interest in the preservation and development of the Tatar language and the Tatar nation. Cultural and political organizations exist in virtually all the former Soviet states and the republics of the Russian Federation, as well as in several Russian *oblasts* and *krais*. In areas with the largest Tatar populations, such as Uzbekistan and the Omsk, Cheliabinsk, and Tiumen *oblasts* of Russia, there are multiple Tatar organizations and local Tatar-language newspapers, as well as Tatar dance troupes and theaters.[25] Even the farthest flung of Volga Tatars have not lost their sense of ethnic belonging. Finnish Tatars have been among the most active in promoting Tatar music in the post-Soviet period, and cultural–linguistic organizations, such as the American Turco-Tatar Association and the Tatar Association of South Australia, have been the focus of much interest and pride in Tatarstan.[26] In recent years a Tatar e-mail discussion list has appeared, with Tatars in the United States, Canada, and Finland making up the majority of the list's participants.[27]

Diaspora Politics in the Soviet Period

While the "creation" of the Volga Tatar diaspora as it must be understood today did not occur until the proclamation of the Republic of Tatarstan in August 1990, the roots of that polity go back to June 16, 1920, when the Tatar ASSR was established by the Bolsheviks. Before the founding of the ASSR, which was at least a nominally Tatar entity, there had not been an autonomous Tatar political formation since the fall of the Kazan Khanate in 1552. In accordance with Bolshevik nationalities policy, the republic had only nominal political and economic autonomy, and only a severely restricted cultural autonomy; the formation of the Tatar ASSR was nonetheless an important event in the evolution of Volga Tatar group consciousness. Even if its borders were not those of the broader "Idel-Ural" state for which Tatars had agitated during the revolutionary period, it was a concretely defined space that at least formally belonged to the Volga Tatars and bore their name.[28]

According to a policy of "national–cultural autonomy," Soviet authorities were formally committed to providing all peoples, even those without their own ethno-federal unit, with cultural outlets and educational opportunities in their indigenous languages.[29] In practice, these opportunities were realized only inconsistently in the highest-level administrative units—the large union republics and the smaller autonomous republics that they contained—and much less so in lower-level autonomous *oblasts* and *krais*. In imperial Russia, the traditional center of Tatar educational and cultural life was the local mosque and medreseh; when anti-religious campaigns began and these mosques and schools were closed and their property expropriated by the Soviet government in the 1920s and 1930s, opportunities for the preservation and development of Volga Tatar language and culture in the Tatar ASSR, and in the rest of the Soviet Union, were severely curtailed.[30]

While there were new, state-sponsored Tatar cultural and educational institutions created in the 1920s and 1930s in places like Moscow and the *oblasts* of the Volga–Urals region (such as national theaters and newspapers in the Tatar language), most of these were closed during the Second World War and never reopened.[31] Even within the Tatar ASSR, there were few national schools by the end of the Soviet period; for example, by 1991 there were only five Tatar-language schools in the three largest cities in Tatarstan, serving only 1.4 percent of the ethnic Tatar students in those cities.[32] The situation regarding Tatar-language schools and cultural institutions outside the ASSR was even more grave.

Intellectuals in the Tatar ASSR were concerned about this lack of cultural and educational opportunities for Tatars both in the republic and throughout the Soviet Union. A group of Tatar writers and linguists registered a formal protest against the dearth of schools and cultural institutions with the Central Committee of the CPSU in 1954, but the appeal went without response.[33] Interest in the fate of Tatars living outside the ASSR increased among intellectuals in the late Soviet period. By the early 1980s, the Tatar intelligentsia had grown tired of writing about the history and culture of the "peoples of the Tatar ASSR," and proposed a multi-volume history of the entire Tatar people, not just those Tatars living in the autonomous republic.[34] However, this project did not receive official support until after the declaration of sovereignty in 1990.

During the earliest stages of perestroika and glasnost, a more wide-spread acknowledgment of the existence of the Tatar diaspora, and the problems surrounding it, began at the societal level in the ASSR.[35] As ethnic consciousness grew, awareness of the existence of the Tatar diaspora and its cultural and educational needs also grew. However, it was only with the transformation of the Tatar ASSR into the Republic of Tatarstan in 1990 that diaspora issues began to receive serious attention from Tatarstani officials.

Immediately following the declaration of state sovereignty, Tatarstan's government found itself faced with the task of giving shape and substance to the newly declared statehood. This process included defining the external aspects of Tatarstan's new autonomy (in particular, its relationship with the Russian central government and with the international community) as well as defining the boundaries of Tatarstan's post-Soviet political community and building a new state and national identity for the republic. One part of the leadership's quest to define the external and internal contours of statehood has included embracing the diaspora and identifying the republic as the homeland and kin-state for all the Tatars of Russia and the wider world. This aspect of Tatarstan's post-Soviet politics has had important repercussions for federal and local politics.

Tatarstan, the Diaspora, and the Politics of a Multi-Ethnic Federation

The Republic of Tatarstan has gained international prominence through its efforts to gain more political and economic autonomy within, and reform the basic structures of, the Russian Federation. The presence of the Tatar diaspora and Tatarstan's decision to identify itself as the definitive Tatar kin-state have influenced both the government's choice of political goals and its political strategy in relations with Moscow and with the international community; it has sought both increased autonomy within Russia and a stronger political and economic presence outside Russia's borders as an autonomous international actor. Throughout the late 1980s and early 1990s, Kazan and Moscow were continually engaged in negotiations on a number of policy issues, including control of natural and economic resources, federal budgetary relations, and the legal status of the republic within the wider federation. The Shaimiev team's main goal throughout these prolonged negotiations was to get Moscow to recognize a special economic and political status for Tatarstan within the Russian Federation, a status that would allow Kazan to pursue its own policies in the international arena.[36]

   Tatarstan refused to sign the Russian federal treaty in 1992, holding out instead to sign an "agreement on the separation of authorities and responsibilities" with Moscow in February 1994. In this agreement, Tatarstan's special status was recognized; the republic was defined as "associated" with Moscow on the basis of this agreement and on the basis of the constitutions of the two signatories.[37] Since the signing of this ground-breaking agreement, similar agreements have been concluded between Moscow and other national republics, *oblasts*, and *krais*, each of them a variation on the founding "Tatarstan model." The Tatarstani example of peaceful, negotiated federal reform has gained notice from the international community, and several international meetings have been held in the Hague in the hopes of using insights from Tatarstan's experience to solve political conflicts in other areas in the Russian Federation and the former Soviet Union.[38] Besides being concerned with increasing its own role and influence within the Russian Federation, Tatarstan has pursued the cause of reforming the federation in general. Tatarstan has sought a decentralization of the Russian Federation based on the "bottom–up" principle, which holds that Russia's national republics, *oblasts*, and *krais* are the primary locus of sovereignty within the federal system and should therefore take on more responsibility for the formulation and implementation of policy in economic, cultural, and other spheres.[39]

   The presence of the Tatar diaspora within and outside Russia has influenced both the choice of Tatarstani political goals and the means by which the republic has pursued them. First, the presence of co-ethnics outside the Russian Federation inspired Tatarstan to increase its own political and economic prominence within Russia and abroad. The Shaimiev administration pursued this goal through the initiation of bilateral, "inter-state" contacts with former Soviet states and other independent countries with large Tatar communities, such as Kazakhstan, Uzbekistan, and Turkey.[40] Through the conclusion of these agreements, which covered a range of political, economic, and cultural matters, Tatarstan sought to create new *de facto* levels of political and economic sovereignty for itself, which in turn strengthened Tatarstan's position *vis–à–vis* Moscow during federal negotiations in the early 1990s.

   Tatarstan used the presence of a large Tatar diaspora in Azerbaijan, Kazakhstan, Uzbekistan, and Turkey, to justify its foreign policy ventures in these states. Defining itself as the "spiritual and historical homeland" for the entire Tatar nation in diaspora, the Tatarstani government argued that the presence of co-ethnics meant that Tatarstan had a "moral obligation" to maintain direct inter-governmental ties with these countries in order to ensure the development of Tatar language and culture among the diaspora.[41] For example, in signing an agreement on cultural and economic cooperation with Uzbekistan in February 1993, Tatarstani prime minister Mohammed Sabirov explained the necessity of the agreement by declaring that, after all, "one in ten Uzbek families contains a Tatar!"[42]

The presence of a Tatar diaspora in areas outside the Russian Federation gave Tatarstan a special connection with certain countries as it took its first steps toward greater involvement in the international political and economic arenas. Summing up the early efforts to develop an international presence in the early 1990s, Tatarstan's foreign policy architect Vasilii Likhachev, the speaker of Tatarstan's republican parliament (the Gossovet, or State Council) and also the vice-chair of the Russian Federation Council, announced that one of the proudest results of the republic's efforts to "increase its image as a state" was its success in fulfilling a moral responsibility to the Tatar diaspora through bilateral contacts with countries with large Tatar populations.[43]

Tatarstan has supplemented these bilateral economic, political, and cultural agreements and strengthened its international presence by the posting of special "authorized representatives" of Tatarstan in the former Soviet republics, the United States, France, Australia, and Turkey, as well as in several Russian cities and republics, including Moscow and St. Petersburg. These representatives are mainly concerned with managing and representing Tatarstan's economic and political interests in the Russian Federation and abroad, but they are also responsible for overseeing the development of the cultural and educational needs of the Tatar diaspora in their respective territories.[44]

The government has developed a special organization to deal with the diaspora question during official bilateral negotiations with other states. The Executive Committee of the World Congress of Tatars (*Vsemirnyi Kongress Tatar*, WCT) was created by the Tatarstani government in June 1992 in Kazan during the convocation of the first world congress. The WCT's Executive Committee serves as the official Tatarstani liaison for Tatar diaspora communities during negotiations with different host-states.[45] Tatarstan's minister of education, minister of culture, and the president of the Academy of Sciences sit on the Executive Committee and often serve as the official WCT representative at these negotiations. Thus, the presence of co-ethnics outside the Russian Federation has provided Tatarstan with both a rationale and an opportunity to increase its own influence and presence in the former Soviet Union and farther abroad. Initial foreign policy contacts with host-states have been expanded to non-host-state countries, such as France, where Tatarstan has also posted a plenipotentiary representative.

The influence of Tatar co-ethnics within the Russian Federation on Tatarstan's federal relations with Moscow, and on Tatarstani local politics, is more complicated. The Shaimiev administration has argued that the presence of co-ethnics in other member units of the federation necessitates a new and direct Tatarstani presence in these places—that Tatarstan is "morally obligated" and "historically predisposed" to help provide for the interests of the Tatar populations in other parts of Russia.[46] Tatarstan thus has pursued bilateral agreements concerning "trade–economic, scientific–technical, and cultural cooperation" with most members of the Russian Federation where significant Tatar populations reside (republics, *oblasts*, and *krais* alike). The republic has also placed "authorized representatives" in places such as Tiumen *oblast'*, Moscow, and St. Petersburg.[47]

The Tatarstani government has also used bilateral and multilateral diplomacy with other Russian Federation member units to try to get the local leadership of these units to take financial and administrative responsibility for the Tatar diaspora on their territory. Besides including members of the Executive Committee in their official delegations to other federal constituents, the government has sponsored seminars in Kazan for library workers, teachers, journalists, and political administrators from other parts of Russia where large Tatar diasporas exist in order to educate them on the problems facing the diaspora and to inspire them to use their own local resources to resolve these problems.[48] In this way Tatarstan has sought both to provide for the needs of the diaspora and to pursue the reconstruction of the Russian Federation "from the bottom up" by getting federal republics and regions to take the initiative in dealing with diaspora problems.

Interestingly, however, the presence of the Tatar diaspora within the Russian Federation has also served as an integrative force, as Kazan has probed the limits of its federal relationship with Moscow. For example, the Tatarstani leadership has taken great pains to clarify that its role is strictly a moral and political one, and that Tatarstan's responsibility to the diaspora does not include economic or other material support. The government has instead argued that both Russian federal institutions and local federation members should take the lead in the actual funding and implementation of programs for the fulfillment of the diaspora's material, educational, and cultural needs. A quote from Likhachev, the speaker of the Tatarstani parliament, illustrates Tatarstan's position:

> Kazan should become a real coordinator of all Russian policy regarding the diaspora. A coordinator in the best and most positive sense. It is important to stress this so that the leaders [of Tatar diaspora groups] do not think that Shaimiev is going to phone up every day to ask how the Tatars

are getting on over there, whether they have been provided with housing, work, etc. It is important that it is by the joint efforts of all the regions of Russia, and I repeat the word "all," that an intelligent, methodical, scientific, and financial center is created to give the Tatar diaspora help, because what we are talking about here is the second largest nation in Russia. Because in essence, the work which is being carried out is currently reliant only on our internal resources.[49]

In another interview, Likhachev announced that the Tatar diaspora's cultural and educational needs could not and would not be fulfilled by Tatarstan alone, but only with the help of the Russian Federation, because of the "serious financial infusions" such programs required.[50]

President Shaimiev has pushed the issue of federal responsibility for the Tatar diaspora on Boris Yeltsin in their personal meetings, while Likhachev has used his influence within the Federation Council to bring the diaspora to the attention of the Russian ministry of nationalities affairs. The WCT, and smaller gatherings of Tatar diaspora representatives that have followed it, have also appealed to federal authorities to develop a federation-wide program of support for Tatars outside Tatarstan.[51]

In response to these requests, a 17-point program, "On the Preservation and Development of the Culture of the Tatars of Russia," was developed by a special joint Russian–Tatarstani commission working through the ministry of nationalities affairs.[52] The program calls for federal support for Tatar cultural institutions, such as short-wave radio programs in Tatar, Tatar-language newspapers and theaters, and new federally supported educational institutions. According to the program, the main financial and administrative responsibility for these new institutions would fall to the federal ministry of education and ministry of culture.

As of 1997, however, no steps toward the implementation of the program had been taken, with the Russian federal government claiming lack of funds for the projects. Tatarstan's government, as well as opposition forces in the republic, instead pointed to a lack of political will and an anti-Tatar bias in the ministry of nationalities affairs.[53] Kazan has argued that the program will never be fully implemented until the perceived anti-Tatar bias and lack of Tatar representation in federal administrative and legislative organs are rectified. Shaimiev and other members of his administration have even suggested quotas for Tatars and other non-Russian nationalities in federal institutions or the creation of a special legislative "House of Nationalities" at the federal level as possible solutions to these problems.[54]

Tatarstan's inability or unwillingness to provide anything but "spiritual and moral" guidance for the diaspora has forced the government to rely on federal organs to perform the functions for the diaspora that Tatarstan itself cannot or will not provide. The presence of Tatar co-ethnics throughout the Russian Federation is thus one of the factors which give Tatarstan an incentive to stay within and pursue the reform of the federation, rather than pursuing secessionist strategies. In this sense, the presence of the diaspora can be said to have acted as an integrative force as Kazan has renegotiated its place within Russia; the diaspora has, in many ways, set limits on Tatarstan's quest for sovereignty. Put another way, the presence of ethnic Tatars throughout the Russian Federation is one of the strongest threads in the web of economic, infrastructural, and political ties binding the Tatar republic to the Russian Federation.

Tatarstan's relationship with its co-ethnics in the Russian Federation has also illustrated one of the classic dilemmas faced by constituents of federal states as they seek to increase their autonomy within federal structures: desiring the benefits that increased autonomy brings while confronting the corresponding increase in responsibility that higher levels of autonomy entail. In Tatarstan's case, this means wanting an independent identity and an increased international role in the post-Soviet world, which the republic's place as the "spiritual homeland" for Tatars helps to give it, but not wanting to adopt the overwhelming financial responsibility and sacrifice that would be necessary to provide Tatars within and outside Russia with cultural centers, schools, textbooks, and teachers.

State Building and Identity Politics

While presenting itself as the "spiritual homeland" of the Tatar people has helped Tatarstan to gain a more independent and distinctive profile internationally and within the Russian Federation, the adoption of a kin-state identity has complicated local politics and the search for a legitimate form of collective identity within Tatarstan. The government's attempts to balance a Tatar, kin-state identity based on ethnic affiliation with a more civic, "Tatarstani" vision of the republic are interesting and instructive for other multi-ethnic states searching for viable collective identities. Tatarstan's experience suggests that multiple state identities, civic and ethnic, may co-exist relatively harmoniously within a single polity.

Tatarstan is a multi-ethnic republic which claims to be the home of more than a hundred nationalities, although only two ethnic groups, Tatars (48.5 percent of the total) and Russians (43.5 percent), make up the majority of the population.[55] In the post-Soviet period, the Shaimiev government has taken pains to cultivate a Tatarstani identity, wherein the republic of Tatarstan defines itself as a "democratic, multi-ethnic society" that adheres to international standards of human and civil rights and provides equal rights and protections for all citizens under the constitution regardless of nationality or religious affiliation.[56] In relations with its own citizens, as well as with the international community, Tatarstan has consistently emphasized the civic and multi-ethnic nature of the republic. Every major public address by President Shaimiev since 1990 has included references to the multi-ethnic nature of the republic, to its long tradition of inter-ethnic harmony, to the equality of all citizens before the law, and to the idea that inhabitants have an equal stake in a successful, sovereign Tatarstan. The government has also issued a number of publications in recent years which discuss Tatarstan's pursuit of sovereignty and statehood in the post-Soviet period and specifically emphasize a non-ethnic, Tatarstani identity.[57]

Convincing its residents of the reality of a civic, multi-ethnic, and democratic Tatarstan (as opposed to an ethnic, ethnocratic one) is important to the Shaimiev administration both as a way of increasing its own legitimacy and as a means of maintaining inter-ethnic harmony within the republic. Obviously, the presence of the Tatar diaspora and the adoption of a Tatar kin-state identity when dealing with it complicate the effort to build a truly "Tatarstani" identity at home. To ensure that the delicate balance between these two roles is maintained, the government has attempted to harness feelings of empathy and support for the diaspora among Tatars in Tatarstan and channel them through quasi-governmental organizations such as the WCT. The events surrounding the first WCT in Kazan in June 1992 highlighted the dilemmas of this dual identity and the strategies that the Tatarstani government has pursued in trying to deal with them.

The early 1990s represented the apogee of popular support among Tatars for social organizations and political parties that advocated political autonomy and cultural revival, such as the Tatar Public Center (*Tatarskii Obshchestvennyi Tsentr*, TPC) and *Ittifak* ("unity" in Tatar).[58] In February 1992 several of the most powerful of these social organizations and political parties held a *kurultai*, or congress, of Tatars from all over the diaspora. Held in Kazan, the *kurultai* elected a 75-member *Milli Medzhlis*, or "national parliament." One-third of the members of the *Milli Medzhlis* were representatives of the Tatar diaspora, and the body proclaimed itself to be the only "official" and legitimate representative of the Tatar nation. Further, the *Milli Medzhlis* declared itself to be in opposition to the Shaimiev government.[59]

Tatarstan's leadership was threatened by this non-sanctioned show of strength and unity by nationalist forces. Claiming that the *Milli Medzhlis* was an "inappropriately and illegally elected organ" which promoted "anarchy and the absence of order" in Tatarstan, and which served to divide the Tatar diaspora from the republic, President Shaimiev called the first WCT in June 1992 as a counter-measure.[60] At the first WCT, over a thousand Tatar representatives from the diaspora gathered in Kazan at the invitation and expense of the republican government to celebrate Tatarstan's independence and their common heritage. During this event, Shaimiev attempted to discredit the *Milli Medzhlis* by describing the WCT Executive Committee as an organ whose structures "conformed to all international democratic norms" and whose goal was to "turn the emotional energy surrounding national issues into real work with the diaspora, so it does not cause harm."[61]

Shaimiev and the Executive Committee chairman, Indus Tagirov, assured the citizens of Tatarstan that despite the holding of the WCT in Kazan and the proclamation of Tatarstan as the "historical and spiritual homeland of all Tatars," the Executive Committee and its activities were fully compatible with the "democratization of social life in Tatarstan;" the republic remained the multinational "homeland of all who live in it."[62] Furthermore, the Executive Committee stated that its primary goal was to develop the sovereignty and statehood of the multinational republic of Tatarstan, a goal which would indirectly lead to national–cultural autonomy for the wider diaspora.[63]

Shaimiev and the government have taken other steps to ensure that the activities of the Executive Committee and the identification of Tatarstan as a kin-state do not overshadow the development of a Tatarstani identity. A "Congress of the Peoples of Tatarstan," celebrating the "historical brotherhood and peaceful co-existence of all the peoples of Tatarstan," was held in May 1992, before the WCT; the two events have since been presented by the president and other members of the government as "the twin bases of civic and multi-ethnic accord in Tatarstan."[64] The president's office has formed its own department of interethnic relations and has also sponsored an "Association of National–Cultural Organizations" in Tatarstan as further measures toward building a truly multi-ethnic state.

The government has in fact been so scrupulous about balancing its roles as promoter of both ethnic and civic conceptions of the state that some Tatar nationalist organizations—such as the *Milli Medzhlis*, the TPC, and *Ittifak* in Tatarstan, as well as diasporic groups such as the *Tugan Tel* (Native Language) society in Moscow and the *Milli Medzhlis* of the Tatars of Bashkortostan—have criticized the government's diaspora policy, claiming that the republic has "turned its back" on its responsibility to the Tatar diaspora.[65] These groups assert that Tatarstan's sovereignty is not being used to benefit the entire Tatar nation, but rather only to benefit Tatarstan's leadership, whom they claim care more about federal authorities in Moscow and other republican leaders than their co-ethnics in Tatarstan and beyond.[66] They claim that the Shaimiev administration has used the presence of the diaspora when it suits its purposes and forgets it when those purposes are not served. For example, when representatives of several Tatar organizations in Bashkortostan appealed to Shaimiev for help in ending discrimination against Tatars in Bashkortostan, they never received a response from Kazan.[67] Further, when the first Congress of the Tatars of Bashkortostan was held in the republic's capital, Ufa, in June 1997, the official delegation from the Republic of Tatarstan did not meet with representatives from the Tatar organizations in Bashkortostan, instead choosing to meet only with high-ranking members of the Bashkortostani government. Tatar groups in Bashkortostan were left feeling that the Tatarstani government was more interested in the concerns of Bashkortostani officials than in the issues facing ethnic Tatars in the neighboring republic.[68] Opposition groups within Tatarstan, especially *Ittifak* and the *Milli Medzhlis*, have strong ties to Tatar groups in the diaspora, particularly with those that are themselves in opposition to their host governments, such as the *Milli Medzhlis* of the Tatars of Bashkortostan. Since the Executive Committee operates only at the level of official inter-governmental contacts and often chooses not to meet with grass-roots Tatar organizations, opposition organizations in Tatarstan have been crucial in highlighting the demands of the diaspora and placing pressure on the Kazan government.

In spite of criticisms from opposition forces and some Tatar diaspora groups, the government has continued to pursue its own relations with the diaspora, such as by holding the Second World Congress of Tatars in Kazan in August 1997. Some critics had earlier claimed that the first congress had not been a meaningful political event, resembling instead the Tatar traditional festival of *Sabantui*, a celebration to mark the end of the planting season which is often accompanied by folk dancing, singing, and traditional sports such as wrestling and horse-racing. The organizational committee for the second WCT therefore stated that the purpose of the congress was to develop "concrete political solutions to the problems of the Tatar diaspora, including discussion of a new official Tatarstani position on the diaspora, and of how to realize the federal program for the Tatar diaspora which was developed in 1994."[69]

Significantly, the second WCT was held in conjunction with the celebrations for the seventh anniversary of Tatarstan's declaration of sovereignty (August 30), a conscious linkage of Tatarstan's most important post-Soviet "civic" holiday with this important Tatar "ethnic" event. The resolutions of the second WCT also directly tied the future preservation and development of the Tatar nation to the "deepening of the sovereignty of the Republic of Tatarstan, the strengthening of its ties with the federal center, the countries of the CIS, and abroad."[70] By insisting that the priority in relations with the diaspora remained the strengthening of the sovereignty of the republic, the Shaimiev administration was able to privilege the civic state identity of Tatarstan while still identifying itself with the diaspora and the enhanced range of influence that relations with the diaspora might bring. In addition, the Russian government's decision in late 1997 to remove the entry for ethnic designation in internal passports gave the Tatarstani leadership the opportunity to reassert publicly its commitment to protecting the interests of ethnic Tatars in other parts of the federation. Tatarstani officials criticized the new passports because they failed to recognize the state sovereignty of Tatarstan and the dual Russian–Tatarstani citizenship of inhabitants of the Tatarstan (affirmed in the republic's constitution). Moreover, Shaimiev and others argued that the omission of ethnic affiliation in the new passports would make it harder for Tatars outside Tatarstan to have their cultural and educational needs met.

While some Tatar nationalist organizations both in Tatarstan and in the diaspora continue to pressure Kazan to adopt a more radical kin-state identity, there has been virtually no public sentiment expressed by the republic's non-Tatar population against the Shaimiev administration's vision of Tatarstan as the "historical, moral, and spiritual homeland" for the world's Tatars.[71] Both Tatar and Russian inhabitants appear to accept the administration's claim that Tatarstan can be both a civic, democratic republic and the historical homeland for the world's six million Tatars. The policy of emphasizing only the moral and spiritual commitment of Tatarstan to the diaspora while avoiding expensive economic commitments likely renders Tatarstan's kin-state identity more palatable to non-Tatars.

This suggests that the dichotomy between "good" civic and "bad" ethnic state identities often stressed by analysts of ethno-nationalism is too simplistic for the reality of the post-Soviet world.[72] The case of Tatarstan illustrates that states may assert different state identities in different arenas of political life, and that multiple state identities can and do exist simultaneously and peacefully in multi-ethnic polities, even when the identities in question represent an uneasy mix of ethnic and civic orientations. Assertions of state identity based on the ethnic affiliation of one population in a multi-ethnic polity may not cause ethnic tension if they are directed, first, in ways that benefit all citizens of the polity (such as increasing the international prestige or autonomy of the state through relations with the diaspora) and, second, in ways that require little sacrifice from citizens that are not part of the primary ethnic community (by avoiding economic responsibility for the community's diaspora).

Conclusion

The presence of the Tatar diaspora has complicated further what is already a complex set of processes: the renegotiation and restructuring of the multi-ethnic Russian Federation, and Tatarstan's place within the federation and within the international community. The experience of Tatarstan provides a useful starting point from which to explore how other multi-ethnic federations are affected by the presence of diaspora communities. Tatarstan's case suggests that the presence of co-ethnics, depending on their location, can provide both opportunities and obstacles for a "homeland" state that is also a member of a multi-ethnic federation. The presence of the Tatar diaspora outside the Russian Federation has helped to inspire the Shaimiev administration to pursue an enhanced international presence for Tatarstan in the post-Soviet period, while the presence of the Tatar diaspora within the federation has functioned as a thread binding Tatarstan to federal structures and as a tool of influence in its efforts to reform them. Moreover, diaspora politics in Tatarstan suggests that multiple discourses about state and national identities can co-exist and that the reality of post-Soviet state building is far more nuanced and complicated than the simple dichotomy of "civic" versus "ethnic" nationalism would allow. Tatarstan's relationship with the diaspora and its search for new forms of communal and state identity since 1991 have indicated that state and national identities, like personal identities, are multiple and highly contextual.[73] The questions of when, how, and why kin-state identities are adopted, and with what other identity discourses they interact, are areas of crucial importance both for understanding the politics of Tatarstan and for assessing the impact of trans-border ethnic groups on state and nation building within ethnically heterogeneous federations.

Notes

Research for this chapter was supported in part by a grant from the International Research and Exchanges Board (IREX), with funds provided by the National Endowment for the Humanities and the United States Department of State, which administers the Russian, Eurasian, and East European Research Program (Title VIII). None of these organizations is responsible for the views expressed here. The author would like to thank Elise Guliano, M. Sean Loftus, and the editors of and contributors to this volume for their helpful comments on drafts of this chapter.

1. All statistical data for the Russian Federation and the former Soviet Union are taken from the 1989 census. Gosudarstvennyi komitet SSSR po statistiki, *Natsional'nyi sostav naseleniia SSSR po dannym vsesoiuznoi perepisi naseleniia 1989 goda* (Moscow: Finansy i statistiki, 1991).

2. "Kolonka glavnogo redaktora," *Tatarstan*, nos. 3–4 (1995): 3.

3. For a detailed account of the early history of the area that is today the Republic of Tatarstan, see Azade-Ayşe Rorlich, *The Volga Tatars: A Profile in National Resilience* (Stanford: Hoover Institution Press, 1986), especially chapters 2–4. Rorlich's book is the most informative and extensive source on early Tatar history available in English.

4. Jaroslaw Pelenski, *Moscow and Kazan: Conquest and Imperial Ideology, 1438–1560* (The Hague: Mouton and Co., 1974).

5. Tatars mark October 15 as the traditional day of remembrance when the forces of Ivan IV attacked Kazan in 1552. Since the late 1980s, opposition nationalist forces in Tatarstan have held rallies and protests on this day, with Tatars from all over the diaspora coming to Kazan for the events of "Remembrance Day." See Ravil Fakhrutdinov, *Zolotaia orda i tatary: chto v dushe naroda* (Naberezhnie Chelny: Gazetno-knizhnoe izdatel'stvo KamAZ, 1993).

6. See Serge Zenkovsky, "The Tataro-Bashkir Feud of 1917–20," *Indiana Slavic Studies*, no. 2 (1958): 37–52; and Daniel Shafer, *Building Nations and Building States: The Tatar–Bashkir Question in Revolutionary Russia, 1917–1920* (Ph.D. diss., University of Michigan, 1995).

7. Maksim Pavlov, "Volga-ural'skii region: konflikt avtonomii," *Idel*, nos. 9–10 (1993): 25–28.

8. Stephen Blank, *The Sorcerer as Apprentice: Stalin as Commissar of Nationalities, 1917–1924* (Westport: Greenwood Press, 1994), 137–38. See also, Ronald Wixman, "Applied Soviet Nationalities Policy: A Suggested Rationale," in S. E. Wimbush, G. Vienstein, and Ch. Lemercier-Quelquejay, eds., *Turco-Tatar Past, Soviet Present: Studies Presented to Alexander Bennigsen* (Paris: Editions de l'Ecole des Hautes Etudes en Sciences Sociales, 1986), 449–68.

9. The idea of a large state in the Volga–Urals region, "Idel-Ural" ("Idel" means Volga in Tatar), was first popularized in the early part of this century by Tatar writer Gayaz Ishaki; there was a movement for founding such a state during the time of the 1905 and 1917 revolutions. Ishaki's book, entitled *Idel-Ural*, was re-released in a new edition by Kazan's Tatarskoe Knizhnoe Izdatel'stvo in 1991, edited and with a new introduction by presidential advisor Rafael Khakimov. For an overview of contemporary views on the Idel-Ural idea, see Ann Sheehy, "Tatarstan and Bashkortostan: Obstacles to Confederation," *RFE/RL Research Report*, May 29, 1992, pp. 33–37.

10. Alan W. Fisher, "Enlightened Despotism and Islam Under Catherine II," *Slavic Review* 27, no. 4 (1968): 542–53. See also Allen Frank, *Islamic Regional Identity in Imperial Russia: Tatar and Bashkir Historiography in the 18th and 19th Centuries* (Ph.D. diss., Indiana University, 1994); and Rorlich, *Volga Tatars*, chapters 5–7.

11. L. Sh. Arslanov and V. M. Viktorin, "Astrakhanskie tatary," in *Materialy po istorii tatarskogo naroda* (Kazan: Akademiia Nauk Tatarstana, 1996), 335–66.

12. The migration of Tatars into the oil-producing regions of western Siberia between 1959 and 1989 was quite dramatic—the Tatar population tripled in these regions during these years. With such intense migration, it is easy to see how clear distinctions between old and new Tatar immigrants to Siberia evolved. See Indus Tagirov, *Tatary i Tatarstan* (Kazan: n. p., 1992), 32. See also S. M. Iskhakova and F. T. A. Valeev, *Sibirskie tatary: etnokul'turnye i politicheskie problemy vozrozhdeniia*, Issledovanie po prikladnoi i neotlozhnoi ethnologii, no. 92 (Moscow: Rossiisskaia Akademiia Nauk, Institut Etnologii i Antropologii, 1996), 11.

13. Iskhakova and Valeev, *Sibirskie tatary*, 11.

14. Tagirov, *Tatary i Tatarstan*. Tagirov, who is the head of Executive Committee of Tatarstan's official organization for work with the diaspora, the World Congress of Tatars, states that "from the late nineteenth century to the beginning of the twentieth century, a process of the consolidation of Middle Volga/Urals Tatars with Astrakhan and Siberian Tatars into a new ethnic society, the Tatar nation, took place." Kazan Tatars serve as the "core" of this nation; Astrakhan and Siberian Tatars are two other "ethno-territorial groups of the Tatar nation" (p. 7). Siberian Tatars, in particular, have rejected this notion. See Valeev and Iskhakova, *Sibirskie tatary*; and also F. T. Valeev, *Siberskie tatary: kul'tura i byt'* (Kazan: Tatarskoe knizhnoe izdatel'stvo, 1993).

15. Mirgaziz Iunus, "Izmailovskii park: moskovskie tatary," *Tatarstan*, nos. 11–12 (1995): 48–57; and Renat Galiullin, "Vozrozhdenie po-peterburzhskii," *Berdemlik/Edinstvo* (paper within a paper in *Rossiiskaia gazeta*, February 22, 1994).

16. Moscow's Tatar organizations are united in an umbrella group, the Union of Tatars of Moscow. The largest organizations in this union are *Tugan Tel* (Native Language) and the Moscow chapter of the Tatar Public Center, headquartered in Kazan. Moscow is also home to several Tatar-oriented newspapers, the largest of which is the Russian-langauge *Tatarskie novosti* (Tatar News).

17. See P. P. Litvinov, "Antitatarskaia politika tsarisma v Srednoi Azii i Kazakhstane," in *Materialy*, 367–87. See also Rorlich, *Volga Tatars*, 39.

18. It is important to note here the divisions in the Tatar population as regards their relationship with the tsarist empire. Some fled its approach, others found favorable places in it. See Litvinov, "Antitatarskaia politika." See also Rim Gil'fanov, "Diaspora: tatarskaia emigratsiia," *Tatarstan*, nos. 5–6 (1995): 80–84.

19. Allen Frank, "Tatarskie mully sredi kazakov i kirgizov, XVIII–XIX vv.," in *Kul'tura i iskusstva tatarskogo naroda: istoki, traditsii, vzaimosviazi* (Kazan: Akademiia Nauk Tatarstana, 1993), 124–30.

20. Of people receiving official status as "resettlers or refugees" in Tatarstan in 1994, for example, 78 percent were Tatars and 12 percent Russians. Of the roughly 25,000 Tatars who arrived in Tatarstan in this capacity in 1994, 22,000 were from the Central Asian republics. "Tatarstan prinimaet bezhentsev," *Tatarskie novosti*, nos. 4–5 (1995): 9. The government of Tatarstan, wanting to stay on good terms with the Uzbek government, has through the voice of its official representative in Uzbekistan explained the exodus of Tatars from the "hospitable" land of the Uzbeks as a "natural strengthening of the tendency for Tatars to migrate to their historical homeland." U. L. Sabirova, "Poisk sovmestnykh reshenii," *Informatstionno-metodicheskii biulleten'*, no. 7 (1996): 41–42. This publication is produced by the Tatarstani president's office, department of interethnic relations.

21. Iakob Grishin, *Pol'sko-litovskie tatary: nasledniki Zolotoi ordy* (Kazan: Tatarskoe knizhnoe izdatel'stvo, 1995). This is an important book which discusses the historical controversy surrounding these Tatar populations and their current situation. See also Gil'fanov, "Diaspora;" and A. G. Karimullin, "Po kontinentam," in *Materialy*, 455–467.

22. I. N. Nadirov, "Tatary v Finlandii," in *Materialy*, 468–85; and Karimullin, "Po kontinentam," 465–66.

23. Karimullin, "Po kontinentam," 456–57; and Gil'fanov, "Diaspora," 83.

24. It is difficult to get concrete numbers on Tatars in China. Some Tatar scholars suggest there are 5,000 Tatars in Xinjiang alone, bringing the total number to around 10,000. Karimullin, "Po kontinentam," 461–62.

25. For a listing of Tatar cultural and educational organizations in the former Soviet Union and world-wide, see *Tatarskii mir: informatsionno-statisticheskii spravochnik* (Kazan: Apparat Prezidenta Respubliki Tatarstan, Otdel po sviaziam s obshchestvennostiu i mezhnatsional'nym otnosheniiam, 1995), 47–57.

26. For example, Tatars in Finland have produced their own original musical works, as well as new recordings of the works of Tatar musicians and composers from Tatarstan, such as the "People's Artist of the Soviet Union" Rustem Yakin. Articles on the Tatar communities and individuals in the United States, Canada, and other countries in the "far abroad" appear quite often in *Tatarskie kraia/Tatar ile* (Tatar Lands), a bilingual Tatar–Russian weekly newspaper for and about the Tatar diaspora sponsored by the Tatarstani ministry of information and the press.

27. Interestingly, the main language of communication in the Tatar expatriate e-mail list is English.

28. See Rogers Brubaker, "Nationhood and the National Question in the Soviet Union and Post-Soviet Eurasia: An Institutionalist Account," *Theory and Society* 23, no. 1 (1994): 47–78; and Philip Roeder, "Soviet Federalism and Ethnic Mobilization," *World Politics* 43, no. 1 (1991): 196–32, on the effects of the Soviet ethno-federal system on national and ethnic consciousness during the perestroika period and earlier. See also Indus Tagirov, "Natsional'noe dvizhenie: ego proshloe, nastoiashchee i budushchee," *Tatarstan*, nos. 3–4 (1995): 4–13.

29. On Bolshevik nationalities policy in general, see Walker Connor, *The Nationality Question in Marxist–Leninist Theory and Strategy* (Princeton: Princeton University Press, 1984). For an interesting article on Tatars and nationalities policy in particular, see Rafael Mustafin, "Enlarged Tataria as a Union Republic?," *Pravda*, January 25, 1989, p. 3, reprinted in *Current Digest of the Soviet Press*, February 22, 1989, pp. 1–3.

30. For the story of just one region and its mosque, see Nikolai Kasimov, "Ai, aul!" *Berdemlik/Edinstvo* (paper within a paper in *Rossiiskaia gazeta*, January 25, 1994).

31. Mustafin, "Enlarged Tataria," 1–3.

32. See *Mnogonatsional'nyi Tatarstan: informatsionno-spravochnyi material* (Kazan: Apparat Prezidenta Respubliki Tatarstan, 1993), 36.

33. Damir Ishakov, "Sovremennoe tatarskoe natsional'noe dvizhenie: pod"em i krizis," *Tatarstan*, no. 8 (1993): 25. See also Damir Ishakov, "Rol' intelligentsii v formirovanii i sovremennom funktsionirovanii samosoznaniia Tatar," in *Sovremennye natsional'nye protsessy v Respublike Tatarstan* (Kazan: Akademiia Nauk Tatarstana, 1994), 15.

34. Ishakov, "Rol' intelligentsii," 16–17.

35. See Azade-Ayşe Rorlich, "Tatars and Azerbaijanis Reach Out to the Disapora," *Radio Free Europe Weekly Report on the USSR*, August 25, 1989, pp. 27–29.

36. For an interesting and detailed account of Tatarstan's negotiations with Russia, see Elizabeth Teague, "Center–Periphery Relations in the Russian Federation," in Roman Szporluk, ed., *National Identity and Ethnicity in Russia and the New States of Eurasia* (New York: M. E. Sharpe, 1994), 21–50.

37. The best English-language source on this treaty is Elizabeth Teague, "Russia and Tatarstan Sign Power-Sharing Treaty," *RFE/RL Research Report*, April 8, 1994, pp. 19–27. This "associated status" is a term inspired by the legal relationship between the United States and Puerto Rico, a relationship that has served as Tatarstan's model for federal relations within the Russian Federation. See the many publications by Tatarstan's most influential presidential advisor on federal issues, Rafael Khakimov, especially the journal he edits, *Panorama–Forum* (Kazan). See also Rafael Khakimov, *Sumerki imperii: k voprosu o natsii i gosudarstve* (Kazan: Tatarskoe knizhnoe izdatel'stvo, 1993) and his *Approaches to Federalism: The Case of Tatarstan* (Kazan: Presidential Apparatus of the Republic of Tatarstan, n. d.). A more recent collection published in Kazan, *Pravovoi status Respubliki Tatarstan* (Kazan: Tatarskoe knizhnoe izdatel'stvo, 1996), also explores these issues.

38. See "Mezhdunarodnyi opyt uregulirovaniia etno-politicheskikh konfliktov," a special issue of *Panorama–Forum* 3, no. 6 (1996).

39. Mintimer Shaimiev, Mikhail Rakhimov, and Mikhail Nikolaev, "Za posledovatel'nuiu demokratizatsiiu i federalizatsiiu Rossii," *Panorama–Forum* 1, no. 1 (1995): 3–6. See also Rafael Khakimov, "Federalizatsiia cherez stabil'nosti," *Panorama–Forum* 1, no. 1 (1995): 34–39.

40. These initiatives are interesting in a discursive sense as well as a material sense. The reference by the government and the mass media in Tatarstan to these

agreements as "interstate" is an integral part of Tatarstan's efforts to construct itself as a "sovereign state" in the post-Soviet period.

41. See the interview with Tatarstan's main federal negotiator, Vasilii Likhachev, in *Respublika Tatarstan*, March 1, 1995, pp. 1–3, also reprinted in *Tatarstan*, nos. 3–4 (1995): 16–18.

42. *Sovetskaia Tatariia*, February 23, 1993, p.1.

43. *Sovetskaia Tatariia*, February 23, 1993, pp. 1–2.

44. President Shaimiev explained the role of these Tatarstani representatives abroad in his report to the first World Congress of Tatars in 1992. Mintimer Shaimiev, "Nashi pomysli chistye, put'—spravedlivyi," *Sovetskaia Tatariia*, June 20, 1992, p. 1. See also Indus Tagirov, "Garantiia sokhraneniia i razvitiia natsii, ili chem dolzhen zanimat'sia Ispolkom VKT," *Sovetskaia Tatariia*, November 26, 1992, pp. 1, 3. For a list of all these representatives, see *Tatarskii mir*, 43.

45. "Informatsiia o deiatel'nosti Ispolkoma vsemirnogo kongressa tatar," *Mnogonatsional'nyi Tatarstan*, 64–67.

46. See the report of the head of the presidency's department of inter-ethnic affairs, Irina Terent'eva, "Po puti aktivnogo sotrudnichestva," *Respublika Tatarstan*, November 11, 1993, p. 4. For list of agreements concluded through 1995, see *Tatarskii mir*, 68–69.

47. The bilateral "Agreements on Trade–Economic, Scientific–Technical, and Cultural Cooperation" that Tatarstan has signed with former Soviet states and the Russian federal republics of Bashkortostan, Marii-El, Chuvashia, and Udmurtia generally contain articles or clauses stating that Tatarstan will undertake responsibility for the "fulfillment of the national–cultural and linguistic requirements" of the counterpart's national minorities in Tatarstan, while the counterpart pledges to do the same for the Tatar national diaspora on its territory. For example, Article 4 of the agreement with Bashkortostan states that "Tatarstan will establish the necessary conditions for the fulfillment of cultural–linguistic and other national requirements of Bashkirs living in Tatarstan, and will promote the achievements of Bashkir culture. Bashkortostan will establish the necessary conditions for the fulfillment of cultural–linguistic and other national requirements of Tatars living in Bashkortostan and will promote the achievements of Tatar culture." See *Sovetskaia Tatariia*, August 21, 1991, p. 1.

48. *Respublika Tatarstan*, November 11, 1993, p. 5; *Respublika Tatarstan*, June 20, 1995, p. 1.

49. See the interview with Likhachev in *Rossiiskaia gazeta*, June 8, 1994, p. 4, in *FBIS-SOV*, June 9, 1994, pp. 43–44.

50. *Respublika Tatarstan*, March 1, 1995, pp. 1–3, in *FBIS-SOV*, March 6, 1995, p. 41.

51. See for example Aiaz Khasanov, "Natsional'nye problemy ne znaiut granits," *Izvestiia Tatarstana*, June 25, 1994, p. 1.

52. The program's main points are reprinted in *Tatarskii mir*, 64–67. See also R. Mirgazizov, "Suverenitet Tatarstana uzhe proglotil, no kul'turno-

natsional'noi avtonomii tatar v Rossii eshche net," *Respublika Tatarstan*, June 8, 1996, p. 4.

53. Mirgazizov, "Suverenitet," 4; and Ildus Zakirov, "Chego ne khvataet tataram v Rossii?" *Altyn urda*, July 10–20, 1996, p. 4.

54. Mirgazizov, "Suverenitet," p. 4; and *Vremia i dengi*, February 13, 1997, p. 2.

55. A prominent Tatar sociologist has argued that recent demographic changes due to increased immigration into Tatarstan have increased the percentage of Tatars in the republic to over 50 percent. Obviously, this is an important and politicized question. Damir Iskhakov, "Nas teper' bol'she," *Idel*, nos. 11–12 (1995): 2–3.

56. These principles are enshrined in Article 1 of Tatarstan's constitution. In addressing the population the day the constitution was adopted, President Shaimiev asserted that the constitution was "both the product of, and expressed the will of, the multinational people of Tatarstan." Mintimer Shaimiev, "Novaia konstitiutsiia—zalog mezhnatsional'nogo i grazhdanskogo soglasiia," *Sovetskaia Tatariia*, November 7, 1992, p. 2.

57. For the most prominent examples, see R. A. Mustafin and A. Kh. Khasanov, *Mintimer Shaimiev: pervyi prezident Tatarstana* (Kazan: Tatarskoe knizhnoe izdatel'stvo, 1995); and R. Kh. Mukhametshin, *Respublika Tatarstan: ot referenduma do dogovora* (Kazan: Tatarskoe knizhnoe izdatel'stvo, 1995). Also see Khakimov, *Sumerki imperii*. For a critical view of this version of Tatarstan's state identity, see Damir Iskhakov, "Tatarstan model: za ili protiv?" *Panorama–Forum* 1 , nos. 1–2 (1995).

58. The Tatar Public Center was one of the first Tatar nationalist organizations formed in Tatarstan in the late 1980s and remains one of the most visible and active Tatar political and social organizations in Kazan and throughout Tatarstan and the rest of the Russian Federation. *Ittifak*, formed shortly after the Center, is a more radically nationalist organization based in the city of Naberezhnie Chelny. Its newspaper, *Altyn urda*, is one of the most interesting opposition newspapers in Tatarstan. For a history of the nationalist movement, see Damir Iskhakov, "Sovremennoe tatarskoe natsional'noe dvizhenie," *Tatarstan*, no. 8 (1993): 25–31.

59. Leonid Tolchinsky, "Tatar Nation Forms Own Ruling Body," *Nezavisimaia gazeta*, January 29, 1992, and also the article in *Izvestiia*, February 3, 1992, in *Current Digest of the Post-Soviet Press* 24, no. 5 (1992): 16–17. Also see Galina Bilialitdinova, "U Tatar kongress: vsemirnyi," *Pravda*, June 6, 1992, p. 2. The *Milli Medzhlis* in Tatarstan is the "All-Tatar" national parliament; the Tatars of Bashkortostan also have their own assembly, the *Milli Medzhlis* of the Tatars of Bashkortostan.

60. Mintimer Shaimiev, "V interesakh mnogonatsional'nogo naroda Tatarstana: obrashchenie Shaimieva v sviazi s Dnem respubliki," *Sovetskaia Tatariia*, August 29, 1992, p. 2. See also Damir Iskhakov, "Kongress ili Sabantui?" *Kris*, February 17, 1997, pp. 1, 3.

61. "Informatsiia o diatel'nosti Ispolkoma," 65–66.

62. "Obrashchenie VKT k gosudarstvam, narodam, i pravitel'stvam mira," in *Mnogonatsional'nyi Tatarstan*, 80; and Shaimiev, "V interesakh," 2.

63. Tagirov, "Garantiia;" and Rimzil' Valeev, "Ispolnaia volia kongressa," *Tatarstan*, nos. 3–4 (1995): 21–24.

64. An especially interesting example of this is *Mnogonatsional'nyi Tatarstan*. See also Shaimiev, "V interesakh;" and Irina Terent'eva, "Glavnoe—sokhranit' stabilnost'," *Tatarstan*, no. 8 (1993): 18–24.

65. This conclusion is based on the author's personal interviews with Rifkat Gabdrakhmanov Galimov, the president of Moscow's largest Tatar cultural organization, *Tugan Tel*, February 27, 1997, and interviews with the leaders of several Tatar cultural and political organizations in the Republic of Bashkortostan, summer 1997. See also Fargat Dauletzhan, "Suverennyi dot biurokratii ili zachem rukovodstvo Tatarstana branitsia s oppozitsii," *Altyn urda*, October 11–20, 1996, p. 1. See also "Zhide el: zhingular hem zhingelular," *Millet: tatar izhitmagyi uzege gazete*, nos. 2–3 (May–June 1995): 1–2.

66. Dauletzhan, "Suverennyi dot," 1.

67. "Obrashchenie k rukovodstvu Tatarstana," *Idel–Ural*, no. 17 (1994): 1.

68. The author was present at the first Congress of Tatars of Bashkortostan and conducted extensive interviews with participants and organizers after the congress.

69. *Kris*, October 4, 1996, p. 1, and February 17, 1997, pp. 1, 3. Personal interview with WCT Executive Committee member Arkadii Fokin, March 18, 1997, Kazan.

70. Part 1, Resolution No. 6, author's copy of "Rezoliutsiia vtorogo vsemirnogo kongressa Tatar."

71. While Russian political and cultural organizations in Tatarstan have criticized other aspects of state building in the republic, especially educational policy, they have never publicly criticized the holding of the World Congress of Tatars in Kazan or the activities of its Executive Committee.

72. One of the clearest expositions of the idea that the states of eastern Europe and the former Soviet Union should be helped to adopt civic, democratic forms of statehood and national identity in the post-Soviet era is Charles Kupchan, "Introduction," in Charles Kupchan, ed., *Nationalism and Nationalities in the New Europe* (Ithaca: Cornell University Press, 1995), 1–14.

73. Dorrine Kondo, *Crafting Selves: Power, Gender and Discourses of Identity in a Japanese Workplace* (Chicago: University of Chicago Press, 1990).

8

The Poles:
Western Aspirations,
Eastern Minorities

Tim Snyder

The predicament of the Polish diaspora reflects the travails of Polish statehood and the travels of Polish state boundaries. Provided that we define the Polish diaspora as Poles who live "abroad" for strict reasons of geopolitics, its vast majority inhabits republics of the former Soviet Union.[1] They are the descendants of Poles whose response to the statelessness, wars, expulsions, and border changes of the past two centuries was to stay put and defend Polishness without the help of a Polish state. They take pride in preserving Polish culture in a hostile environment, and often see themselves as better Poles and better Catholics than their kindred within Poland's frontiers. Yet these eastern Poles have been left behind, in several senses, by the complicated and continuing journey westward of the Polish state.[2]

Millions of Poles chose the opposite response to the trials of the past two centuries of Polish history, leaving Polish lands for the west. More than ten million people of Polish descent thus inhabit western Europe and the Americas, but their relation to the Polish state is manifestly different from that of their eastern kindred. While eastern Poles form communities which self-reproduce over generations, Polish immigrants to the west are quickly assimilated to their new societies. The Polish state traditionally cultivates western emigrants and their children for their wealth and influence, tactically treating them as a unitary group which it grandly calls "Polonia." While "Polonia" is a time-tested construction designed to serve Warsaw's interests, "Poles in the east" (as they are officially known) constitute a new foreign policy problem for a newly sovereign Polish state.

In this chapter, the three dimensions of this problem will be examined in turn: the interests of the Polish state, the position of Polish minorities in the former Soviet Union, and relations among Poland, its minorities, and their host-states. After specifying just what is meant by a "westerly Poland" and an "easterly diaspora," this examination will allow us to draw conclusions about the aims and effects of Poland's eastern policy, the present situation of Polish minorities, the patterns of relations between Poland and its eastern neighbors, and the importance (or lack thereof) of the diaspora to Polish state building. The basic argument will be that Poland's western identity and aspirations restrict its interest in its eastern minorities, while supplying its diplomats with tools to protect the diaspora in their dealings with post-Soviet republics.

A Westerly Poland

The early history of Polish statehood was one of eastern expansion, crowned by the formal union of the Polish Republic with the Grand Duchy of Lithuania, Rus', and Samogitia in 1569. In the seventeenth century, Polish dominion reached as far north as present-day Estonia and as far south as the Black Sea. In the eighteenth century, Poles migrated east, as local elites assimilated to Polish culture. The history of Polish statelessness, which followed the third partition of the Polish–Lithuanian Commonwealth in 1795, is also quite distinctly eastern. Although Prussia and Austria joined the partitions, most Poles were subjects of the Russian tsars. Interestingly, Polish culture and Polish national identity remained attractive in parts of Poland's former eastern dominions in the nineteenth century, even though the Polish state had been removed from the map. The Roman Catholic church, repressed but not outlawed by the tsars, survived in the Russian empire as the "Polish faith." Vestiges of Polish culture would remain, into the twentieth century, wherever the Polish state had once reached.[3]

The twentieth century has seen Poland move west in three distinct phases, beginning in 1918, 1945, and 1989. The end of the First World War brought to Europe an independent Poland, which won for itself eastern boundaries stretching far into present-day Lithuania, Belarus, and Ukraine. Inter-war Poland was thus an independent state with a self-consciously western national identity, yet also home to five million Ukrainians and a million Belarusians. Its eastern marches were graced by Vilnius, Hrodna, and Lviv, presently important urban centers of independent Lithuania, Belarus, and Ukraine. Even so, about 600,000 Poles remained beyond Poland's eastern borders in the new Soviet Union. Moscow administered autonomous republics in the Belarusian and Ukrainian Soviet Socialist Republics, designed to attract Poles across the border to Soviet communism. These were eliminated by Stalin, and the majority of their inhabitants killed or exiled in 1937 and 1938.[4]

In 1945 the Soviet victory in the Second World War moved Poland west at the expense of Germany, and extended the Belarusian, Ukrainian, and newly absorbed Lithuanian Soviet Socialist Republics into formerly Polish lands. Poland gained Gdansk and Wroclaw, but lost Vilnius and Lviv. In 1939 perhaps 3.3 million Poles had lived in these eastern lands. Hundreds of thousands of ethnic Poles were exiled to Siberia and Kazakhstan during the first Soviet occupation of 1939–41.[5] When the Red Army once again secured these territories in 1944, hundreds of thousands more were exiled east to Siberia and Kazakhstan and well over one million "repatriated" (effectively expelled) west to People's Poland.[6] Most Poles left alive in Ukraine accepted "repatriation," not least because Ukrainian nationalists had slaughtered tens of thousands of Polish civilians during the course of the war. Ukrainians living in Poland were likewise brutally "repatriated" east or dispersed in Poland's newly gained western territories, and the Holocaust destroyed the huge majority of Poland's Jewish minority of three million.[7] Post-war Poland was thus geographically far more westerly, and ethnographically far more homogenous. Its own minorities were few, but some two million Poles remained beyond its eastern borders.

Yet the obvious challenges posed by this new diaspora to Polish foreign policy could not be met. Post-war Poland was a communist state, whose limited sovereignty was circumscribed by the interests of the Soviet Union. This simple fact of history was of enormous importance to the relationship between the Polish state and Polish diasporas to the east. Most obviously, Poles who remained in the Soviet Union faced enormous discrimination and efforts at denationalization, while Polish intervention on their behalf was unthinkable. The consequences of two generations of isolation from the mainstream of Polish life will be treated in greater detail below. More interesting, however, is the effect of fifty years of international impotence upon the attitudes of Poles in Poland to their co-ethnics in the east. In three ways, the subjugation of Poland to the Soviet Union, and the response of the Polish opposition to that subjugation, reframed the question of Polish minorities for both the Polish population and its elites.

First, the immediate priority of Polish communist authorities from 1945 was to secure popular acceptance of Poland's new borders. Previous Polish rule over eastern lands was ignored or criticized, and Poland's new acquisitions in the west were associated with the happy times of Poland's medieval Piast kingdom. Polish schoolchildren were taught that the "recovered territories" in the west were a natural Polish inheritance, while the lost lands of the east had been forever alien. This lesson, though falsified history, was well learned.[8] Polish communist authorities ignored the existence of Poles in the Soviet Union; to have done otherwise would have been to raise taboo questions about their origins and their plight. When mentioned at all, they were associated with prominent Polish communists of the past (such as Felix Dzerzhinsky, founder of the Cheka, and Julian Marchlewski, who would have administered Poland for Moscow had Russia won the Polish–Soviet war). Such a practice only discouraged an already dwindling interest.[9]

Second, the achievement of the Polish opposition of the 1970s and 1980s was to accept Poland's new borders as the verdict of history, while taking a friendly interest in Lithuanian, Belarusian, and Ukrainian national movements. Rather than rejecting Poland's new borders in the name of historical claims, oppositionists accepted a westerly Poland while reposing the taboo eastern question. The published reflections of emigres (especially Juliusz Mieroszewski and others writing in *Kultura*, the outstanding political and cultural review published by the Polish emigre Jerzy Giedroyć in Paris) and Solidarity intellectuals created an elite consensus in favor of Lithuanian, Belarusian, and Ukrainian independence.[10] These activists argued that historical disputes between Poland and its eastern neighbors had only served the cause of Russian expansion, and that Poland should treat Lithuania, Belarus, and Ukraine as equals.[11] This did not mean that patriotic Poles lost all interest in the Polish diaspora, but rather that they accepted that another goal of a future Polish eastern policy could supersede the protection of Poles abroad.

Third, for Poles who remained untouched by the preferences of their communist rulers and the innovations of opposition elites, isolation from Poles in the Soviet Union and the simple passage of time between 1945 and 1989 were very important. The majority of Poles alive today do not remember Polish dominion in the east, and the descendants of Poles "repatriated" after the Second World War generally have no desire to return. Nostalgia for the old borderlands has not yet expired, but actual returns to the east are extremely rare. Indeed, the average Pole cultivates a certain snobbery with respect to lands and peoples to their east, which very often extends to Poles from the former Soviet Union.[12] To take one telling example, although the polite Polish word for a Russian is *rosjanin*, a Russian will likely be called a *ruski*, a mildly pejorative term often extended to all Slavs from the east.

Ironic as it may seem, in these three ways the communist era laid the foundations for Poland's third step westward, the "return to Europe" which followed the revolution of 1989. Krzysztof Skubiszewski, foreign minister of Poland from 1989 through 1993, took part in this elite consensus and took advantage of these changes in popular attitudes.[13] He treated the fate of Polish minorities as an important but tertiary motivation of Poland's eastern policy. Poland's first motivation was the "return to Europe," or integration with European institutions. This required that Poland maintain good relations with its eastern neighbors and avoid disputes over ethnic minorities. Its second motivation was the independence and territorial integrity of newly independent eastern neighbors, which provided an historically unprecedented barrier to Russian power. Its third and final motivation was the protection of the rights of the Polish diaspora.

Skubiszewski crafted what might be called a policy of state interest rather than national interest, in which the security of Poland was defined to the benefit of the Polish state rather than the Polish ethnos. Eastern Poles were to be treated first and foremost as citizens of the states in which they reside.[14] They would be protected by the inclusion of "European standards" in state–to–state treaties, and Poland would offer itself as a bridge to "Europe" to its eastern neighbors. The fundamental "European standards" were the preservation of the national life of minorities within existing state borders; this implied opposition to all forms of territorial claims by Polish minorities, but support of their cultural development. The idea of "Europe" resolved some of the intellectual and practical problems involved in Poland's eastern policy: It supplied Polish diplomats with ideological and legal support as they pressed for the protection of Polish minorities, and it suggested to Poland's neighbors that good relations with Poland could bring them, too, closer to "Europe."

The plight of Poles abroad has exerted some influence on Polish domestic politics, and public interest has from time to time forced the foreign ministry to give the issue greater than this tertiary priority. Outbursts of public sympathy have led to dramatic action, though public attention to the eastern diaspora has been sporadic. Parliamentarians, often prompted by meetings with Polish groups visiting from the east, have issued statements contradicting Polish foreign policy. The Polish foreign ministry has thus been forced on occasion to place greater emphasis upon the minority issue than it might have, but in general this has not much affected the course of policy, or overridden the higher goals of striving for integration with the west while trying to secure the sovereignty of neighbors in the east. Although Skubiszewski resigned after the defeat of the former opposition by the former communists in the parliamentary elections of 1993, the main lines of his policy were followed by left-wing governments from 1993 to 1997. The treatment of Poles abroad was not an issue in these elections, or indeed in any Polish national elections after 1989.

From the outset, however, the execution of Polish eastern policy has been less than coherent, as the foreign ministry has been joined by a variety of other official and quasi-official actors: the Polish Community Association (*Stowarzyszenie "Wspólnota Polska"*), a quasi-nongovernmental body associated with the Polish Senate; the Foundation to Aid Eastern Poles (*Fundacja Pomocy Polakom na Wschodzie*), formed in 1994 by the council of ministers as a rival to the Polish Community; the ministries of culture and education; and parliamentary commissions. The most apparent problem is that while the foreign ministry is tasked with setting Polish policy toward its eastern diaspora, other agencies receive 90 percent of the funds designated for its implementation.[15] The Polish Community tends to regard the interests of ethnic Poles as synonymous with the interests of the Polish state. It is run by patriots with roots in the east and by Roman Catholic clergymen with a natural interest in spreading their own religion.[16] Although the Roman Catholic church is not an agent of the Polish state, it is often viewed as such by Poles and their neighbors alike. Because religion is a sensitive issue in the national revivals of Poland's eastern neighbors, as well as the main constituent of the national identities of Poles in the east, this has created significant problems. Specific instances will be discussed below.

Poland's eastern policy is rendered complex enough by the distribution of responsibility among several policy actors. It is complicated further still by the widely varying situations of ethnic Poles dispersed throughout the republics of the former Soviet Union. Before examining Polish eastern policy in greater depth, we must therefore take stock of this dispersion, establish in which republics ethnic Poles constitute an ethnic minority of politically significant size, and focus on the history and present position of the major concentration of Poles in the lands of the former Soviet Union, along the Lithuanian–Belarusian border. Polish policy toward its minorities in Lithuania and Belarus, and toward the newly independent states of which they are citizens, will provide the important case studies for an assessment of the importance of the Polish diaspora to state building both in newly sovereign Poland and in the newly independent states of the former Soviet Union.

An Easterly Diaspora

Since 1989, Polish policy has had to contend with three sorts of diasporas in the former Soviet Union (see Table 8.1). Perhaps best known and most dramatic is the situation of Poles in the first group, those who live far beyond the reaches of any historic Polish state in Russia and Kazakhstan.

These amount to about 13.7 percent of the total population of Poles in the former Soviet Union: Of the 1,126,334 Poles counted in the Soviet census of 1989, some 59,956 inhabited Kazakhstan and some 94,594 inhabited the Russian Federation.[17] These Poles are almost entirely descendants of exiles, about evenly divided between those deported from the western Soviet Union in the 1930s and those deported from formerly Polish territories annexed by the Soviet Union to the expanded Ukrainian, Belarusian, and new Lithuanian Soviet Socialist Republics during the Second World War. Some trace their lineage to heroes of the 1863, 1830, or even 1794 Polish risings against Russian rule. A small percentage is also descended from Polish engineers and workers who moved east in search of work during Russia's nineteenth-century industrialization, or from still older Polish communities in such cities as Kyiv or Odessa.[18] Between 1945 and 1989, these Poles were totally isolated from Poland and Polish culture. In Russia and Kazakhstan, Poles were dispersed throughout enormous territories and denied access to schooling in Polish.[19] The result was a near total loss of the Polish language and high rates of intermarriage with Russians. The status of ethnic Poles has not become an important issue in Polish–Russian relations since the end of the Soviet Union in 1991, despite the odd visit by Polish officials to Siberian towns.[20] In the rare cases where Poles have organized themselves and sought to establish Polish schools, Polish consulates have provided funds and advice.[21]

The Polish minority in Kazakhstan has likewise created no problems in Polish–Kazakh relations. The minority is vanishingly small (especially in comparison to the Russian presence in Kazakhstan), and Kazakh authorities have generally welcomed attempts to revive Polish culture.[22] An ethnic Pole was named bishop for Polish communities in Central Asia in 1992, Polish volunteers are sent to Kazakhstan to teach Polish, and a Polish school is planned in the new Kazakh capital of Akmola.[23] But the main interest of the impoverished mass of ethnic Poles in Kazakhstan is repatriation. In 1992 the Union of Poles in Kazakhstan pressed Polish authorities to allow them to return to their homes—in Ukraine. Unsurprisingly, the Polish government did not prevail upon Ukraine to return land to these Poles.[24] Then, rather by accident, Poland reopened the question of repatriation in 1996. The government's Foundation to Aid Eastern Poles surveyed Poles in Kazakhstan, asking them to inform the Polish embassy and the speaker of the Polish Senate if they wished to emigrate to Poland. As the embassy in Almaty and the Senate in Warsaw were flooded with petitions, the media picked up the issue, and Polish politicians fell over each other in their eagerness to show their interest in Kazakhstan. Not to be outdone by the government Foundation, the Polish Community announced its plans to settle Kazakhstani Poles in

TABLE 8.1   Polish Minorities in the Former Soviet Union

	Population	% of Total Pop.	Majority Polish-Speakers	Native to Area	Claims to Territory	Opposed Independence
Belarus	417,700	4.0	No	Yes	No	No
Lithuania	258,600	7.0	Yes	Yes	Yes	Yes
Ukraine	219,200	0.5	Yes	Yes	No	No
Latvia	60,400	2.3	No	Yes	No	No
Russia	94,600	0.06	No	No	No	No
Kazakhstan	59,900	0.4	No	No	No	No

Source: Population figures based on 1989 Soviet census.

every Polish locality. The Polish government prepared a repatriation ordinance, which the Polish embassy in Almaty began to implement in July 1996.[25] Polish policy underwent a radical change with no real consideration of how repatriation might best be achieved and whether or not the entire process was in the interests of the state. Though the issue was a minor one, the policy change was a triumph of patriotism over calculation, and of the methods of the Polish Community and the Foundation to Aid Eastern Poles over those of the foreign ministry. It remains to be seen how many Kazakhstani Poles will wish to "return" to Poland: It is, after all, much easier to send a petition than to leave home.

Poles in Russia and Kazakhstan not only found themselves outside the boundaries of Polish states; they were also deported into far reaches where Polish power had never extended. More than 80 percent of Poles in the former Soviet Union, however, inhabit territories which were Polish in 1939 (before the Molotov–Ribbentrop pact) or in 1772 (before the partitions). This is the situation of Poles in Latvia, Ukraine, Belarus, and Lithuania. Poles in Latvia and Ukraine should be distinguished from the rest, because they constitute a very small percentage of the populations of independent Latvia and Ukraine, and have created no significant problems in Polish–Latvian or Polish–Ukrainian relations. The 60,416 Poles in Latvia (2.3 percent of the Latvian population) continue a tradition of Polish presence in these lands which dates from the 1560s, when Livonia's German nobility sought the protection of the Polish crown against Russian invaders. In the twentieth century their numbers have remained steady, and since Latvian independence they have suffered no discrimination.[26] A Union of Poles in Latvia was founded in 1988, and by 1989 had initiated Polish courses in Latvian schools.[27] Poland and Latvia are traditionally friendly neighbors, and the Polish minority in Latvia has done nothing to alter this state of affairs.

Poles in Ukraine constitute an even smaller percentage of the total population (0.5 percent), although in absolute terms they are quite numerous (219,179). The numbers were an order of magnitude greater in the inter-war period: Poles in western (Polish) and eastern (Soviet) Ukraine together numbered some 2.3 million.[28] The Polish presence in Soviet Ukraine was virtually eliminated by deportations in the 1930s. Deportations between 1939 and 1941 removed hundreds of thousands of Poles from western Ukraine. In 1942 and 1943 Ukrainian nationalist forces massacred Polish civilians in an attempt to drive the remaining Polish population west. Estimates of civilian deaths range from fifty thousand to five hundred thousand, and the nationalists boasted of driving half a million Poles out of Ukraine.[29] Poles in Ukraine were therefore much more likely than their counterparts in Belarus and Lithuania to choose "repatriation" from the Soviet Union to Poland after 1944. Some 784,500 Poles left Ukraine at this time.[30] The result of this wartime suffering and destruction was a tremendously reduced Polish presence in Ukraine. Cities once dominated by Poles and Jews, such as Lviv, became thoroughly Ukrainian in the post-war period.[31] In the perestroika period of the late 1980s, Polish organizations in Ukraine supported the Ukrainian national movement, and since independence ethnic Poles have profited from a liberal nationalities law.[32] In western Ukraine there have been bitter local quarrels over the ownership of churches expropriated in Soviet times, disputes about the relationship between the Ukrainian Catholic (Uniate) and Roman Catholic churches, and incidents where Poles have been prevented from honoring their war dead as they wished. Radically different estimations of wartime events have also cast some pall on Polish–Ukrainian relations.[33] Because such quarrels involve property, faith, and the memory of war and ethnic cleansing, no political act by central authorities can resolve them. Nevertheless, the joint declaration on historical reconciliation signed by Ukrainian and Polish presidents Kuchma and Kwaśniewski in May 1997 was an impressive gesture, and at the very least signaled that local disputes are unlikely to escalate into problems of international relations.[34] Generally speaking, the existence of a Polish minority in Ukraine has not created problems for the Polish state, not least because its members have followed the advice of Polish officials and behaved as loyal Ukrainian citizens.[35]

Like Poles in Latvia and Ukraine, Poles in Belarus and Lithuania are heirs to a long tradition of Polish settlement. Poles in Belarus and

Lithuania are, however, far more numerous relative to local majority populations than are their kindred north and south. There are 257,994 Poles in Lithuania (7 percent of the population) and 417,720 in Belarus (4 percent of the population), according to the 1989 Soviet census. Exactly 60 percent of the Poles in the former Soviet Union inhabit these two small republics. Moreover, the vast majority of Poles in Lithuania and Belarus inhabit a corridor which runs along the Belarusian–Lithuanian border, from the point where the border reaches Poland near Hrodna to the point where it touches Latvia near Daugavpils. Thus at least fifty percent of the Poles in the former Soviet Union (an area of 22,272,000 square kilometers) inhabit an area of only 30,000 square kilometers along the edges of two small republics. In other words, half of the Poles in the former Soviet Union inhabit one one-thousandth of its surface area. In addition, unlike their counterparts elsewhere in the former Soviet Union, Poles in Belarus and Lithuania live along a state border, inhabit relatively concentrated communities, and have founded large organizations which make serious political demands (see Table 8.1).

Poles in Belarus and Lithuania Before 1989

The question of the origin of the Polish minority in Lithuania and Belarus is hotly disputed, though these ethno-historical quarrels reveal more about the assumptions of their participants than they do about the national identity of eastern Poles. Extreme Lithuanian nationalists insist that the people in question are racially Lithuanian, and should be forced to rediscover their lost identity.[36] The most common Lithuanian view is that these Poles are actually Belarusians who confuse their Roman Catholic religion with Polish national identity. Belarusian nationalists are generally of the same opinion, and thus unwittingly strengthened Gorbachev's hand as he attempted to use Belarusian claims to Vilnius to deter Lithuania from declaring independence in the period 1989–91.[37] Lithuanian president Vytautas Landsbergis and Belarusian president Stanislav Shushkevich were even able to agree in 1992 that Poles in Lithuania are in fact Belarusians.[38] Shushkevich wished to bolster a weak Belarusian state with all available demographic resources, while Landsbergis much preferred to deal with a Belarusian than with a Polish minority. However, newly independent Belarus then used the ostensible predominance of Belarusians in eastern Lithuania to press revisionist claims in 1992.[39] Accepting the same logic, Belarus in 1994 asked the United Nations to investigate the situation of "Belarusians" in Lithuania.[40]

Yet the people in question self-identify as Poles and stubbornly maintained this identity under Soviet communism.[41] (Although Polish identity has become more attractive since 1989—with the acceleration of Poland's reforms and the consequent accentuation of differences between Poland and its eastern neighbors—the populations considered here already declared Polish identity in the Soviet period.) In this important sense, the question of their origins is beside the point. Their ancestors were probably Lithuanian-speaking peasants who in early modern times absorbed the Belarusian language, the Roman Catholic religion, and then Polish culture, supplemented by Poles who migrated east under the old Polish–Lithuanian Commonwealth. Despite great national oppression, these Poles maintained their national identity during the rule of the tsars, which followed the end of the Polish state in 1795 and lasted until the First World War. The preservation of a Polish university in Vilnius until 1832 certainly helped. In 1900 there were approximately 1.3 million Poles in lands presently Lithuanian and Belarusian. Indeed, during the first decade of the twentieth century, the dominance of the Polish language in Vilnius and the eastern part of present-day Lithuania strengthened.[42]

After the revival of Polish statehood in 1918 and the establishment of Poland's eastern borders after the Polish–Soviet war in 1921, the majority of these Poles found themselves citizens of a Polish state. Ethnic Poles constituted perhaps one-third of the populations of the northeastern Polish districts of Wilno, Nowogród, and Białystok, where Belarusians constituted a majority. Poles and Jews dominated the cities, and Poles constituted an absolute majority of about 70 percent in Vilnius. Native Poles were joined by settlers and soldiers, and access to Polish schooling and mandatory military service strengthened Polish identity and spread the use of the Polish language. Interestingly, the religious criterion of national identity was reinforced by the return of Polish political power: Belarusian-speakers of the Roman Catholic faith learned Polish quickly, while Belarusian-speakers of the Orthodox faith treated it as a foreign language. Poland meanwhile suppressed the Belarusian schools and organizations which would have provided a rival identity. By 1939 there were perhaps 1.5 million Poles in the territories which are presently part of Belarus and Lithuania.[43]

By the Second World War, then, the distinctive crescent of Polish ethnic predominance—from Hrodna to Daugavpils through Vilnius—was well established. The war deaths, political executions, and ethnic cleansings of the war and its aftermath reduced the Polish presence by perhaps half, but did not change its general shape.[44] Poles did lose their dominance in cities, most notably in Vilnius. The Polish intelligentsia was singled out for repression by Germans and Soviets, and after the war was more likely to accept "repatriation" to Poland. The Poles of the former regions of Wilno, Nowogród, and Białystok were thereby left a peasant people, now ruled by communists in Moscow rather than compatriots in Warsaw.[45] The vast majority of these districts was transferred to Soviet Belarus. A thin sliver, which included Vilnius, was joined to newly Soviet Lithuania. From 1945, the fates of Poles in this formerly coherent region began to diverge, since from the Polish point of view the Lithuanian and Belarusian versions of communism turned out to be surprisingly different.[46]

The first and crucial difference was language. Lithuanian is a Baltic language, while Polish, Belarusian, and Russian are Slavic languages. Poles in Belarus, many of whom had never spoken Polish in any case, found themselves swamped by local Belarusians and migrant Russians.[47] Every Polish school in Soviet Belarus was closed by 1948, so post-war generations of Poles were educated in Russian or Belarusian. Perhaps one in ten Belarusian Poles speaks Polish at home.[48] In Lithuania, on the other hand, Polish schools continued to function, and the Baltic–Slavic linguistic divide created a clear barrier between Poles and Lithuanians.[49] About 85 percent of Poles in Lithuania consider Polish their native language. Poles educated in Russian (which was more frequent) could still contrast themselves with the Lithuanian majority. Russian is much easier for Poles to learn and was the most useful language in the Soviet Union. Only 15.5 percent of Poles could speak Lithuanian in 1989, whereas 57.9 percent could speak Russian.[50]

Second, this difference in Soviet educational policy reflected a clear political goal of Soviet central authorities. In Belarus local nationalism was weak, and a post-war policy of russification was quite successful. This rendered the Poles the least trustworthy nationality in Soviet Belarus, and they were effectively forced to assimilate. In Lithuania, on the other hand, local nationalism was very strong, and the Lithuanian authorities resisted Russian migration and preserved Lithuanian as the language of education and culture. From Moscow's point of view, Poles in Lithuania were more trustworthy than Lithuanians. They were thus allowed to study in Polish, and their national identity was supported as a card to be played against Lithuania.

That Moscow could envisage such a strategy suggests the third difference between the experience of Poles in Lithuania and Poles in Belarus. Poles in Belarus faced the prospect of russification, but never the threat of a local nationalism. Surveys record a generally positive attitude toward Belarus and Belarusian national aspirations.[51] Poles in Lithuania, on the other hand, experienced direct Lithuanian rule from 1939 to 1940, and associate Lithuanian officials with the German occupation and the extermination of local Jewry from 1941 to 1944. In the waning years of the Soviet Union, Poles in Lithuania still treated the Lithuanian presence in their lands as alien, regarded Lithuanians with more antipathy than any other nationality (save the Jews and the Roma), and feared that Lithuanians would use independence to settle old scores against Poles.[52] Whereas Poles in Belarus saw Belarusian independence as an opportunity to revive Polish culture, many Poles in Lithuania would have preferred Russian hegemony to continue. As Lithuania pressed for independence in 1990 and 1991, Moscow sought to turn the suspicions of local Poles to its advantage.[53] As the Soviet Union fractured and collapsed, the linguistic and political differences between Poles in Lithuania and Poles in Belarus became manifest in their attitudes and aspirations, which in turn necessitated different policies from the newly sovereign Polish state.

Poles in Lithuania and Polish Policy Since 1989

Most Poles in Lithuania did not experience Lithuanian independence as a liberation.[54] The years preceding the recognition of Lithuanian independence in 1991 saw a number of campaigns directed against Poles and Polish national identity. Influential nationalist groups such as Vilnija tried to persuade Poles that they were racially Lithuanians; the press began to carry pseudo-historical "proofs" that Poles with certain surnames were actually Lithuanian; Lithuanian officials created problems for Poles who wished to use Polish names in legal documents; and prominent Lithuanian intellectuals denigrated proud events in Polish history.[55] Poles in Lithuania tended to believe that Lithuanian nationalists had pursued a conscious policy aimed at forcing them to either assimilate or immigrate.[56] The Union of Poles in Lithuania (*Związek Polaków na Litwie*), heavily infiltrated by trusted communists, announced on several occasions in 1989, 1990, and 1991 its intention to create a Polish "national–territorial unit" on Lithuanian soil. One of its leaders, the former lecturer on Marxism Jan Ciechanowicz, advocated the creation of a second Polish state, drawn from territories along the Lithuanian–Belarusian border.[57] Although these declarations must be seen as part of Gorbachev's plans to intimidate Lithuania in the period 1989–91, they nevertheless resonated with a Polish population which feared Lithuanian nationalism. The Union of Poles in Lithuania was in large measure a creature of the Communist party, but its mass support was very real.

This dispute between the Lithuanian national movement and the Polish minority drastically reduced Poland's influence in Lithuania between 1989 and 1991. Although Poland was more supportive of Lithuania's aspirations than any other state, Lithuanians suspected that the Polish state supported the territorial aspirations of the Polish minority. Lithuanians generally discouraged contact between Solidarity delegations and local Poles, believing that in so doing they were preventing a conspiracy against them. In fact, intellectuals and diplomats from Poland sought to discourage territorial claims and urge Poles in Lithuania to support the movement for Lithuanian independence.[58] Their lack of influence increased the isolation of the Polish minority and its dependence upon Moscow. Poles from Lithuania, however, were able to travel freely in Warsaw and win a few parliamentarians over to their view.[59] This had the effect of reinforcing Lithuanians' belief that Warsaw stood behind the demands of the Polish minority and of reducing the credibility of Polish diplomats in Lithuania. The August 1991 coup effectively removed the Moscow axis of this dispute. But when Lithuanian independence was recognized in September 1991, all three remaining parties—Lithuanians, the Polish minority, and the Polish state—were alienated from one another.

The first years of Lithuanian independence posed numerous challenges to Polish foreign policy. Independent Lithuania, having acquired its capital Vilnius from Poland by way of the Molotov–Ribbentrop pact and Soviet domination of eastern Europe, was extremely sensitive to the Polish question. Whereas Polish officials were operating according to a new foreign policy paradigm which emphasized the future interests of the Polish state, Lithuanian leaders such as Vytautas Landsbergis (chairman of parliament and effectively head of state) tended to view Poland as a culture bound to continue certain trends of national history. There was great fear that Poland would once again occupy Vilnius, as it had in 1920: Lithuania's defense minister went so far as to call Poland his country's greatest security threat.[60] Given this set of assumptions, Lithuania's new leaders were bound to strike against local Poles who had dared to reduce the country's unity at its most urgent moment. In September 1991, Lithuania dissolved the regional governments of the two regions in which Poles constituted a majority (Vilnius region, 63.8 percent, and Šalčininkai region, 79.8 percent), suspended local elections, and began the sensitive processes of reform by sending in ethnic Lithuanian officials.

This effectively froze Polish–Lithuanian relations. The Polish foreign ministry took the position that new elections should be held immediately, so that Poles in Lithuania could democratically replace the leaders who had proven unworthy. Lithuania extended direct rule through 1992, and Polish leaders in Lithuania complained that Poland was unwilling to protect their interests. Leaders of the Union of Poles in Lithuania said that Foreign Minister Skubiszewski came to Lithuania "walking on his knees," and complained that Polish foreign policy amounted to "paper actions."[61] They again took their case to Polish parliamentarians and caused momentary scandals. Their most dramatic success was persuading deputies of a governing party (the Christian–National Union) to declare that Poland should demand autonomy for Poles in Lithuania as a price for Vilnius, which clearly contradicted Poland's foreign policy of unconditionally recognizing existing borders.[62] Though these delegations were never able to win significant support, such public statements and proposed resolutions were enough to convince Landsbergis that Poland was swamped in "nationalism and chauvinism."[63] Polish diplomats were thus caught between extreme positions: Their compatriots called them cowards, while their neighbors called them imperialists. Foreign Minister Skubiszewski explained to parliament that the rights of Poles in Lithuania was only one of several Polish interests in the east, while Polish diplomats argued that they were holding Lithuania to "European standards," and offered Polish help in European integration.[64] In 1992 and 1993, Lithuanian officials resisted Polish help, preferring a "Scandinavian road" to Europe. Indeed, diplomatic problems deepened in 1993, as Lithuania demanded that Poland officially apologize for its "occupation" of Vilnius in 1920 and accept that Vilnius was "legally" part of Lithuania during the inter-war period. Poland refused, partly on the grounds of historical accuracy (Vilnius was demographically a Polish–Jewish city in 1920), and partly because they feared that such an apology would prejudice the rights of Poles still residing in Lithuania.[65]

From late 1993, changing Lithuanian perceptions of Europe brought a thaw to relations with Poland. In the wake of the success of Zhirinovsky's chauvinist Liberal Democrats in Russian parliamentary elections, Poland's successful courting of western institutions, and the announcement of NATO's Partnership for Peace, Lithuania shifted from a balanced foreign policy to a distinctly western orientation. Poland was finally seen as a bridge to the west, even by the very defense minister who had called Poland a threat to Lithuania in 1991.[66] The Democratic Labor Party of Algirdas Brazauskas, in power from late 1992 to late 1996, yielded to opposition pressure to announce NATO membership as a foreign policy goal, but in so doing persuaded the nationalist conservative opposition (including Landsbergis's Fatherland Union and a number of other parties) that this would require compromises in negotiations with Poland. (As late as October 1993 the opposition, including Landsbergis, was calling for draconian measures to be taken against the Polish minority.)[67] A treaty with Poland containing an article on the free development of national life by minorities was signed in April 1994 and ratified (unanimously in Poland and with a few votes against in Lithuania) six months later.

This began a period of steadily improving Polish–Lithuanian ties, and a new pattern in relations within the triad of the Polish state, the Lithuanian state, and Poles in Lithuania. Poland could appeal to the treaty in its attempts to protect the rights of Poles in Lithuania, and was able to blunt Lithuanian attempts to deny Poles their rights to expropriated property, to prevent the use of Polish in schooling, and to gerrymander electoral districts to reduce the Polish minority's political power.[68] Polish presidents have soothed tensions by ritually visiting Lithuania and urging local Poles to be loyal citizens, while Polish officials assure Lithuania of their intent to help Lithuania join Europe.[69] Though nationalist stereotypes have by no means disappeared, since 1994 Lithuania has seen in Poland its "most important strategic partner" and the key to its future integration into Europe.[70] The Union of Poles in Lithuania has ignored these successes, and has generally worked to keep Poles in Lithuania fearful of Lithuanian nationalism.[71] (Its various undertakings, including the inflammatory newspaper *Nasza Gazeta* [Our Gazette] are nevertheless sponsored by the Polish Community and the Foundation to Aid Eastern Poles.) The Union has been joined in Lithuanian political life by the moderate and liberal Congress of Lithuanian Poles, which has concentrated its energies on winning seats in parliament.[72] In sum, after 1994 relations between Poland and Lithuania greatly improved; relations between Poland and the Polish minority remained troublesome; and relations between Lithuania and its Polish minority continued to be difficult. Lithuania, though, has been subject to Polish leverage, because Lithuanians believe their stake in Europe depends upon Polish good will and good offices.

Poles in Belarus and Polish Policy Since 1989

The situation of Poles in Belarus (417,700 of 10,151,900 citizens of the republic, according to the 1989 census) and the evolution of Polish policy designed to protect them have passed through three distinct phases. From 1989 Poles in Belarus published a widely read newspaper in Hrodna (*Głos znad Niemna*, or Voice from Beyond the Niemen River) and pressed several cultural, educational, and political demands. The most controversial political demand was for dual citizenship, which Polish authorities declined to support after Belarus became an independent state.[73] After its foundation in 1990, the Union of Poles in Belarus (*Związek Polaków na Białorusi*) also requested that Belarusian authorities carry out a new census, in the belief that it would record at least a million Poles.[74] This the Belarusian Supreme Soviet flatly refused to do. By 1991 the Union of Poles in Belarus had settled on the two major goals which it would henceforth consistently pursue: the return of Polish schools (abolished in 1948) and the legal equality of the Roman Catholic church *vis-à-vis* the dominant Orthodox church. The first public demonstration of Poles in Belarus in the post-war period, a march in Hrodna in September 1990, pressed the demand for Polish schools. Significantly, the Poles were joined by representatives of the Belarusian National Front and other Belarusian national organizations.[75] Though no support was forthcoming from the Belarusian Supreme Soviet, the number of local Polish classes mushroomed, and the study of Polish spread from Hrodna and the northeastern borderlands as far as Minsk.[76] Meanwhile, a religious revival was underway among Belarus's 2.5 million Roman Catholics. In 1990 a seminary was founded in Hrodna,[77] and Pope John Paul II named Tadeusz Kondrusiewicz, a Pole from Hrodna, apostolic administrator for Minsk and Belarus.[78]

During 1992 and 1993, the first two years of Belarusian independence, Poland and Belarus enjoyed moderately good relations. In contrast to Lithuania, where the Polish minority had immediately posed problems for good relations between neighbors, in Belarus concerns were relatively muted. The Union of Poles in Belarus had supported Belarusian independence in 1990 and 1991, as its leaders consciously sought to avoid the "Lithuanian model," in which Poles and local patriots found themselves on opposite sides of the barricades.[79] In 1992 and 1993, the Union of Poles in Belarus was considered part of the democratic front which pressed for the protection of Belarusian independence, a clear separation from Russia in foreign affairs, and support of Stanislav Shushkevich (chairman of the Supreme Soviet and effectively head of state) against the conservative–communist majority in parliament.[80] Some representatives of the Belarusian National Front minimized the number of Poles in Belarus, and protested that Polish priests were spreading Polish national identity by delivering sermons in Polish and decorating churches with symbols of the Polish state. But these quarrels did not prevent them from meeting regularly with the Union.[81]

Shushkevich expressed the same reservations about Polish priests in his dealings with the Polish state.[82] Though only about 15 percent of the 2.5 million Roman Catholic Belarusians self-identified as Poles in the 1989 census, a Roman Catholic in Belarusian lands is traditionally viewed as a Pole, by himself and by his Orthodox neighbors.[83] Belarusian nationalists, and Shushkevich, thus feared that a Roman Catholic revival carried out by Polish priests would drain their fragile national movement of demographic resources. Polish activists estimate that 1 million to 1.25 million Belarusian citizens will declare themselves Poles in the next census, which confirms this fear.[84] In January 1992 the pope named

Kazimierz Świątek archbishop of Minsk, replacing Kondrusiewicz. Though another Pole, Świątek was far more sensitive to Belarusian concerns and forbade priests from decorating churches with "the attributes of a neighboring state." This muted but did not end the controversy. Most Roman Catholic priests in Belarus are Poles, and their Polish parishioners fiercely desire that mass be said in Polish. For older generations of Poles, the church was their one link to Poland during Soviet times.[85] In some cases older Polish parishioners insist on the use of Polish over the objections of Polish priests, who wish to reach a younger generation by using Russian or Belarusian.[86] In this sense the problem is internal to Belarusian society, and no action by the Polish state or the pope can resolve it. In January 1993 the Belarusian Council for Religion requested that the Vatican recall all Polish priests from Belarus.[87]

The Polish state nevertheless showed good faith on this issue and had much to offer Belarus in these early years of independence.[88] In 1992 and 1993, Polish prime minister Hanna Suchocka and president Lech Wałęsa visited Belarus and emphasized to Shushkevich their support for Belarusian independence.[89] Wałęsa made a point of telling ethnic Poles to be good citizens of Belarus.[90] While Shushkevich tried to move Belarus toward European institutions, Poland offered itself as a bridge to the west. Polish diplomats argued, with success, that good Polish–Belarusian relations were essential to both countries' "return to Europe."[91] Polish negotiators pressed for guarantees of the cultural rights of the Polish minority and Belarus and the Belarusian minority in Poland in accordance with "European standards."[92] Shushkevich swallowed his reservations and in June 1992 signed a treaty with Poland which guaranteed minorities the free development of national culture without discrimination.[93]

Shushkevich lost a no-confidence vote in January 1994, and in July 1994 Alexander Lukashenka was inaugurated as Belarus's first directly elected president. Lukashenka quickly directed Belarusian foreign policy to the east, seeking integration with Russia. As Lukashenka surrendered the attributes of Belarusian state independence in the name of union with Russia, the Union of Poles in Belarus and other democratic organizations tended to unite against the common threat. Belarusian Poles joined the rousing, but ineffectual, protests against Lukashenka's policy in 1995, 1996, and 1997. Meanwhile, Poland's "western" credentials hindered rather than helped Belarusian–Polish relations, as Lukashenka saw Poland as the *avant-garde* of a threatening imperialist bloc rather than as a bridge to a friendly and prosperous Europe. He and other Belarusian officials trotted out standard nationalist complaints against Poland, but did so to distract the Belarusian nationalist opposition rather than to press concrete demands.[94] As Lukashenka progressively dismantled the institutions of Belarus's new democracy from 1994 to 1996, simple contact with Poles and Polish organizations (especially the Solidarity labor union) was deemed dangerously contaminating.

Under Lukashenka, Poles in Belarus suffered no greater deprivations of rights than Belarusian citizens in general, and the Union of Poles in Belarus was repressed in the same measure as other democratic organizations. Referenda and parliamentary elections were marred by massive fraud, which worked against Poles just as it worked against Belarusian democrats generally. Natural Polish electoral districts were divided, and a military garrison was added to the district of the leader of the Union of Poles in Belarus.[95] In September 1996, Poles in Hrodna did finally receive a single Polish school, built with funds from the Polish Community as well as private donations.[96] (It was the only school in Belarus with Polish as the language of instruction. Lukashenka had promised to build Polish schools during his electoral campaign, but in office he not only failed to do this, but banned all textbooks not printed in the Soviet Union.[97] The ban of non-Soviet textbooks was urged upon Lukashenka by Zhirinovsky's Russian Liberal Democrats, who argued that alien reading matter would corrupt the pure Slavic youth of Belarus.)[98] The school was inaugurated by a high-level Polish government delegation, in order to insure that it was not immediately converted to a Belarusian or Russian school.[99] The Polish foreign ministry hunkered down, opening a consulate in Hrodna and asking that Belarus hold to its treaty obligations with respect to its Polish minority.[100] But while Lukashenka's authoritarianism drove Poles and Belarusian nationalists together, his policy of union with Russia reduced the leverage of the Polish state, and threatened a future in which Belarusian and Polish culture alike would be swamped in a state dominated by Russia.

Conclusion

Poland's integration with western institutions has marked a new stage in a long and tangled historical journey in which the geographical location and the political aims of the Polish state have shifted from east to west. Since 1989 "Europe" has been both the end and the means of Polish eastern policy. "Europe" is the end, since the protection of Poles in the east has been subordinate to the goals of furthering European integration and affirming the sovereignty and territorial integrity of eastern neighbors. "Europe" is also the means, since Polish diplomats have tried to include "European standards" of minority rights within bilateral treaties with eastern neighbors and offered Poland as a bridge to "Europe" as an incentive for these neighbors to sign them. In some sense the idea of "European standards" was a shell game, for the European Union has been unable to establish a coherent definition of minority rights.[101] Polish diplomats were nevertheless quite right to argue that westerners would look askance at obvious abuses of minorities and unresolved disputes over state boundaries. While this approach has eased historical conflicts over Polish minorities, its execution has also brought to light the very different ways the Polish eastern diaspora is perceived by all parties concerned.

For instance, Poland's pursuit of a policy of state interest rather than national interest has left the more radical representatives of the eastern minorities disappointed. These eastern Poles see themselves as defenders of embattled outposts of a higher culture, deserving of the full support of the Polish state. It is not surprising that Lithuanians and Belarusians see matters differently: They may agree that Poles represent a different culture, but decline to acknowledge its superiority. Or alternatively, they deny that the Poles in their countries are in fact Poles at all and seek to "return" to them their lost Lithuanian of Belarusian nationality. As we have seen, these local disagreements about identity created international conflicts of interest between newly sovereign Poland and newly independent Lithuania and Belarus, which Polish officials addressed with the aid of "Europe."

Poland's European strategy has been effective in so far as its interlocutors desire to rejoin "Europe." Polish–Belarusian relations were good in 1992 and 1993, so long as Belarus was interested in a rapprochement with western institutions. After Lukashenka turned Belarusian foreign policy eastward, Poland's western credentials became a positive barrier to good relations. By that time, Poland had signed a treaty with Belarus, to which it could refer when the rights of Poles in Belarus were violated. Lithuania, on the other hand, was uninterested in Polish help in 1992 and 1993, as it believed it could balance its foreign policy between east and west, and pursue a "Scandinavian road to Europe" in any case. Once Poland began to seem like an essential partner in European integration, Lithuania became willing to accept a treaty which protected the rights of its Polish minority.[102] The association of Poland with "Europe" works against traditional stereotypes of Poland as aggressor and thereby eases suspicions and fosters cooperation. Because the myth of a prosperous European future can counteract the myth of an imperialist Polish past, the success of Poland in protecting its eastern minorities depends upon the appeal of the west to Poland's eastern neighbors.

For most representatives of the Polish state, "Europe" has been the end as well as the means of Poland's eastern policy. While the Polish foreign ministry and other Polish officials have sought to protect the eastern diaspora, this goal has been a tertiary priority: less important than European integration, and less important than helping eastern neighbors consolidate their independence. It is true that the plight of Polish minorities has attracted sufficient attention to momentarily derail official Polish policy in an area of interest (as in Lithuania) and fundamentally alter Polish policy in an area of little importance (as in Kazakhstan). Such cases are to be expected, as Poles in Poland certainly regard (in the abstract, at least) the eastern diaspora as part of the Polish nation, and in times of crisis will rally to support eastern Poles. In such circumstances, conservative parliamentarians and the Polish Community come to the fore and take actions which countervail the general direction of Polish policy. But these moments are rare and fleeting, because few Poles in Poland regard the position of eastern minorities as a significant political issue, and fewer still recognize non-Polish-speakers as co-nationals when they meet them in Poland. Whereas politically aware eastern Poles regard themselves as exemplars of Polish tradition, eastern lands and history are no longer deeply implicated in the national identity of Poles in Poland.

This cultural reorientation allowed reforming Polish elites to realize a new foreign policy paradigm after 1989, one which stressed the return to Europe and the independence of eastern neighbors rather than the national uniqueness of Poland and the historical rights of Poles abroad. Growing recognition of the desirability of membership in the European Union and NATO has rendered this set of priorities the common property of most of the Polish political class, and refined the historically emerging popular vision of a westerly Poland to include Poland's membership in western institutions.[103] The promise of a west European future outshines the gilded but fading memories of Poland's eastern mission, and neither the definition of the Polish nation nor that of the Polish state requires a diaspora. Although Poles can still be roused to aid their kindred in the east, and although Polish officials will continue to protect eastern minorities, in this sense today's Poland is a post-diasporic state.

Notes

The author would like to thank the U.S. embassies in Vilnius and Minsk for their kind help, and representatives of the Polish, Lithuanian, Belarusian, and Ukrainian governments, press, and academy for their willingness to be interviewed. Thanks also to Steve Burant for a characteristically close reading. This essay was written while the author was a postdoctoral fellow at the Olin Institute for Strategic Studies, Harvard University. Much of the research was carried out during a stay at the Institut für die Wissenschaften vom Menschen, Vienna.

1. There are also small Polish minorities in the Czech Republic and Slovakia, which fall beyond the scope of this analysis.

2. For a subtler account which distinguishes six phases in the creation of the Polish diaspora in the east, see Hieronim Kubiak, "Polacy i Polonia w ZSRR: kwestie terminologiczne, perodyzacja, rozmieszczenie przestrenne, szacunki ilościowe," in Hieronim Kubiak et al., eds., *Mniejszości Polskie i Polonia w ZSRR* (Wroclaw: Ossolineum, 1992), especially pp. 20–21.

3. It has been argued that russification in Belarusian lands actually favored Polish culture, in that politically active Belarusians chose the Polish cause as more likely to succeed than the Belarusian one. See M. Dovnar-Zapolsky, "The Basis of White Russia's State Individuality," Hrodna 1919, reprinted in Vitaut Kipel and Zora Kipel, *Byelorussian Statehood* (New York: Byelorussia Academy of Arts and Sciences, 1988), 47–48.

4. See J. S. Pawłow, "Represje wobec osadników polskich w zachodnich odwodach Białorusi," in Małgorzata Giżejewska and Tomasz Strzembosz, eds., *Społeczeństwo białoruskie, litewskie i polskie na ziemach północno-wschodnich II Rzeczypospolitej w latach 1939–1941* (Warsaw: Instytut Studiów Politycznych, 1995), 370; Piotr Eberhardt, "Przemiany narodowościowe na Białorusi," *Przegląd wschodni* 2, no. 3 (1992–93): 541.

5. The dispute among Polish historians as to the number actually deported during this period continues, with estimates ranging from 300,000 to one million. For the debate, see "Sprawozdanie z dyskusji dotyczającej liczby obywateli polskich wywiezionych do Związku Sowieckiego w latach 1939–1941," *Studia z Dziejów Rosji i Europy Środkowej* 30, no. 1 (1996): 117–48. For an excellent account of the first Soviet occupation, see Jan T. Gross, *Revolution from Abroad: The Soviet Conquest of Poland's Western Ukraine and Western Belorussia* (Princeton: Princeton University Press, 1988).

6. On the basis of agreements of September 9 and 22, 1944, 1,227,000 Poles were "repatriated" from Poland's former eastern territories. Another 256,000 left in a second wave of "repatriations" in 1956 and 1957. Philipp Ther, taking into account eastern Poles who were in Siberia or Germany during the war, reaches an estimate of 2.1 million. See his "The Integration of Expellees in Germany and Poland after World War II: A Historical Reassessment," *Slavic Review* 55, no. 4 (1996): 779.

7. For sources related to the "repatriation" and dispersal of Ukrainians, see Volodymyr Serhiichyk, *Etnichni mezhi i derzhavnii kordon Ukrainy* (Ternopil': Vydavnytstvo Ternopil', 1996), 143ff.

8. Antonina Kłoskowska, *Kultury narodowe u korzeni* (Warsaw: PWN, 1996), 300.

9. Mikołaj Iwanow, "Stan i potrzeby badań nad polską mniejszością narodową w Związku Radzieckim," in Kubiak et al., eds., *Mniejszości Polskie*, 35.

10. For accounts of oppositionists, see Jacek Kuron, *Wiara i wina: do i od komunizmu* (London: Aneks, 1989), 347; and the interview with Adam Michnik in

Roman Solchanyk, *Ukraine: From Chernobyl to Sovereignty. A Collection of Interviews* (New York: St. Martin's Press, 1992), 59–64. For western summaries, see Ilya Prizel, "The Influence of Ethnicity on Foreign Policy: The Case of Ukraine," in Roman Szporluk, ed., *National Identity and Ethnicity in Russia and the New States of Eurasia* (Armonk: M. E. Sharpe, 1994), 108; and Stephen Burant, "Overcoming the Past: Polish–Lithuanian Relations, 1990–1995," *Journal of Baltic Studies* 37, no. 4 (1996): 313–18. For further references, see Włodzimierz Brylewski, "Kronika białoruska," *Kultura*, no. 416 (May 1982): 130; Józef Darski, "Kronika białoruska," *Kultura*, no. 471 (December 1986): 96; and Antoni Pospielaszki, "Kościół katolicki i białoruskie odrodzenie," *Kultura*, no. 505 (October 1989): 99.

11. For influential examples see Kazimierz Podlaski, *Białorusini, Litwini, Ukraińcy*, which was published illegally several times from 1983 and received Solidarity's cultural award in 1985; and Juliusz Mieroszewski, "Polska 'ostpolitik,'" *Kultura*, no. 309 (June 1973); as well as Juliusz Mieroszewski, "Rosyjski 'kompleks polski' i obszar ULB," *Kultura*, no. 324 (September 1974). See also Józef Darski, "Kronika białoruska," *Kultura*, no. 471 (December 1986): 95–97.

12. For some survey data which is consistent with this observation, see "Spoleczenstwo polskie wobec otwartych granic," *CBOS serwis informacyjny*, March 1993, p. 12. For the personal recollections of eastern Poles, see Thomas Szayna, "Ethnic Poles in Lithuania and Belarus: Current Situation and Migration Potential," *Rand Corporation Report*, August 1993, p. 26; Andrzej Ratkiewicz, "Cztery tysiące studentów," *Rzeczpospolita*, April 16, 1996, p. 3.

13. For example, "Współpraca na Zachodzie, życzliwość na Wschodzie," *Rzeczpospolita*, April 30–May 1, 1993; and "Polityka nie musi być w kolizji z moralnoscią," *Życie Warszawy*, June 15, 1993, p. 11. On this point generally see Ilya Prizel, "Warsaw's Ostpolitik: A New Encounter with Positivism," in Ilya Prizel and Andrew Michta, eds., *Polish Foreign Policy Reconsidered* (New York: St. Martin's Press, 1995), 96–102.

14. Examples will be developed in context below. For statements which suggest this order of priorities, see "Skubiszewski Briefs Sejm on Eastern Policy," Warsaw PAP in English, November 18, 1992, in *FBIS-EEU*, November 24, 1992, p. 23; "Wystąpienie Pana Ministra Dariusza Rosatiego na sesji Senatu RP poświęconej Polonii i Polakom zagranicą," unpublished document, Polish Ministry of Foreign Affairs, March 4, 1997; and "Polska polityka zagraniczna a Polonia i Polacy zagranicą," unpublished document, Polish Ministry of Foreign Affairs, March 1997. These documents and others listed in the notes below are available at http://www.urm.pl/mszdpi.html.

15. "Wystąpienie Pana Ministra Dariusza Rosatiego," 5.

16. Janina Paradowska, "Wspólnota Polska," *Polityka*, November 2, 1996, p. 6.

17. V. A. Tishkov, ed., *Narody Rossii: entsiklopediia* (Moscow: Bol'shaia Rossiiskaia Entsiklopediia, 1994), 268. The practice in Poland since the 1920s has been to assume that Russian counts of ethnic Poles must be multiplied by a factor of two to two and a half. I will make no such systematic adjustments for three reasons. First, in my estimation the correction for the Soviet Union as a whole

would be more like a factor of one and a half. Second, it makes very little difference for my purposes whether or not the actual number of Poles in Russia, Kazakhstan, Latvia, or Ukraine is larger than official estimates. The number will remain exceedingly small in comparison to other nationalities in these republics. Third, the use of these low estimates for Lithuania and Belarus, where Poles are numerous, insulates the argument from certain criticisms. It is often contended that people in these republics who call themselves Poles do so for conjunctural reasons of self-interest. Relying upon the Soviet census ensures that the populations in question not only chose Polish identity before the revolution in Poland, but in a Soviet Union which strongly discouraged this choice.

18. Some small number are also more recent migrants from Lithuania, Belarus, or Ukraine. On the history of forced migration of Poles to Kazakhstan, see Artur Kijas, "Polacy w Kazachstanie: Przeszłość i teraźniejszość," *Przegląd wschodni* 2, no. 1 (1992–93): 33–47. Detailed treatment of the fate of Poles deported from Soviet Ukraine to Kazakhstan in the 1930s can be found in Henryk Stroński, "Polska droga do Kazachstanu," *Przegląd wschodni* 3, no. 2 (1994): 145–64. On deportations from Soviet Belarus, see Pawłow, "Represje," 372–74. The literature on Polish deportees to Siberia is enormous. On the period before the Second World War, see Mikołaj Iwanow, *Pierwszy naród ukarany: Polacy w Związku Radzieckim 1921–1939* (Warsaw–Wrocław: PWN, 1991). For a reliable treatment of the history of formerly Polish eastern territories and their inhabitants during the Second World War, see Piotr Eberhardt, *Polska granica wschodnia, 1939–1945* (Warsaw: Editions Spotkania, 1993).

19. On Polish language and culture in Kazakhstan, see Tadeusz Samborski, "Polonia sowiecka" (interview with Polish consul–general Roman Brzoż), *Kultura*, nos. 496–97 (January–February 1989): 108–12.

20. See for example Jan Skorzyński, "Z polakami na Syberii," *Rzeczpospolita*, April 12, 1996, p. 6.

21. Andrzej Kaczyński, "Lekcja polskiego," *Rzeczpospolita*, August 12, 1996, p. 3.

22. The Poles are not even mentioned in demographic studies, such as M. Kh. Asylbekov and A. B. Galiev, *Sotsial'no-demograficheskie protsessy v Kazakhstane (1917–1980)* (Almaty: Gylym, 1991).

23. On Polish teachers in Kazakhstan, see Barbara Pietkiewicz, "Pan Jurek, bez nas zginiesz!" *Polityka*, August 24, 1996, pp. 24–25.

24. "Kazakhstan Poles Want to Return to Ukraine," Warsaw PAP in English, March 23, 1992, in *FBIS-EEU*, March 27, 1992, p. 27; "Poles in Kazakhstan Seek Return to Homeland," Warsaw PAP in English, August 10, 1992, in *FBIS-EEU*, August 14, 1992, p. 14.

25. This account is drawn from Paradowska, "Wspólnota Polska;" "Wystąpienie Pana Ministra Dariusza Rosatiego;" and "Polska polityka zagraniczna."

26. Eryk Jekabson, "Stosunki polsko-łotewskie na przestrzeni dziejów," in Edward Walewander, ed., *Polacy na Łotwie* (Lublin: Katolicki Uniwersytet Lubelski, 1993), 23–43.

27. Wanda Krukowska, "Działalność Związku Polaków na Łotwie," in Walewander, ed., *Polacy na Łotwie*, 303–4.

28. For an excellent history of Polish colonization of Ukrainian lands, see Daniel Beauvois, *La bataille de la terre en Ukraine, 1863–1914* (Lille: Presses Universitaires de Lille, 1993).

29. The best source on these events is Ryszard Torzecki, *Polacy i Ukraińcy: Sprawa ukraińska w czasie II wojny światowej na terenie II Rzeczypospolitej* (Warsaw: PWN, 1993). For a provocative and controversial Ukrainian account see Viktor Polishchuk, *Hirka pravda: zlochynnist' OUN–UPA* (Toronto: n. p., 1995).

30. Kubiak, "Polacy i Polonia," 30.

31. For a personal account of the felt absence of Polishness in Lviv, see Krzysztof Masłoń, "Lwowskie klimaty," *Rzeczpospolita*, April 6–8, 1996, pp. 6–8. That noted, it should be added that it is not difficult to find Ukrainians from western Ukraine who speak very good Polish.

32. Bohdan Osadczuk, "To były najszczęśliwsze dnie w moim życiu" (interview with Polish ambassador in Kyiv, Jerzy Kozakiewicz), *Kultura*, nos. 532–33 (January–February 1992): 21; Susan Stewart, "Ukraine's Policy toward its Ethnic Minorities," *RFE/RL Research Report*, September 10, 1993, pp. 55–62.

33. These problems in Polish–Ukrainian relations are considered in Tim Snyder, "The Polish–Lithuanian Commonwealth Since 1989: National Narratives in Relations among Poland, Lithuania, Belarus, and Ukraine," in Jeffrey Kopstein and Adam Seligman, eds., *Recasting Political and Social Identities in Eastern Europe* (forthcoming 1998).

34. For more on the declaration, see Steve Burant, "Ukraine and Poland: Toward a Strategic Partnership," paper prepared for the conference "Intellectuals, Culture, and Politics," Kyiv, June 5–7, 1997.

35. "Pomoc dla Polaków," *Rzeczpospolita*, October 10, 1996, p. 6.

36. For a sophisticated example, see Algirdas Budreckis, "Demographic Problems of Vilnius Province," in Algirdas Budreckis, ed., *Eastern Lithuania: A Collection of Historical and Ethnographic Studies* (Chicago: Lithuanian Association of the Vilnius Region, 1985), 314–15.

37. Józef Darski, "Kronika litewska, białoruska i ukraińska," *Kultura*, no. 512 (May 1990): 87–88; Stephen Burant, "Belarus and the Belarusian Irredenta in Lithuania," *Nationalities Papers* (forthcoming): 5–6.

38. Jan Zaprudnik, *Belarus: At a Crossroads in History* (Boulder: Westview, 1993), 221. This view is also widely held by Belarusian intellectuals. See Burant, "Belarus and the Belarusian Irredenta," 7–9.

39. For the view of the secretary of the Belarusian National Front in 1991, see "Interview with Vintsuk Vyachorka," *Uncaptive Minds* (Fall 1991): 211. See also Józef Darski, "Z lektury czasopism białoruskich," *Kultura*, no. 505 (October 1989): 106. For the revanchist claims, see Józef Darski, "Kronika litewska i białoruska," *Kultura*, no. 535 (April 1992).

40. "Country Asks UN Help for Ethnic Belarusians in Baltics," Moscow Segodnya in Russia, April 9, 1994, in *FBIS-SOV*, April 11, 1994, p. 45.

41. For the ethnographic accounts, see Lech Mróz, "Problemy etniczne w Litwie wschodniej," *Przegląd wschodni* 1, no. 3 (1991): 496; Jacek Kuśmierz, "Między 'wschodem' a 'zachodem:' stosunki etniczne na Wileńszczyźnie w wypowiedziach jej mieszkanców," *Przegląd wschodni* 1, no. 3 (1991): 507–8.

42. However, there were also notable concentrations in major cities beyond this area. This number is based upon Piotr Eberhardt's adjustments of the 1897 Russian census. Eberhardt, "Przemiany narodowościowe na Białorusi," 530; Piotr Eberhardt, "Przemiany narodowościowe na Litwie w XX wieku," *Przegląd wschodni* 1, no. 3 (1991): 454–57.

43. Piotr Eberhardt, "Struktura narodowościowa Polski północno-wschodniej w latach trzydziestych XX wieku," in Giżejewska and Strzembosz, eds., *Społeczeństwo*, 48 (on religion and language), 53 (for population estimates).

44. For a Belarusian view of these events, see Wasilij Kusznier, "Wybrane problemy stosunków białorusko-polskich w latach 1920–1944 we współczesnej historiografii białoruskiej," in Giżejewska and Strzembosz, eds., *Społeczeństwo*, 14; see also Alexander Chackiewicz, "Aresztowania i deportacje społeczeństwa zachodnich obwodów Białorusi (1939–1941)," in the same volume, p. 136.

45. Poles had the lowest educational attainments and were least well represented in the professions in both Lithuania and Belarus.

46. This point is perceptively made in Anne Applebaum, *Between East and West* (London: Macmillan, 1995), 94.

47. Poles in Belarus were less likely than their Belarusian or Russian neighbors to join the communist party. Zdzisław Winnicki, "Polacy na Białorusi," in Jacek Pietraś and Andrzej Czarnocki, eds., *Polityka narodowościowa państw Europy Środkowowschodniej* (Lublin: Instytut Europy Środkowo-Wschodniej, 1993), 199.

48. Juozis Lakis, "Ethnic Minorities in the Postcommunist Transformation of Lithuania," *International Sociology* 10, no. 2 (1995): 179.

49. In 1953, 27,000 students studied in Polish schools or studied Polish in non-Polish schools. By 1987 this number had fallen to 10,133. Grzegorz Błaszczyk, "Polacy na Litwie. Zarys problematyki historycznej i współczesnej," *Przegląd wschodni* 1, no. 1 (1991): 156. On the preference of Polish children to study in Polish, see Lakis, "Ethnic Minorities," 180.

50. Eberhardt, "Przemiany narodowościowe na Litwie ," 478.

51. Szayna, "Ethnic Poles," 35.

52. Kuśmierz, "Między 'wschodem' a 'zachodem'," 512–13; Mróz, "Problemy etniczne w Litwie wschodniej," 496; Szayna, "Ethnic Poles," vii.

53. On Moscow's strategy, see Anatol Lieven, *The Baltic Revolution: Estonia, Latvia, Lithuania and the Path to Independence* (New Haven: Yale University Press, 1993), 167; and Szayna, "Ethnic Poles," 15. For Landsbergis's reaction, see "Landsbergis on Relations with Poland," Lithuanian Radio, September 25, 1991, *SWB-SU*, September 27, 1991.

54. Problems of Lithuanian–Polish relations between 1989 and 1994 are treated at greater length in Tim Snyder, "National Myths and International Relations: Poland and Lithuania, 1989–1994," *East European Politics and Societies* 9, no. 2 (1995): 317–44.

55. Piotr Lossowski, "The Polish Minority in Lithuania," *Polish Quarterly of International Affairs* 1, nos. 1–2 (1992): 73.

56. Szayna, "Ethnic Poles," vii. See also Kuśmierz, "Między 'wschodem' a 'zachodem,'" 513.

57. Nikolaj Iwanov, "Die Polen Weissruslands," *Osteuropa* 44, no. 5 (1994): 473.

58. For Skubiszewski's position in 1990, see Leon Brodowski, "Niepodległość in statu nascendi," *Lithuania*, no. 2 (1991).

59. Józef Darski, "Kronika litewska, białoruska i ukraińska," *Kultura*, nos. 520–521 (January–February 1991).

60. "Poland Termed 'Greatest Threat,'" Warsaw Słowo Powszechne in Polish, in *FBIS-SOV*, November 27, 1991, p. 36. Another source of Lithuanian insecurity is a long term concern over low birth rates. See V. Stankuniene and A. Sipaviciene, "Evolution de la population et problèmes démographiques en Lithuanie," *Populations* 47, no. 1 (1992): 216.

61. "Skubiszewski Criticized Over Lithuanian Visit," Warsaw PAP in English, January 15, 1992, in *FBIS-EEU*, January 22, 1992, p. 20; "Visiting Delegation Discusses Poles in Lithuania," Warsaw PAP in English, March 20, 1992, in *FBIS-EEU*, March 23, 1993, pp. 15–16.

62. See Edward Krzemień, "Dwa nacjonalizmy," *Gazeta wyborcza*, January 18, 1992, p. 1.

63. For this incident, see "Problems Over Polish Minority's Status Noted," Moscow Interfax in English, December 24, 1991, in *FBIS-SOV*, December 26, 1991, p. 36; "Landsbergis Attacks 'Impermissable Remarks' About Lithuania in Polish Sejm," Lithuanian Radio, in *SWB-SU*, December 23, 1991.

64. For example, "Skubiszewski Briefs Sejm on Eastern Policy," Warsaw PAP in English, November 18, 1992, in *FBIS-EEU*, November 24, 1992, p. 23; Zygmunt Fura, "Polska mniejszość ma prawo do samorządu" (interview with Mariusz Maszkiewicz), *Czas krakowski*, May 26, 1992, pp. 3–4.

65. This is the major subject of Snyder, "National Myths and International Relations."

66. "Defence Minister on Russian Army Withdrawal, Lack of Policy Towards Poland," Lithuanian Radio in Russian, July 23, 1993, in *SWB-SU*, July 27, 1993. He had come around to advocating NATO membership very early in the game. "Butkevicius Favors Joining NATO," Vilnius Radio in Lithuanian, September 3, 1993, in *FBIS-SOV*, September 8, 1993, p. 105.

67. See "Lietuvos Respublikos politinių partijų pareiškimas dėl padėties rytų Lietuvoje," *Atgimimas*, October 27, 1993, reprinted as "Lituaische Politiker und Parteien zur aktuellen Situation der Polen in Litauen," *Dokumentation Ostmitteleuropa* 20, nos. 1–2 (1994): 116–19.

68. "Polska polityka zagraniczna w 1996 roku," unpublished document, Polish Ministry of Foreign Affairs, 1997; "Szkoły polskie na Litwie," unpublished document, Polish Foreign Ministry, February 1997; "Polish–Lithuanian Relations," *OMRI Daily Digest*, January 2, 1997.

69. Olena Skwiecińska, "Kochamy Litwinów," *Gazeta wyborcza*, April 28, 1994, p. 6; Alexander Kwaśniewski, "Address to the Lithuanian Parliament in Vilnius," March 16, 1996; "Polish Sejm Speaker Discusses Relations," Tallinn BNS in English, October 25, 1994, in *FBIS-SOV*, October 26, 1994, p. 57; Joźef Oleksy, "Toast at the official dinner given in his honour by Mr. Adolfas Slezevicius, Prime Minister of the Lithuanian Republic," September 16, 1995.

70. "Lithuanian Foreign Minister Visits Poland," *OMRI Daily Digest*, January 7, 1997.

71. Maja Narbutt, "Niepokój o traktat," *Rzeczpospolita*, April 27–28, 1996, p. 23.

72. "New Polish Organization Formed in Lithuania," *OMRI Daily Digest*, October 17, 1995.

73. Tadeusz Gawin, *Ojcowizna. Odrodzenie polskości na Białorusi* (Hrodna and Lublin: Fundacja Pomocy Śzkołom Polskim na Wschodzie im. Tadeusza Goniewicza, 1993), 38. Gawin is the leader of the Union of Poles in Belarus.

74. Iwanow, "Die Polen Weissrusslands," 474.

75. Dariusz Rostkowski, "Polski po pół wieku," *Polityka*, October 5, 1996, p. 40; Gawin, *Ojcowizna*, 63.

76. On the spread of Polish-language instruction, see Rostkowski, "Polski po pół wieku," 40; Iwanow, "Die Polen Weissrusslands," 480; Iwona Kabzińska-Stawarz, "Polacy na Białorusi: relacja z badań nad wspołczesnym procesem kszałtowania się świadomości etnicznej," *Przegląd wschodni* 2, no. 3 (1992–93): 684; Waldemar Preckajło, "Pierwsza w pierwszej szkole," *Głos znad Niemna*, May 29–June 4, 1995, p. 2; Waldemar Preckajło, "Chcemy rozmawiać po polsku," *Głos znad Niemna*, January 2–14, 1996, p. 1.

77. Liliana Urbanowicz, "Wyświęcenie kaplanów," *Głos znad Niemna*, July 3–9, 1995, p. 1. *Głos znad Niemna*, the newspaper of Poles in Belarus, has the highest circulation of newspapers in the Hrodna (Grodno) region.

78. Józef Darski, "Kronika litewska, białoruska i ukraińska," *Kultura*, no. 512 (May 1990): 86.

79. Gawin, *Ojcowizna*, 88, 104, 119, 123, 136, 158.

80. For examples of joint meetings and demonstrations of Poles and Belarusians, see Gawin, *Ojcowizna*, 81, 90.

81. Poles surveyed cited religious issues as harming otherwise good relations with Belarusians. See Szayna, "Ethnic Poles," 38–39. One Belarusian National Front deputy, Markevich, consistently defended the rights of his Polish constituents. See Stanisław Wojna, "Opozycjoniści mogą być dumni z swej działalności," *Głos znad Niemna*, May 8–14, 1995, p. 3. For the views of a representative of the Hramada party on Polish priests, see "Nie zgadzamy się z taką oceną," *Głos znad Niemna*, January 9–15, 1995, p. 4.

82. Gawin, *Ojcowizna*, 27–28; "Chairman Shushkevich Reviews Ties With Poland," Wrocław Gazeta Robotnicza in Polish, June 13–14, 1991, in *FBIS-EEU*, June 25, 1992, p. 63.

83. This is not to say that there were previously no Belarusian Catholics. Many of the leading lights of the Belarusian national revival of the turn of the century were Roman Catholics.

84. Winnicki, "Polacy na Białorusi," 201–2; Gawin, *Ojcowizna*, 149.

85. See Applebaum, *Between East and West*, 100–6, for an illuminating anecdote.

86. Mróz, "Problemy etniczne w Litwie wschodniej," 688, 691.

87. Szayna, "Ethnic Poles," 52.

88. Jan Krauze, "Foreign Ministry on Establishing Eastern Policy," *Le Monde*, March 8-9, 1992, in *FBIS-EEU*, April 10, 1992, p. 27.

89. Tadeusz Kossobudzki, "Stracone szansy," *Kultura*, no. 560, May 1994, p. 21. See also "Suchocka Signs Economic Agreements With Belarus," Warsaw PAP in English, November 19, 1992, in *FBIS-EEU*, November 19, 1992, p. 16.

90. "Holds News Conference With Shushkevich," Minsk Radio in Belarusian, June 28, 1993, in *FBIS-SOV*, June 29, 1993, p. 61; "Polish Leader Addresses Supreme Soviet," Minsk Radio in Belarusian, June 29, 1993, in *FBIS-SOV*, June 30, 1993, p. 64; "Says Poland Has 'No Territorial Claims' on Belarus," Moscow Itar-Tass in English, June 29, 1993, in *FBIS-SOV*, June 30, 1993, p. 64.

91. For an example from Wałęsa, see "Cooperation Agreements Signed with Byelarussia," Warsaw PAP in English, April 24, 1992, in *FBIS-EEU*, April 28, 1992, p. 15.

92. For an example from Skubiszewski, see "Diplomatic Relations Established," Warsaw TVP Television, March 2, 1992, in *FBIS-EEU*, March 3,1992, p. 11.

93. Stephen R. Burant, "International Relations in a Regional Context: Poland and its Eastern Neighbors—Lithuania, Belarus, Ukraine," *Europe–Asia Studies* 45, no. 3 (1995): 407.

94. "Poland's Struzik Discusses NATO, Priests, Trade," Warsaw Polskie Radio, April 4, 1995, in *FBIS-SOV*, April 5, 1995, p. 63; Maja Narbutt, "Nie ufać Warszawie," *Rzeczpospolita*, May 4–5, 1996, p. 1; Tadeusz Gawin, "Jak długo będziemy wierzyli w dobrego cara?" *Głos znad Niemna*, July 31–August 6, 1995, p. 3. For a Polish argument that Lukashenka's talk of "polonization" conceals an attack on Belarusian nationalism, see Julian Czapla, "Jeszcze raz o tak zwanym 'opalaczywaniju,'" *Głos znad Niemna*, May 8–14, 1995, p. 4.

95. "Poles Accuse Authorities of Discrimination," Warsaw TVP Second Program in Polish, February 9, 1995, in *FBIS-SOV*, February 10, 1995, p. 56; Tadeusz Gawin, "Pod naciskiem dyktatu," *Głos znad Niemna*, December 4–10, 1995, p. 1; Ryszard Karaczun, "Jak rodak z rodakiem," *Głos znad Niemna*, November 20–26, 1995, p. 1.

96. "W obronie naszych racji," *Głos znad Niemna*, February 17–23, 1997, pp. 1–2; Rostkowski, "Polski po pół wieku."

97. Ryszard Karaczun, "Z drogi odrodzenia nie zejdziemy" (interview with Tadeusz Gawin), *Głos znad Niemna*, September 23–29, 1996, p. 1.

98. Cezary Goliński, "Prezydent Łukaszenko przepisuje historię," *Gazeta wyborcza*, August 17, 1995, p. 9.

99. Paradowska, "Wspólnota Polska," 5.

100. "Konsulat Generalny RP już działa," *Głos znad Niemna*, June 26–July 2, 1995, p. 1.

101. See for example Marcel Scotto, "Paris rechigne à signer la convention européenne sur les minorités," *Le Monde*, February 23, 1995, p. 2.

102. The argument about the leverage provided by the promise of future European integration is a major theme of Milada Vachudová, *Systemic and Domestic Determinants of East Central European Foreign Policies* (D.Phil. thesis, University of Oxford, 1997).

103. For a summary of related survey data see Kłoskowska, *Kultury narodowe*, especially p. 386. See also "Polska–NATO," *CBOS serwis informacyjny*, June 1996, p. 24.

9

Conclusion: Diasporas, International Relations, and Post-Soviet Eurasia

Neil J. Melvin and Charles King

The demise of the Soviet Union produced a dramatic reconfiguration of political space across eastern Europe and Eurasia. In place of the vast regions unified under a single set of party and state institutions, an array of independent states was established. The creation of these new political entities involved a fundamental redrawing of the political, economic, and strategic contours of the former Soviet lands. What were once administrative boundaries suddenly became interstate frontiers. A single, centralized economic system was transformed by the creation of separate national economies, which were in turn reshaped, in greater and lesser degrees, by market reforms. Once-dominant social and ethnic groups, whose positions rested on their privileged relationship with the structures of political and economic power within the Soviet system, were replaced by new networks controlled by rival political elites. Cultural and linguistic boundaries shifted in response to the policies of the newly independent governments aimed at "nationalizing" or "indigenizing" the territories under their control and rectifying what many saw as decades of dominance by "foreign" political actors. In place of a system of political legitimation based on the leading role of a Marxist–Leninist party, the new political entities turned to varying admixtures of nationalism, democracy, and the market to justify the monumental changes initiated in the late 1980s and consolidated after 1991.

The effort to erect a distinct set of political–cultural markers between the post-Soviet states has, however, been challenged by the presence of ethnic communities whose patterns of settlement stretch across the newly established international borders. The existence of these trans-border ethnic populations has raised a number of critical questions for the new states of eastern Europe and Eurasia: Should the identities of the post-

Soviet states be constituted according to territorial or ethnic criteria? What relationship should exist between the recognized political frontiers of the state and the amorphous, cultural boundaries of the nation that the state claims to represent? What place should ethnic or linguistic minorities occupy within both state and nation? And, most problematically, how should these states develop relations with elements of their national community resident beyond their territorial boundaries?

The issue of diasporas is not new in the former Soviet territories, for over the centuries the region has been characterized as much by the migration of borders as by the migration of populations, and indeed the former has often been the impetus for the latter. What in the 1990s has been termed "ethnic cleansing"—the effort to make coterminous the boundaries of nations and states—is a familiar project to the peoples of eastern Europe, Russia, the Transcaucasus, and Central Asia. In these areas demography has long been seen as the handmaiden of politics, with political leaders wielding a variety of ethnic, cultural, linguistic, and religious arguments to justify claims to territory.

But since 1991 the issue of trans-border ethnic groups has taken on a special significance in the political development of the post-Soviet republics. The current volume was conceived as a vehicle to explore the complex features of diaspora politics in the former Soviet Union. The essays were not envisaged as a comprehensive account of all the diaspora policies of the Soviet successor states, but rather as an investigation of the major factors that underlie diaspora politics in the region and the remarkable diversity of outcomes that these common factors have produced.

Moreover, although the principal task of *Nations Abroad* has been to provide an introduction to diaspora issues in the post-Soviet territories, this book also aims to contribute to wider debates about the role of transnational—or, more accurately, trans-state—actors in international politics, in particular the role of what we term "internationalized ethnicity:" the roots and ramifications of solidary and self-conscious ethnic populations acting beyond the boundaries of individual states. Above all, the task of these essays has been to examine the sources of diversity within diaspora relations and to move toward an analysis of the patterns of interaction among trans-border ethnic groups, their traditional ethnic homelands, and the states in which they reside.

The Dynamics of Diaspora Politics

The overriding impression that emerges from the studies in this volume is the enormous diversity of relationships among kin-states, host-states, and diasporas in the former Soviet Union. Some states have engaged in an active policy of encouraging diasporic return, while others have feared that reaching out to co-ethnic populations might produce a massive and unwelcome influx of immigrants. Some states have created high-level government institutions to maintain links with co-ethnic communities, while others have made work with the diaspora a secondary or even tertiary policy priority. Some states have eagerly promoted themselves as the homelands of distinct ethnic populations, while others have been engaged in the uncertain process of constructing identities based on both mono-ethnic and multi-ethnic visions of the state. The preceding chapters have cautioned against easy generalizations about the form and function of diaspora politics, for each case has illustrated rather different dimensions of internationalized ethnicity.

Russians

The sudden collapse of the Soviet system had a dramatic effect on the Russian populations of the region. The nature of the Russian community, notions of Russianness, and the geographical settlement of Russians across Eurasia had developed over the course of more than four hundred years in conjunction with the expansion of the Russian and Soviet empires. The disintegration of the imperial state in the late 1980s and its replacement with a set of (at least nominal) nation-states struck directly at the leading position of Russian communities within the republics; the establishment of a set of new state borders erected political barriers to these communities' acting in concert. With titular nations ascendant within the new states and with Russian language and culture in retreat, the future of the Russian populations in the early 1990s seemed uncertain.

Within this context, the emergence of diaspora politics served a number of purposes. First, it provided a means for the political elite within the Russian Federation to regroup following the disorientation of the perestroika years. In an environment with very few markers to indicate future policy directions, the discovery—or invention—of a Russian diaspora served as the basis for developing a consensus about Russia's new identity: Russia became defined as an ethnic homeland, a diasporic state with responsibilities toward a diaspora beyond its frontiers. Second, diaspora politics created an apparently legitimate basis for an active Russian engagement with the internal and external affairs of the new states of Eurasia. At a time when many of the non-Russian successor states and the international community were harshly critical of Russia's "neo-imperial" designs, the Russian government was able to couch its interests in the "near abroad" in broadly humanitarian terms. Concern for the cultural, linguistic, educational, and political rights of the Russian diaspora became an important component of Russian official discourse, even if the meaning of "Russian" itself remained the subject of considerable debate in Moscow.

However, as Neil J. Melvin argued, the process of diasporization was not without its difficulties. Identifying an obvious and clearly bounded Russian community resident outside the Russian Federation that could legitimately be called a "diaspora" was problematic. Patterns of settlement and the history of Russian imperial expansion since the sixteenth century had produced a multi-ethnic, multi-confessional, and multilingual population whose sense of Russianness and attachment to the Russian Federation were mutable and contingent. The notion of a Russian diaspora, therefore, emerged from a hybrid of ethnic, linguistic, historical, political, and crypto-spiritual definitions. This hybridity—which included, at one point, a definition of the diaspora as the "ethnic citizens" of Russia—permitted the Russian Federation to claim a legitimate right to speak on behalf of its diaspora, but it provided little basis for concrete policy programs. By the late 1990s, the meaning of Russianness, both at home and abroad, remained as ill-defined as before, and Russia's policy pronouncements concerning its diaspora, while provoking strong reactions from nervous post-Soviet governments, had produced little in the way of practical assistance to Russian settler communities.

Jews

The Jews have historically been seen as the archetypal diaspora community, but the Holocaust and the creation of the state of Israel altered the significance of dispersal for many Jews. The demise of the Soviet Union marked another important moment for the Jewish diaspora, both within the former Soviet territories and elsewhere. The events of the late 1980s and early 1990s opened the way for an unprecedented level of contact between Soviet and world Jewry, and between Soviet Jews and Israel. This increased contact, however, brought to light the highly variegated nature of a diaspora that is nevertheless united by a common identity, religion, and historical narrative of dispersal.

The most significant component of diaspora politics in the Jewish case has been migration from the Soviet Union to Israel and, to a lesser degree, the United States. Like the case of Kazakhstan considered below, the "return" of Jews from the diaspora to Israel provided a much-needed infusion of new co-ethnics to a homeland threatened by the demographic strength of other ethnic groups (Russians/Slavs in the case of Kazakhstan and Arabs/Palestinians in the case of Israel). Soviet Jewry represented the last sizable diaspora resource available to the Israeli state, and the emigration of Jews from the Soviet Union was broadly embraced by the homeland, at least at an official level.

Interestingly, though, the pattern of Jewish migration has also led to the emergence of a sub-diaspora—"a diaspora within a diaspora," in Zvi Gitelman's terms—of Russian-speaking Jews in Israel, the United States, and elsewhere, a new community that is more closely linked than other diaspora returnees to the Jews who have remained behind in the former Soviet Union. While Israel has remained the principal point of reference for Jews in the Soviet successor states, identities and loyalties continue to be influenced by a variety of factors beyond the Israeli kin-state and the states of Jewish settlement. Unlike the other cases examined in this volume, Soviet Jews lacked a commonly accepted homeland within the former Soviet bloc (the effort to establish a "Jewish territory" in the Russian Far East notwithstanding). Diaspora relations in this context have thus been different from those of most other communities in this study. Diaspora politics has primarily been conducted between agents beyond the states of the former Soviet Union. The governments of Israel and the United States, and former Soviet Jewish communities in both these states, have been far more important actors within the diaspora than the former Soviet republics. Intra-diaspora dynamics, rather than relations between states and ethnic communities, have been the motor of Jewish diaspora politics.

Armenians

For the Armenians the relationship between diaspora and homeland was considerably complicated by the establishment of an Armenian republic within the Soviet Union. The Armenian Soviet Socialist Republic represented a nominal homeland for Armenians, but it was a homeland located outside the traditional Armenian heartland in Anatolia. After the 1920s the Armenian republic and the Armenian diaspora, therefore, became alternative and often rival agents for developing and sustaining Armenian national consciousness.

From the 1960s the consolidation of Soviet Armenians within the Armenian SSR and the increasing assertiveness of the Armenian state in its relations with the diaspora gradually challenged the leading role that diaspora organizations, such as the Dashnaks, had previously held within the Armenian national community. The collapse of the Soviet

Union intensified this development and exposed a number of new dimensions in homeland–diaspora relations, including the uneasy rapprochement between the Armenian state and its territorially dislocated but highly organized diaspora. As Razmik Panossian showed, the form of diaspora politics that emerged from this contact was, following an initial honeymoon, characterized by tension and even conflict. Kin-state and diaspora became engaged in a competition for leadership of the national community both within the homeland and abroad, as the initial enthusiasm for diaspora returnees and their responsibility toward the kin-state gave way to disillusionment and a sense that the gulf between diaspora and homeland was greater than many had anticipated. Although many diaspora Armenians retain a sense of allegiance to "Armenia" as an abstract concept, and may feel a sense of duty to help co-ethnics within the Armenian state, the degree to which the homeland of the imagination is coterminous with the kin-state has remained questionable.

Ukrainians

Significant numbers of Ukrainians have lived in the west for many decades. During the Soviet years, these Ukrainian communities constituted a powerful lobby group promoting Ukrainian national ideals and calling for an independent Ukrainian state. The collapse of the Soviet system allowed elements of the western diaspora to influence developments within Ukraine directly and openly. At the same time, though, the emergence of an independent Ukraine also meant that Kyiv was in a position, for the first time, to address the question of its "eastern" diaspora. In this new environment, some Ukrainian political actors have sought to develop a form of diaspora politics that aims to "diasporize" proto-Ukrainian communities within the newly independent states of the former Soviet Union and eastern Europe.

However, engagement with the eastern diaspora has been restrained by the problem of sorting out the complex forms of interaction, assimilation, and engagement that have developed over the centuries between Ukrainians and Russians, Belarusians, Romanians, and Slovaks along the borderlands of eastern Europe. Who counts as a Ukrainian, as Andrew Wilson argued, has been extremely difficult to ascertain. Further, the factors shaping diaspora politics have frequently been contradictory. On the one hand, Ukraine's own weakly developed sense of nationhood has prompted some Ukrainian politicians to seek to build bridges to the eastern diaspora as a way of reinforcing nationalist credentials in the homeland. National revival abroad, some argue, is a key component of national revival at home. On the other hand, the multi-ethnic and multilingual character of Ukraine, with its large Russian and russified settler minorities who continue to form important segments of the political and economic elite, has provided a check on the state's ability to build links to a mono-ethnically defined diaspora. Concerned that an active diaspora policy might establish a precedent for interference from states with co-ethnics within Ukraine (primarily Russia) and constrained by the weak national identification of the potential diaspora and by the needs of civic nation building at home, Ukraine has normally sought to limit its engagement with the eastern communities. Calls for cultural renewal and the signing of cultural and educational agreements with neighboring host-states have been the primary forms of diaspora politics in Ukraine.

Kazakhs

The experience of Kazakhstan since the late 1980s suggests yet another form of diaspora politics. Independence for Kazakhstan took place against a background of relatively low nationalist mobilization. However, diaspora relations soon emerged as an important element of the new political regime. Significant numbers of Kazakhs had emigrated from Central Asia long before the establishment of a modern Kazakh national identity during the Soviet period. Within these communities, there was little affinity for Kazakhstan as a national homeland. Nevertheless, following independence the Kazakhstani government moved quickly to forge links with this newly discovered diaspora and to encourage the "return" of these populations to their newly independent Kazakh kin-state.

While the diasporization of Kazakhs outside Kazakhstan was in part prompted by a desire to bolster the legitimacy of Kazakhstani independence, the principal rationale for this policy was the need to alter the country's demographic balance in favor of ethnic Kazakhs. For the Kazakhstani leadership, national revival abroad was the *sine qua non* of national survival at home. However, the state's diasporization of Kazakhs outside Kazakhstan was highly selective, concentrating principally on Kazakhs resident in Turkey and elsewhere beyond the former Soviet Union and territorially contiguous states. Although Kazakhs located farther afield were less numerous than co-ethnic communities closer to Kazakhstan—such as in Russia or China—Kazakhstan's diaspora policy was constrained by the desire not to be perceived as meddling in the internal affairs of powerful neighbors.

As Sally N. Cummings argued, Kazakhstan thus faced an intriguing dilemma: On the one hand, encouraging diasporic return seemed the only way of rectifying the disadvantageous demographic situation of the titular nationality, and the populations with the clearest sense of loyalty to Kazakhstan were those that lived in adjacent states. But on the other hand, building bridges to co-ethnic communities in neighboring states (such as Russia) might encourage those states to take a more active interest in their own co-ethnic populations within Kazakhstan—populations that were likely to suffer as a result of the government's emphasis on "kazakhifying" the economic and political institutions of the newly independent state. The very policy that sought to redress the internal demographic problem, then, seemed destined to exacerbate the state's external political problems. By the late 1990s, however, other demographic and political dynamics within Kazakhstan had begun to alter the relative power balance between Kazakhs and Slavs in favor of the former. The "return" of ethnic Kazakhs continued to have an important symbolic function, but diaspora politics lost much of its earlier salience.

Volga Tatars

The case of the Tatars offers an experience very different from the other communities examined in this volume. Tatar diaspora politics illustrates the interrelationship between diasporization and the exigencies of nation and state building, even among the constituents of federations. Since the perestroika period, diaspora politics has been central to the Tatarstani political elite's strategy for wresting power from Moscow. The Tatarstani leadership sought to develop ties not just with Tatars living outside Tatarstan and within the former Soviet territories, but also with co-ethnic communities in Turkey, the United States, and Finland. The presence of Tatars outside the Russian Federation was used by Tatarstan to justify the establishment of inter-governmental relations with various Tatar host-states, an implicit acknowledgment of Tatarstan's sovereignty and its right to conduct a relatively autonomous foreign policy.

The diasporization of ethnic Tatars, the development of Tatarstan as a Tatar homeland, and the struggle for power with Moscow did not, though, lead to ethnic conflict or separatism. While diaspora politics permitted Kazan to present Tatarstan as the homeland for all Tatars, the Tatarstani leadership has argued that responsibility for the diaspora should be divided between Kazan and Moscow—with the former providing political and "moral" leadership and the latter underwriting the economic support for Tatar linguistic, educational, and cultural programs. In Tatarstan diaspora politics became an integral element of the republic's effort to claim greater power for itself within a political system undergoing a massive transformation in center–region relations. However, as Katherine E. Graney concluded, the establishment of connections with the diaspora also helped bind Tatarstan to Russia, providing a stimulus to reform the Russian state and encouraging the development of the multiple personal and political identities critical to the successful operation of both a multi-ethnic federation and a markedly multi-ethnic Tatarstan.

Poles

As with the Russians, the Polish case illustrates the degree to which the notion and significance of a diaspora are contingent upon the domestic politics and external ambitions of the homeland. The form of diaspora politics that emerged with respect to Polish populations after 1989, though, does offer one important contrast to the Russian experience. The geographical migration of Polish borders westward over the last two centuries, along with communist nationalities policy after 1917, created Polish communities in a variety of different locations across the former Soviet lands. Most significantly, important Polish populations are found in territories adjacent to Poland in Lithuania and Belarus, many of which are self-consciously Polish and see Poland as a legitimate kin-state.

These communities might have become an important lever for Poland's foreign relations with the former Soviet republics and a political resource for nationalist politicians in Warsaw. But the goal of pan-European integration, focusing on Polish accession to the major economic, political, and defense structures of the Euro-Atlantic space, has overridden any emotive attachment to the Polish diaspora and the "lost Polish lands" of the east. The Polish political elite has sought to cast Polish identity as fundamentally territorial and inclusively pan-European. There is little place in this vision of Poland's destiny for Poles left behind by the progressive westward movement of Polish borders. Poland has, therefore, sought to minimize its engagement with and responsibilities toward Poles living outside Poland, except for those communities in the west that can act as important lobbying groups for the Polish state. For the present, at any rate, Poland appears to operate as what Tim Snyder calls a "post-diasporic state," a state that—unusual in eastern Europe—has traded its obligations to a territorially dislocated nation for the prospect of integration into a territorially united Europe.

Patterns in Diaspora Politics

The collapse of the Soviet federation and the division of Soviet territory into new states challenged the populations of the region to reformulate basic notions of "home" and "abroad." As a result, new political relationships have developed between states, between states and their majority and minority populations, and between states and their newly identified diaspora communities. The evidence of the post-Soviet cases contained in this volume highlights the varied and complex nature of these developments. Some states have sought to downplay the significance of their diasporas or even to avoid a relationship with some co-ethnic populations abroad (Poland). Other states have struggled to foster a diaspora identity on the basis of communities with little notion of a link to an external homeland and with poorly defined diaspora boundaries (Russia). Some states have defined the diaspora primarily on the basis of communities "external" to the Soviet Union and have ignored "internal" diasporas within the post-Soviet republics themselves (Armenia and Kazakhstan). Others have defined the diaspora entirely in terms of "internal" groups, ignoring more affluent communities living in the west (Russia). Still others have sought to combine internal and external definitions of the diaspora (Ukraine and Tatarstan).

The specific policies pursued in relation to diaspora populations have also been diverse. While some states have focused on cultural and political ties (Ukraine and Tatarstan), others have encouraged the "return" of the diaspora to the homeland, even if the connection between diaspora and kin-state is tenuous (Israel and Kazakhstan). The extension of citizenship to diaspora communities has become the centerpiece of diaspora politics in some cases (Russia), while other states have deliberately avoided granting blanket citizenship or creating provisions for dual citizenship (Armenia and Ukraine). In some cases, the diaspora has been closely tied to broader foreign policy aims (Russia), while in other cases a clear distinction between the kin-state's international relations and its obligation to the diaspora has been established (Poland).

Overall, the essays in this volume suggest that there is nothing inevitable in the process of diasporization or in the actions of diasporic states; indeed, it is diversity that characterizes both the definition of "diaspora" and the types of policies pursued in relation to diaspora populations. This complexity has been the focus of a major contribution to the study of ethnicity and nationalism by Rogers Brubaker.[1] Offering a framework within which to analyze diaspora politics, Brubaker has identified a "triadic nexus" at work among kin-state, host-state, and diaspora. Brubaker stresses the "relational" character of the elements within this triad—the fact that the political activities of each of the elements cannot be understood outside their relationship to the activities of (and perceptions about the activities of) all the others. On Brubaker's reading, the array of relations among states and trans-state ethnic populations are part of a web of interdependent "representational struggles," efforts to define the boundaries and nature of membership in a given political or cultural community.

The work in this volume confirms that these relationships are at least as complex as Brubaker argues. Clusters or nests of "triadic" relationships among kin-states, host-states, and diasporas operate interdependently, making it extremely difficult to disentangle the causal connections that exist among the policies of states and the identities and activities of territorially dispersed nations. For example, the location of russified settler populations at the core of the Russian and Soviet empires ensured that Ukrainian and Belarusian communities both within their homelands and beyond developed in relation to and along with a community broadly defined as "Russian." In the immediate post-Soviet period, the cultural and geographic interpenetration of these communities provided an important check on the ability of the homeland states to develop clear diaspora policies. Whom exactly the Russian, Ukrainian, and Belarusian states should target as "their" diaspora has been uncertain, and the projects of defining the frontiers of Russian, Ukrainian, and Belarusian identity—especially beyond the borders of Russia, Ukraine, and Belarus—have emerged as both cause and consequence of these states' foreign policies.

The experience of the post-Soviet states therefore illustrates that to understand relations between kin-states, host-states, and diaspora communities, one must recognize that such relationships operate within the context of numerous and overlapping interactions: between states, between states and ethnic groups, between ethnic groups, and even between factions within a single ethnic group. The terrain of diaspora politics, in other words, is far more complicated than one might imagine, and mapping the complex, multi-directional, and interdependent connections that can arise among ethnic groups whose identity and sense of solidarity extend beyond international frontiers is a task that is still only in its initial stages.

But despite the diversity of outcomes, the evidence presented here does point to common patterns in diaspora relations and a common set of causal factors that seem to have produced the perplexing lattice of relationships among kin-states, host-states, and diasporas in the former Soviet Union. A major theme of this volume has been the highly situational and mutable nature of the "diaspora" label. However, we do not argue that the effectiveness with which states engage in the diasporization of ethnic communities abroad is randomly determined. Indeed, to say that "diaspora" is an identity negotiated among a variety of actors does not tell us why efforts to instrumentalize such an identity become prominent in some states but not in others, or why some attempts to build bridges between kin-states and co-ethnic communities prove successful while others fail. In other words, we are intellectually liberal about how one defines a diaspora, but we are rather more conservative in our conclusion that the ability of kin-states to define co-ethnic populations as diasporic is determined by an identifiable set of factors, some of which have been uncovered in the case studies in this volume.

The studies collected here have highlighted several factors that help explain both the sources and effectiveness of diaspora policies. Domestic politics within the kin-state, the organization and resources of the diaspora, the foreign policy priorities and constraints of the kin-state, inter-ethnic relations within the host-state, and the economic resources available to the kin-state have all shaped diaspora politics in the former Soviet republics. Identification of these factors is a first step toward cutting through the tangled web of interactions that seem, on Brubaker's reading, to defy the attempt to mark out genuinely causal connections within the "relational fields" of diaspora politics. The boundaries of nationhood may indeed be negotiable, but as these studies have shown, the outcome of this process of negotiation is conditioned by a variety of discernible, and sometimes rather pedestrian, domestic and international factors.

Domestic Politics in the Kin-State

The single most important factor affecting the development of diaspora politics and the process of diasporization is domestic politics within the kin-state—above all, the role that nationalism has played within the kin-state since the late 1980s. Some states have embraced or fostered their identity as a diasporic state to help strengthen domestic and international legitimacy or sovereignty. The adoption of a diasporic identity draws upon nationalism by helping post-independence elites with the task of constructing a legitimate locus of political power: the national homeland and its capital. The presence of sizable and powerful ethnic minorities within the kin-state has, however, served as an important constraint on the ability of political elites to use diaspora issues as a major domestic political resource (e.g., Tatars in the Russian Federation and Russians in Ukraine). Moreover, like all domestic political issues, relations with the diaspora have rarely been a subject of universal agreement among political actors. Diaspora policy on the part of kin-states has emerged as a result of domestic wrangling among actors with divergent visions of the homeland and its ties to territorially displaced co-ethnic communities.

Kin-states with the most far-reaching diaspora policies have been those that have been able to develop a domestic political consensus on the need for stronger ties with the diaspora and to mobilize domestic resources for such a project. Most often, such a consensus has arisen not in response to a strongly felt sense of national identity and "obligation" toward the diaspora within the kin-state, but in response to specific domestic concerns.

In Russia nationalist and neo-communist politicians found the status of russified settler communities in the "near abroad" to be a powerful emotive issue on which to attack the record of the Yeltsin leadership and to challenge the dominance of the "Atlanticist" school within the Russian foreign policy establishment. As other questions took center stage after 1991, such as the pace of economic reform and relations among Russia's constituent units, the domestic utility of the diaspora question quickly receded. Likewise, in Kazakhstan encouraging diaspora "return" was a direct response to the disadvantageous demographic position of ethnic Kazakhs within their own republic, but by the late 1990s, as the demographic balance began to look more favorable, Kazakhstani policy toward the diaspora became a secondary concern. In both instances, the domestic uses of the diaspora were ultimately one of the key variables in determining the strength and shape of the state's diaspora policy.

In contrast, in states where the diaspora presented a direct threat to domestic political actors, the state's "duty" toward the diaspora did not arise as a major issue. In Armenia, for example, the influence of diaspora returnees immediately after independence created rifts with indigenous elites and led to the eventual banning of the most powerful representative of diaspora Armenians, the Dashnaks. While Armenia continued to portray itself as the homeland of all Armenians, it has been the diaspora itself that has felt the greatest sense of obligation in the kin-state–diaspora relationship, rather than the other way around.

Organization and Resources of the Diaspora

Diaspora communities have themselves been key actors in the diaspora politics of the post-Soviet period, both in active and passive roles. A major factor determining the nature of diaspora activity has been the institutional strength and resources within these communities: the strength of political organizations, the level of economic resources, and degrees of communal solidarity. Diasporas with well-developed internal organizations, extensive financial resources, and a strong inter-generational sense of ethno-national identity—such as the Armenian and Ukrainian diasporas in the west—have been most effective in challenging the leading role of indigenous elites within the homeland and in becoming powerful independent actors both within the kin-state and in the international arena. The relative weakness of other diaspora groups, such as the russified settler communities, has allowed the kin-state a greater role in determining the shape of diaspora politics. In other cases, such as post-Soviet Jews, intra-diaspora relations have emerged as a political sphere separate from state activity. In each of these instances, though, the degree to which the diaspora is a relatively solidary entity, with political and economic resources independent of the kin-state, has been an important determinant of the shape of diaspora politics.

Foreign Policy Priorities and Constraints

Apart from domestic politics and the resources of the diaspora, the priorities of and constraints on foreign policy making in the kin-state have also influenced relations among homelands, co-ethnics abroad, and host governments. The emphasis of Ukraine and Kazakhstan upon contact with the "external" diaspora in the west rather than the "internal" diaspora in other post-Soviet republics has been driven not simply by a perception that the former constitute "more genuine" Ukrainians and Kazakhs than the latter. Important has also been the consideration that engagement with the "internal" diaspora would involve setting an unwelcome precedent, a precedent that the Russian Federation might use to argue for closer engagement with Russian communities in Ukraine and Kazakhstan. Similarly, Polish reluctance to make the situation of its co-ethnics in the east a major priority was prompted by Poland's overriding foreign policy goal of "rejoining" Europe. A more concerted effort to reach out to ethnic Poles in Lithuania and Belarus would have contradicted Poland's broader goal of underscoring its commitment to European integration and civic conceptions of national identity. In contrast, Russia's desire to embrace a diaspora has been used to bolster the Russian Federation as a "great power" and to underscore Russia's special foreign policy role throughout the former Soviet Union.

The degree to which kin-states focus on diaspora issues is thus determined in part by the broader foreign policy agendas to which political elites are committed and the particular constraints that those elites face in crafting policies toward host-states. All the states in eastern Europe and the former Soviet Union are, to some degree, self-defined diasporic states; that is, both political elites and majority populations see the state as constituted by and for a particular nation whose demographic boundaries stretch beyond the territorial boundaries of the state. At the same time, however, translating this notion into actual foreign policy always competes with an array of other policy priorities and the constraints of the international environment in which political elites must operate, including their obligations as members of international organizations such as the Council of Europe and the Organization for Security and Cooperation in Europe (OSCE). There is thus no direct correspondence between the rhetoric of political elites concerning the "duties" toward an ethnically defined diaspora beyond the state's frontiers and the willingness of those elites to take concrete actions in defense of co-ethnic communities abroad.

Inter-Ethnic Relations Within the Host-State

Another dimension that has emerged from the preceding chapters is the crucial importance of inter-ethnic relations in the host-state. Relations between diaspora populations and other ethnic communities within the host-state (including the titular nationality) can have an impact on both the kin-state's willingness to engage with the diaspora, as well as on the receptiveness of the diaspora to overtures from the kin-state. For example, the indistinct cultural and linguistic boundaries between Ukrainians and Russians, Belarusians, and other groups in the western borderlands of the former Soviet Union have made any efforts by Ukraine to "diasporize" these communities extremely difficult. The overlapping and often situational identities of communities in this region have also helped to prevent conflict around diaspora questions; even if Kyiv were in a position to launch an aggressive diaspora policy among its eastern diaspora, there are few clearly identifiable groups that the Ukrainian state could target and even fewer that would express enthusiasm for Ukraine as an ethnic homeland.

In other cases, such as Russians in Central Asia, where interaction between titular and minority groups has been relatively limited, it has been far easier for kin-states to conduct a policy of diasporization. In addition, where the diaspora has been clearly targeted by the host-state as the object of discriminatory policies, calls within the kin-state for protecting the interests of the diaspora are likely to meet with more support. This has been the issue that has sparked the greatest worry in the post-Soviet period: Many observers in the west have been concerned that policies in the former Soviet republics aimed at reducing the influence of russified settler communities and increasing the power of indigenous elites might prompt the Russian Federation to intercede on behalf of "its" embattled minority. But the picture that emerges from these studies is rather more complex. While the political and economic status of the diaspora within the host-state may be important in conditioning the homeland's policies, in many instances it is unclear exactly which communities the kin-state should define as "its" minority abroad. The solidarity of the diaspora, its relations with neighboring ethnic communities, and the degree to which clear cultural lines separate it from other, closely related ethnic groups within the host-state are vital in influencing the kin-state's willingness to make the diaspora a foreign policy priority.

Economic Resources of the Kin-State

The availability of economic resources has affected all actors in the diaspora politics of the post-Soviet period. The economic collapse faced by most states and populations of the former Soviet Union has placed clear constraints on the ability of the kin-states to engage with potential diasporas. The costs of developing contacts with the diaspora—and the limited economic gains that such contacts are likely to bring—have meant that relations between kin-state and diaspora have often been more a matter of rhetoric and "moral support" than concrete policies buttressing the cultural or economic development of co-ethnic communities. Indeed, the kin-states of the former Soviet Union have been most willing to engage with their diasporas in instances in which the homeland has been the beneficiary and the diaspora the benefactor, rather than the other way around. This pattern is likely to persist, even with improvements in the economic performance of countries in the region. In fact, the important economic assistance that "external" diaspora communities can provide has often made retaining links with these communities of lasting importance, even when (as in Armenia and Ukraine) these relations have become conflictual.

Malleable Identities and Internationalized Ethnicity

As the introductory chapter argued, defining "diaspora" in terms of a set of rigid sociological or historical criteria can blind researchers to the range of ways in which states and trans-border ethnic groups negotiate the meaning of a diasporic identity. Whether the diaspora label is analytically useful should therefore be determined by the degree to which both states and ethnic groups act as if a diasporic relationship exists, not by the degree to which a distinct ethno-cultural community possesses a prescribed list of traits associated with archetypal diasporas such as Jews or Armenians. The chapters in this volume have underscored the malleability of the diaspora label. With the exception of the contributions by Zvi Gitelman and Razmik Panossian, all have dealt primarily with transborder ethnic communities that until 1991 were in no real sense considered diasporic, either by the communities themselves or by policy makers in their ostensible homelands. After the emergence of independent states in the former Soviet Union, however, political elites set about (in various capacities and with variable zeal) "diasporizing" co-ethnic populations abroad that had previously felt little attachment to the homeland. Some states have been more successful in this endeavor than others, just as some have attached a higher priority to relations with the diaspora than other post-Soviet republics. But the emergence of diaspora politics since the late 1980s has illustrated the point that the very term "diaspora" can become part of a foreign policy project targeting transborder populations that have little in common with archetypal diasporic groups.

We have been most concerned here not with establishing whether or not these groups "really" are diasporic, but rather with charting (1) the processes via which political elites within newly independent states come to see themselves as the legitimate spokespersons for a mobilized political community that extends beyond the boundaries of the state, and (2) the major determinants of the effectiveness of such attempts at diasporization. The former Soviet Union provides a remarkably rich environment for the study of what we have come to call "diaspora politics:" the effort by political leaders to secure their domestic legitimacy and assert their power in the international arena not through legal instruments stemming from the state's right to protect its own citizens, but rather through more vaguely identified connections with a displaced co-ethnic population. It is this international dimension of ethnicity that we have sought to uncover in this work.

While the various dimensions of diaspora politics are indeed complex, we have sought to identify several factors that seem to account for the uneven salience of diaspora issues within the former Soviet republics and the variable success that the newly independent states have had in reaching out to co-ethnic communities. We are convinced of the semantic malleability of the diaspora label, but it is not our contention that all efforts to use it as a tool of international politics will ultimately prove successful. In other words, to say that identities are fluid does not explain why they appear so immutable in some instances and so patently protean in others. The case studies collected here have brought to light several factors which help explain the variable outcomes in the diaspora politics of the post-Soviet space, including most importantly the degree to which diaspora issues can be instrumentalized in the domestic politics of the kin-state.

It is worth stressing two important implications of this argument. First, while both scholars and policy makers worry that the "nationalizing" tendencies of the new states of Eurasia and eastern Europe may lead both to discrimination at home and an aggressive policy abroad, our research has shown that these worries are sometimes unfounded. Indeed, the issue of trans-border ethnic populations only becomes a foreign policy priority under a rather specific set of conditions, which include at least the following: the issue must be of some utility to domestic elites within the kin-state; the diaspora must be relatively well-bounded and solidary; relations with the diaspora must not compete with other major foreign policy priorities on the part of the kin-state; inter-ethnic relations within the host-state must either present an imminent threat to the diaspora or at least encourage the maintenance of a separate identity tied to the kin-state; and the kin-state must have the economic and other resources necessary to engage in a policy designed to influence both the host-state and the diaspora. These are high hurdles indeed, and that there has not been *more* conflict over trans-border ethnic groups since 1991 is testimony to the fact that all these conditions very rarely obtain.

Second, even if political elites define their states as diasporic, stressing the duty to protect the interests of "their" co-nationals abroad, there is little reason to believe that such an identity will necessarily find expression in actual state policy. Here we take issue with the view that the "nationalizing" policies of east European and Eurasian states is necessarily a bad thing. While the rhetoric of nationalism may at times prove unpalatable to western observers, in the foreign policy arena there is no guarantee that such rhetoric will automatically translate into concrete policies. Once again, it is only under a complex and rather rare set of conditions that diaspora politics can lead to overt foreign policy moves; while reaching out to co-ethnics may be an important component of building a national identity within the kin-state, the threat that such a project presents to the host-state is normally rather limited. Hence, in contrast to those scholars who focus exclusively on the "constructed" nature of ethno-national identity, we have asked why states engage in the project of constructing a vision of a territorially dislocated nation in the first place and, moreover, why such projects succeed in some instances and fail in others.

There is one final dimension to diaspora politics in the former Soviet Union. Beyond the co-ethnic populations that were "left behind" by the transformation of the Soviet Union's internal borders into international frontiers, there is also another locus of diaspora politics that may become even more significant in the future. All of the states or regions covered in this volume are now diaspora-producing entities, sending co-ethnic individuals and families abroad not because of war, conquest, or famine— the three great generators of diasporas in the past—but because of independence and democratization. These are by and large younger and often well-educated co-ethnics who fully embrace the independence of their homelands and who are likely in the future to feel a greater connection to these kin-states than older emigres who arrived abroad when their homelands were still part of the Soviet Union. Indeed, these new diasporas are likely to be the most vocal advocates of the consolidation of their kin-states' independence, since it was independence that allowed them to leave in the first place. In the future, the states of Eurasia may find it more beneficial to reach out to this new, "post-Soviet," and largely "external" diaspora for political support and economic assistance than to the older and poorer co-ethnic communities located in neighboring republics. While attention in the 1990s has been focused on the plight of trans-border ethnic groups within Eurasia, in the coming decades the venue of diaspora politics for the Soviet successor states is likely to be far broader than the territory of the former Soviet Union.

Notes

1. Rogers Brubaker, *Nationalism Reframed: Nationhood and the National Question in the New Europe* (Cambridge: Cambridge University Press, 1996).

Further Reading

The references below provide a very brief selection of some of the most important works in English on the themes addressed in this volume. In some instances especially significant works in other languages have been included as well.

Diaspora Politics

Brubaker, Rogers. *Nationalism Reframed: Nationhood and the National Question in the New Europe.* Cambridge: Cambridge University Press, 1996.

Chaliand, Gérard, and Jean-Pierre Rageau. *The Penguin Atlas of Diasporas.* New York: Viking, 1995.

Cohen, Robin. *Global Diasporas: An Introduction.* London: UCL Press, 1997.

Constas, Dimitri C., and Athanasios G. Platias, eds. *Diasporas in World Politics: The Greeks in Comparative Perspective.* London: Macmillan, 1993.

Ducháček, Ivo D. *The Territorial Dimension of Politics: Within, Among, and Across Nations.* Boulder: Westview Press, 1986.

Sheffer, Gabriel, ed. *Modern Diasporas in International Politics.* London: Croom Helm, 1986.

Sowell, Thomas. *Migrations and Cultures: A World View.* New York: BasicBooks, 1996.

Ethnicity, Communism, and the Soviet System

Bremmer, Ian, and Ray Taras, eds. *New States, New Politics: Building the Post-Soviet Nations.* 2nd edition. New York: Cambridge University Press, 1997.

Dawisha, Karen, and Bruce Parrott, eds. *The End of Empire? The Transformation of the USSR in Comparative Perspective.* Armonk: M. E. Sharpe, 1997.

Kaiser, Robert J. *The Geography of Nationalism in Russia and the USSR.* Princeton: Princeton University Press, 1994.

Lapidus, Gail W., Victor Zaslavsky, with Philip Goldman, eds. *From Union to Commonwealth: Nationalism and Separatism in the Soviet Republics.* Cambridge: Cambridge University Press, 1992.

Motyl, Alexander J., ed. *The Post-Soviet Nations: Perspectives on the Demise of the USSR*. New York: Columbia University Press, 1992.

Pipes, Richard. *The Formation of the Soviet Union*. New revised edition. Cambridge: Harvard University Press, 1997.

Simon, Gerhard. *Nationalism and Policy Toward the Nationalities in the Soviet Union*. Boulder: Westview Press, 1991.

Suny, Ronald Grigor. *The Revenge of the Past: Nationalism, Revolution and the Collapse of the Soviet Union*. Stanford: Stanford University Press, 1993.

Russians

Chinn, Jeff, and Robert Kaiser. *Russians as the New Minority: Ethnicity and Nationalism in the Soviet Successor States*. Boulder: Westview, 1996.

Harris, Chauncy. "The New Russian Minorities: A Statistical Overview." *Post-Soviet Affairs* 34, no. 1 (1993): 1–27.

Kolarz, Walter. *Russia and Her Colonies*. New York: Praeger, 1952.

Kolstø, Pål. "The New Russian Diaspora—An Identity on Its Own? Possible Identity Trajectories for Russians in the Former Soviet Republics." *Ethnic and Racial Studies* 19, no. 3 (1996): 622–32.

Kolstoe, Paul. *Russians in the Former Soviet Republics*. London: Hurst, 1995.

Kory, William Boris. "Spatial Diffusion of the Russians in the USSR." In *Ethnic Russia in the USSR: The Dilemma of Dominance*, edited by Edward Allworth, 285–91. New York: Pergamon Press, 1980.

Melvin, Neil. *Russians Beyond Russia: The Politics of National Identity*. London: Pinter, 1995.

Rudensky, Nikolai. "Russian Minorities in the Newly Independent States." In *National Identity and Ethnicity in Russia and the New States of Eurasia*, edited by Roman Szporluk, 58–77. Armonk: M. E. Sharpe, 1994.

Shlapentokh, Vladimir, Munir Sendich, and Emil Payin, eds. *The New Russian Diaspora: Russian Minorities in the Former Soviet Republics*. London: M. E. Sharpe, 1994.

Smith, Graham, and Andrew Wilson. "Rethinking Russia's Post-Soviet Diaspora: The Potential for Political Mobilisation in Eastern Ukraine and North-east Estonia." *Europe–Asia Studies* 49, no. 5 (1997): 845–64.

Zevelev, Igor. "Russia and the Russian Diaspora." *Post-Soviet Affairs* 12, no. 3 (1996): 265–84.

Jews

Gitelman, Zvi. *Immigration and Identity: The Resettlement and Impact of Soviet Immigrants on Israeli Politics and Society*. Los Angeles: Wilstein Institute, 1995.

———. *Jewish Nationality and Soviet Politics*. Princeton: Princeton University Press, 1972.

———. "Recent Demographic and Migratory Trends among Soviet Jews: Implications for Policy." *Post-Soviet Geography* 33, no. 3 (1992): 139–45.

Kagedan, Allan Laine. *Soviet Zion: The Quest for a Russian Jewish Homeland.* New York: St. Martin's Press, 1994.

Pinkus, Benjamin. *The Soviet Government and the Jews, 1948–1967.* Cambridge: Cambridge University Press, 1984.

Ro'i, Yaacov, ed. *Jews and Jewish Life in Russia and the Soviet Union.* London: Frank Cass, 1995.

———, ed. *Russian Jews on Three Continents.* London: Frank Cass, 1997.

Armenians

Bakalian, Amy. *Armenian-Americans: From Being to Feeling Armenian.* New Brunswick: Transaction Publishers, 1993.

Björklund, Ulf. "Armenia Remembered and Remade: Evolving Issues in a Diaspora," *Ethnos* 58, nos. 3–4 (1993): 335–60.

Bournoutian, George A. *A History of the Armenian People.* Vol. 2, 1500 A.D. to the *Present.* Costa Mesa: Mazda Publishers, 1994.

Matossian, Mary. *The Impact of Soviet Policies in Armenia.* Leiden: E. J. Brill, 1962.

Mouradian, Claire. "L'Arménie soviétique et la diaspora." *Les temps modernes,* nos. 504–505–506 (July–August–September 1988): 258–304.

Shirinian, Lorne. *Armenian–North American Literature: A Critical Introduction. Genocide, Diaspora, and Symbols.* Lewiston: Edwin Mellen Press, 1990.

Suny, Ronald Grigor. *Looking toward Ararat: Armenia in Modern History.* Bloomington: Indiana University Press, 1993.

Tölölyan, Khachig. "Exile Governments in the Armenian Polity." In *Governments-in-Exile in Contemporary World Politics,* edited by Yossi Shain, 166–87. New York: Routledge, 1991.

Ukrainians

Cipko, Serge. "The Second Revival: Russia's Ukrainian Minority as an Emerging Factor in Eurasian Politics." *Harriman Institute Review* (March 1996): 70–80.

———. *Ukrainians in Russia: A Bibliographic and Statistical Guide.* Edmonton: CIUS, 1994.

Kuropas, Myron. *The Ukrainian Americans: Roots and Aspirations, 1884–1954.* Toronto: University of Toronto Press, 1991.

Luciuk, Lubomyr, and Stella Hryniuk. *Canada's Ukrainians: Negotiating an Identity.* Toronto: University of Toronto Press, 1991.

Pawliczko, Ann Lencyk, ed. *Ukraine and Ukrainians Throughout the World: A Demographic and Sociological Guide to the Homeland and Its Diaspora.* Toronto: University of Toronto Press, 1994.

Sossa, Rostyslav. *Ukraïntsi: skhidna diaspora.* Kyiv: Mapa, 1993.

Subtelny, Orest. *Ukrainians in North America: An Illustrated History*. Toronto: University of Toronto Press, 1991.
Vynnychenko, Ihor. *Ukraïntsi v derzhavakh kolyshn'oho SRSR: istoryko-heografichnyi narys*. Zhytomyr: L'onok, 1992.
Wilson, Andrew. "The Donbas between Ukraine and Russia: The Use of History in Political Disputes." *Journal of Contemporary History* 30, no. 2 (1995): 265–89.
———. *Ukrainian Nationalism in the 1990s: A Minority Faith*. Cambridge: Cambridge University Press, 1997.
Zastavnyi, Fedor. *Skhidna ukraïns'ka diaspora*. Lviv: Svit, 1992.
———. *Ukraïn'ski etnichni zemli*. Lviv: Svit, 1993.

Kazakhs

Akiner, Shirin. *Islamic Peoples of the Soviet Union: An Historical and Statistical Handbook*. 2nd edition. New York: Kegan Paul International, 1987.
Benson, Linda, and Ingvar Svanberg, eds. *The Kazaks of China: Essays on an Ethnic Minority*. Studia Multiethnica Upsaliensia 5. Uppsala: Almquist and Wiskell International, 1988.
Bezanis, Lowell. "Soviet Muslim Emigres in the Republic of Turkey." *Central Asian Survey* 13, no. 1 (1994): 59–180.
Istoriia Kazakhstana. 4 vols. Almaty: Atamura, in press.
Olcott, Martha Brill. *The Kazakhs*. 2nd edition. Stanford: Hoover Institution Press, 1995.
Svanberg, Ingvar. *Kazak Refugees in Turkey: A Study of Cultural Persistence and Social Change*. Studia Multiethnica Upsaliensia 8. Uppsala: Almquist and Wiksell International, 1989.
Syroezhkin, Konstantin L. *Kazakhi v KNR: ocherki sotsial'no-ekonomicheskogo i kul'turnogo razvitiia*. Almaty: Kazakhstan Institute of Strategic Studies, 1994.
Teufel Dreyer, June. "Ethnic Minorities in the Sino-Soviet Dispute." In *Soviet Asian Ethnic Frontiers*, edited by William O. McCagg, Jr., and Brian D. Silver, 195–226. New York: Pergamon Press, 1979.

Volga Tatars

Karimullin, Abrar. *Tatarii: etnos i etnonim*. Kazan: Tatarskoe knizhnoe izdatel'stvo, 1988.
Materialy po istorii tatarskogo naroda. Kazan: Akademiia Nauk Tatarstana, 1996.
Mnogonatsional'nyi Tatarstan: informatsionno-statisticheskii spravochnik. Kazan: Apparat Prezidenta Tatarstana, 1993.
Rorlich, Azade-Ayşe. *The Volga Tatars: A Profile in National Resistance*. Stanford: Hoover Institution Press, 1986.

Schafer, Daniel. *Building States and Building Nations: The Tatar–Bashkir Question, 1917–1921.* Ph.D. Dissertation. University of Michigan, 1995.

Tagirov, Indus R. *Tatary i Tatarstan.* Kazan: n. p., 1993.

Tatarskii mir: informatsionno-statisticheskii spravochnik. Kazan: Apparat Prezidenta Tatarstana, 1995.

Wixman, Ronald. "The Middle Volga: Ethnic Archipelago in a Russian Sea." In *Nations and Politics in the Soviet Successor States,* edited by Ian Bremmer and Ray Taras, 421–47. Cambridge: Cambridge University Press, 1993.

Zenkovsky, Serge. *Pan-Turkism and Islam in Russia.* Cambridge: Harvard University Press, 1960.

Poles

Applebaum, Anne. *Between East and West: Across the Borderlands of Europe.* London: Macmillan, 1995.

Burant, Stephen. "International Relations in a Regional Context: Poland and Its Eastern Neighbors—Lithuania, Belarus, Ukraine." *Europe–Asia Studies* 45, no. 3 (1995): 395–418.

———. "Overcoming the Past: Polish–Lithuanian Relations, 1990–1995." *Journal of Baltic Studies* 27, no. 4 (1996): 309–29.

Eberhardt, Piotr. *Między Rosją a Niemcami: przemiany narodowościowe w Europie środkowo-wschodniej w XX w.* Warsaw: PWN, 1996.

Giżejewska, Małgorzata, and Tomasz Strzembosz, eds. *Społeczeństwo białoruskie, litewskie i polskie na ziemach północno-wschodnich II Rzeczypospolitej w latach 1939–1941.* Warsaw: Instytut Studiów Politycznych Polskiej, 1995.

Lossowski, Piotr. "The Polish Minority in Lithuania." *Polish Quarterly of International Affairs* 1, nos. 1–2 (1992): 69–88.

Prizel, Ilya. "Warsaw's Ostpolitik: A New Encounter with Positivism." In *Polish Foreign Policy Reconsidered,* edited by Ilya Prizel and Andrew Michta, 94–116. New York: St. Martin's Press, 1995.

Snyder, Tim. "National Myths and International Relations: Poland and Lithuania, 1989–1994." *East European Politics and Societies* 9, no. 2 (1995): 317–44.

———. "The Polish–Lithuanian Commonwealth since 1989: National Narratives in Relations among Belarus, Lithuania, Poland, and Ukraine." In *Recasting Political and Social Identities in Postcommunist Europe,* edited by Jeffrey Kopstein and Adam Seligman. In press.

Szporluk, Roman. "The Soviet West—or Far Eastern Europe?" *East European Politics and Societies* 5, no. 3 (1991): 466–82.

Index